Contents

KU-134-367

COMMUNITY ACTION AND PLANNING

Contexts, drivers and outcomes

Edited by Nick Gallent and Daniela Ciaffi

First published in Great Britain in 2016 by

Policy Press
University of Bristol
1-9 Old Park Hill
Bristol BS2 8BB
UK
t: +44 (0)117 954 5940
pp-info@bristol.ac.uk
www.policypress.co.uk

North America office:
Policy Press
c/o The University of Chicago Press
1427 East 60th Street
Chicago, IL 60637, USA
t: +1 773 702 7700
f: +1 773 702 9756
www.press.uchicago.edu
sales@press.uchicago.edu

British Library Cataloguing in Publication Data
A catalogue record for this book is available from the British Library

Library of Congress Cataloging-in-Publication Data
A catalog record for this book has been requested

ISBN 978-1-4473-1517-9 paperback

Cover design by Qube Design Associates, Bristol
Front cover image: Getty
Printed and bound in Great Britain by Lavenham Press Ltd, Suffolk
Policy Press uses environmentally responsible print partners

Lists of images, figures and tables

Images

Figures

Tables

Notes on contributors

Editors

Nick Gallent is professor of housing and planning and head of the Bartlett School of Planning at University College London, UK. He is a chartered town planner and a chartered surveyor. His research focuses on UK planning policy as it pertains to housing delivery and as it affects rural communities. He has conducted research for a wide range of funding bodies and is the author or editor of several previous works on planning, housing and communities.

Daniela Ciaffi is professor of urban sociology in the Faculty of Political Science at the University of Palermo, Italy. She has published widely in the fields of strategic and inclusive planning, participative planning and urban sociology. She is a chartered architect and town planner who has been engaged in several international and national projects looking at social and spatial urban sustainability over the last decade.

Contributors

Jørgen Amdam is professor of local and regional planning and development and head of the Department of Public Administration and Planning at Volda University College, Norway. He is the author of more than 20 internationally published articles and book chapters as well as five books (in Norwegian) and more than 200 national research publications on local and regional planning. He has led national research programmes addressing regional development as well as municipal strategic planning, gender concerns in local planning and planning for local development. He was previously rector of Volda University College and is now an elected member of the municipal parliament in Volda.

Mustapha Berra is an architect and urban planner and currently director of the Centre de Ressources pour la Politique de la Ville (CRPV-PACA), France.

Hemalata Dandekar is professor and department head of City and Regional Planning, California Polytechnic State University San

Luis Obispo, USA. She holds a PhD in urban planning from the University of California, Los Angeles, and is a licensed architect, State of California. Her research interests include comparative issues of rural development, housing, vernacular architecture and planning methods and has been involved in work in India, on the US–Mexico border, South Africa and in Michigan, and Arizona. She has been a consultant for the World Bank, UNESCO, UN Habitat and APA and is the author of numerous books and articles.

Wulf Daseking was director of planning for the City of Freiburg (Germany) between 1984 and 2012 during which time he oversaw the city's emergence as an internationally recognised environmental leader. In 2010, he accepted the Academy of Urbanism's European City of the Year award which recognised Freiburg's exemplary sustainable urbanism. Educated at the Technical University of Hannover and ETH Zürich, he is a professor in the University of Freiburg's sociology department, and is a visiting professor at the Bartlett School of Planning, University College London.

Pierre Filion is a professor at the School of Planning at the University of Waterloo, Canada. His research interests include the relationship between land-use and transportation planning, the evolution of planning models and attempts at changing the course of urban development. His present research work concerns efforts at recentralising growth at the metropolitan scale, with special attention to obstacles in the way of intensification, mixed-use patterns and transit-oriented development in dispersed suburban areas. Common to these research themes is a focus on the political economy of planning and the city.

Iqbal Hamiduddin is a lecturer in transport planning and housing at the Bartlett School of Planning, University College London, UK. His research specialisms are in transport, housing and particularly the interface of transport and housing policies in residential design. His PhD thesis on the social implications of residential car reduction was based largely on detailed comparative field research undertaken in different neighbourhoods of Freiburg. He has also investigated different elements of transport planning and housing delivery separately in a variety of projects for organisations including the Royal Institution of Chartered Surveyors, the Regional Studies Association and the European Union.

Sue Kilpatrick is pro vice-chancellor (students) and previously director of the Centre for University Pathways and Partnerships, University of Tasmania, Australia. She was formerly pro vice chancellor (rural and regional) at Deakin University, Australia. Professor Kilpatrick holds a PhD in the economics of education and a Master of Economics in labour economics. She has had a diverse career in higher education, including research in education and learning in rural and regional Australia, rural workforce, social capital, rural health systems and community and regional development. She is the author of over 180 papers and has led more than 50 research projects

Sophie Lewis is a postdoctoral research associate at the Faculty of Health Sciences, University of Sydney. Her research involves exploring the health needs and experiences of consumers and how culture and society affect people's health behaviour. Her PhD used qualitative interviews and provided a better understanding of the experience of being overweight in Australian society. Her broad interests include qualitative research methods, obesity, breast cancer and the impacts of stigma on health. She is currently contributing to research exploring how Australians make choices about their healthcare, and the resources they draw on when making health choices.

Kelly Main is an associate professor of city and regional planning at California Polytechnic State University, San Luis Obispo, USA. She holds a PhD in urban planning from the University of California, Los Angeles. Her research interests and teaching focus include community planning in culturally diverse and transnational communities, community outreach and participation methods, place attachment, place identity and public space planning. She has conducted research in southern and central California and in Mexico. Prior to completing her doctorate and joining Cal Poly, she was a public planner in Southern California for more than 15 years.

Peter Matthews is a lecturer in social policy at the School of Applied Social Science, the University of Stirling, UK. With a background in urban planning and urban studies, his research focuses on community empowerment and spatial inequality, both socio-economic and in terms of equalities and diversity. He is particularly interested in bringing theorisations of time into understanding community and community-based processes, particularly through co-produced research with communities. He completed his PhD at the University of Glasgow.

Maha Messaoudène holds a PhD in urban spatial planning from Paul Cézanne University, France. Her doctoral research looked at urban renewal processes in two social housing areas in the northern suburbs of Marseille. She currently teaches at the l'Ecole Polytechnique d'Architecture et d'Urbanisme in Algiers.

Gavin Parker is chair of planning studies in the School of Real Estate and Planning at University of Reading, UK. He is a chartered planner with research and teaching interests covering a range of planning topics, including community-led planning and citizenship. In the period 2012–14 he was director of professional standards at the Royal Town Planning Institute, where he oversaw Planning Aid England in delivering support to neighbourhood planning groups across England. Gavin also chaired the Community Council for Berkshire (2006–11), an early pioneer of community-led planning in England. He has produced numerous academic and practice-oriented publications, including the books *Citizenships, contingency and the countryside* (Routledge, 2002) and *Key concepts in planning* (SAGE, 2012) and a string of papers on community-led planning.

Ton van der Pennen is senior researcher at the Delft University of Technology, the Netherlands. He lectures in the Architecture department and at Erasmus University Rotterdam, in urban sociology.

Daniel Pinson holds a PhD in urban sociology and is an architect. He is the author of several books and numerous articles on the city, the suburbs and urban renewal. He is currently professor of urban planning at the Aix-Marseilles University, France.

Yvonne Rydin is professor of planning, environment and public policy at University College London's Bartlett School of Planning (UK). She specialises in urban and environmental planning, governance issues and sustainable cities. This includes attention to the role of social capital and excursions into social network analysis. She has recently worked on sustainable urban energy initiatives and planning for sustainable construction and design. Her current project is on low carbon commercial property: measurement, planning and the market. Her latest three books are *Governing for sustainable urban development* (published by Earthscan), *The purpose of planning: creating sustainable towns and cities* and *The future of planning: beyond growth-dependence* (both published by Policy Press).

Madhu Satsangi is a senior lecturer and head of housing studies in the School of Applied Social Science, University of Stirling, UK. His research publications are in the social relations of rural housing provision; community land ownership; epistemology and social research; housing, planning and land markets; and the operation of housing subsidy systems. Madhu is qualified in environmental science and town and regional planning; his doctorate looked at the structures of housing provision in rural Scotland. Madhu is convenor of the Rural Housing Service, vice chair of Positive Action for Training in Housing (PATH Scotland) and was an advisor to the Scottish Parliament's Land Reform Review Group.

Hanneke Schreuders is a project leader at Platform31, a Dutch national knowledge centre for social and urban economic issues.

Gemma Vilà is professor of urban sociology at the Department of Sociological Theory and Methodology in Social Science at the University of Barcelona and coordinator of the Research Group Territory, Population and Citizenship. She is a member of the Spanish Network for Urban Sociology and of the European Network City Times (ENCiTi). She has completed more than 30 research projects (European Framework Programme, R+D National Programme, and Local and Autonomic Government applied researches) in the field of housing, urban planning, sustainability, and civic participation over the last 13 years and is an expert in the field of urban planning, urban participation and the social effects of urban regeneration.

Karen Willis is associate dean (learning and teaching) in the Faculty of Health Sciences at the Australian Catholic University. She holds a PhD in sociology and is a health sociologist with expertise in qualitative research methods. Her research examines the connections between health behaviours, social ideas and social structure. She has a particular interest in how rurality is implicated in the health choices that people make. She has published widely on health behaviour and on achieving best evidence using qualitative methods.

Laura Wolf-Powers is an assistant professor in the graduate City and Regional Planning programme at the University of Pennsylvania School of Design (USA), where her teaching and research centre on economic development policy and finance, workforce development, and the political economy of neighbourhood revitalisation. She is a faculty fellow at the University of Pennsylvania's Institute for Urban

Preface

The desire of community groups to take greater control and responsibility for their own lives and neighbourhoods is a long-term and fundamental trend. It pre-dates all recent concern for government and governance. It is bigger than periodic episodes of community activism, and it is certainly much bigger than local concerns over the planning system and what that system should look like. The case studies assembled in this book attempt to capture something of the diversity, across the Global North, of the local experiences of community action and planning and how these experiences are embedded within different societies, different political and government traditions and in different urban or non-urban contexts. The book is divided into four parts. The first part is *predominantly* about foundational thinking on communities, planning and collaborative action; the second part is predominantly about the contexts in which community action and planning takes root; the third part is about the actions that communities take and, in some instances, about the plans they make; and the final part is predominantly about the desire of some, but not all, communities to shape the political environment outside of their immediate neighbourhoods and overcome the barriers of 'scale'. The word 'predominantly' is crucial; readers will quickly realise that *all* of the case studies deal, to some degree, with the contexts, drivers and outcomes of community action and planning. They each analyse outcomes born of different contexts, which set in train alternative processes. And they all deal with the fundamental trend of communities (defined in different ways) wanting to take control and shape an outcome, occasionally because of frustration with higher authority, but always because taking control – of their everyday lives and of the neighbourhood they call home – is an important way in which the notion of 'community' finds practical expression.

Edited books are one of the most challenging ways to disseminate research. We, as editors, are hugely indebted to the book's contributors who have each offered their own perspectives on the processes and outcomes of community action and planning in their own countries and in places where they have conducted primary research. However, the overall responsibility for this edited collection, and its ability to make sense of this diverse and complex field, is that of the editors alone. Besides our debt to the contributors, many other colleagues and friends have helped steer and support this project. Sandra Mather drew all the figures that appear in this book, with the obvious exception of Figure 12.1. Emily Watt, Laura Vickers and Laura Greaves from Policy Press have helped us keep the project on track. One of the great advantages of publishing with Policy Press is the care its staff take in helping authors and editors shape and improve their projects: we are grateful for that and to the reviewers who provided comments on the original proposal and also to those who found the time to read the first manuscript during January and February 2014. Their insightful suggestions have been of huge value and we hope they can detect some improvements in this final version. Finally, to Manuela, Marta, Elena, Alessandro and Lisa: your love and support makes these projects possible.

Nick Gallent, London
Daniela Ciaffi, Palermo
March 2014

Part 1
Framing community-based planning

In many instances and in response to various triggers, communities simply mobilise. Their trust in the state to solve problems or grasp the opportunities around them, has either been eroded, or they see the virtue and wisdom in doing some things for themselves. In many instances, the local actions taken by community groups and the projects they deliver themselves are hugely successful. Observing this success, governments that have for many years been seeking the means to revitalise parliamentary democracy – or simply find more effective mechanisms for delivering local services – see an opportunity to rebuild their own legitimacy. They connect to community action where it arises, nurturing it and claiming it as their own. Where it does not arise naturally, they try to make it happen. National governments – through a variety of means – may attempt to seed or incentivise community action and seek to bring the traditional users and consumers of, for instance, planning decisions (businesses, affected residents and communities) and those advising on, or making, decisions (consultants or other 'experts', local officials and elected representatives) together in a process that aims to achieve a co-production of plans and other frameworks and results in greater participation in planning systems. An attempt is made to substitute administration and remoteness with active engagement and proximity, sometimes unsuccessfully (Pasqui, 2011) but occasionally with positive results (Laville and Gardin, 1999).

Therefore, community action and planning have their roots in two places: in communities themselves and in the desire to find local solutions; and in established forms of government, which sees a need to reconnect to the citizenry or lose totally its legitimacy (although reconnections of this type may have positive long-term governance outcomes, participatory effort seldom translates into immediate electoral success; Allegretti and Herzberg, 2004). Where communities themselves take the lead, this leadership may be driven either by ideological counter-culture (Bookchin, 2005) or by a desire to complement established models of government (Benedikter, 2008). Community action may challenge authority, or work with it. This book takes an international perspective on community action. It looks to the commonalities between contexts in different places, but also seeks to explain the form and success of community action as a function of place (Ciaffi and Mela, 2011). Written from a governance-planning perspective, it is concerned in particular, with the interaction (and complementarity) between established models of government and community projects and planning. The many case studies presented in this book collectively narrate the life-cycle of community action and planning, exploring the contexts in which actions and projects arise, examining the act of planning from a community perspective, and dissecting issues of scale in planning and more specifically, attempts by government at all levels to embrace the tide of community action that is now evident in many countries and is becoming a critical component of national planning systems and local practice.

The purpose of this book is to position community-based action in different planning and local government contexts and ask how different systems are harnessing community energies and with what effect. A closely related goal is to consider how and whether community groups can become part of a wider governance and leadership system that delivers benefits for a range of interests, from communities themselves, to policy-makers and private enterprise. To that end, the chapters contained in this volume, and in its concluding parts, analyse the extent to which planning at the community scale adds value to the necessarily broader process of strategic spatial planning.

The more specific purpose of this opening chapter is to offer initial answers to some of the contextual questions that this book needs to address. First, it poses and offers a broad answer to the basic question of *what is a community*. In considering the evolution of thinking on the nature and constitution of communities, it looks at the move away from viewing community as a *passive* consequence of residential proximity to seeing it instead as a product of *active* exchange across social networks. The dynamism of community, expressed in the vibrancy of those networks, then provides a backdrop to the second question. Is an inclination towards social action, in response to various triggers (for example, dissatisfaction with existing political processes, an aspiration towards betterment, or perception of an extraneous threat), an innate feature of communities, particularly those where social exchange – and the power of relationships – is strong? One of the potential outcomes of this action is the inclination to plan: to express dissatisfaction with a current state of affairs and to (occasionally) offer alternatives; to express future aspiration; and to outline how threats may be mitigated. Planning at a community scale may bear little resemblance to the normative processes of the state, being driven by local interest rather than abstract notions of the public good, which connect local actions to regional and national priorities. The third contextual question is, therefore, *what does planning look like and what does it mean for communities?* An important aspect of this question is whether the plans that communities draw up are primarily for internal consumption (a guide for local action/self-help, or an articulation of shared values around which the community coalesces) or intended to influence up-stream plans and strategies and/or signal key concerns, grievances and priorities to local politicians. In addressing these three questions – what is community, why do communities mobilise behind projects and plans, and what is planning for at a community scale – we hope to establish some of the basic principles for later chapters. It is inevitable, and essential, that those chapters will challenge some of the answers offered here, giving more nuanced perspectives on the community and planning processes with which this book is centrally concerned.

The community question

On the face of it, the community question is a simple one. Communities tend to be self-selecting. Individuals linking with each other, through live contact or through virtual networks, tend to identify themselves as a group or community of some description. They do this because they have something in common, either residential proximity (or proximity in a workplace) or a shared interest which leads them to interact on a regular basis. However, even this simple description points to an important distinction in the constitution of community. Residential 'place communities' (that is, communities which are socio-spatial) comprise individuals or families who share a physical space, but it does not automatically follow that the bonds between residents are strong or that they even have a reason or desire to interact (see Bell and Newby, 1976). On the other hand, a shared interest providing a basis and rationale for interaction gives purpose to a community, potentially generating real strength and vibrancy. Delanty (2003) has argued that socio-spatial notions of community imply 'static' and fixed relationships that are merely an accident of residency and lack any deeper motivation. He contrasted this view with alternate conceptions of community which are 'identity-driven' (formed along sexuality, cultural beliefs or lifestyle choices), 'politically mobilised' (formed around the need to collectively address social injustice) and 'technological' (formed around new technologies and the internet such as chat rooms and social network websites) all of which are 'fluid' and free from spatial fixity. In recent years, the rapid mobilisation of protest groups, comprising individuals linked together through social media, has become indicative of the power of virtual networks to bring like-minded and like-motivated people together. These particular groups may dissolve as quickly as they form – as a threat recedes or an aim is achieved – but other virtual networks appear to enjoy longevity, focused on longer-term urban transformations for instance and attempts to shape policies (Cremaschi, 2008). Over time, network members self-select and de-select other nodes creating virtual communities of individuals with shared interests, shared agendas or shared politics on social media. Whether communities are socio-spatial or virtual, however, their coherency will depend on the strength of shared values, on which responses to different challenges are built.

There has been a long debate surrounding the meaning of 'community' and even the earliest contributions to that debate accept that shared interests or beliefs – what Tönnies (1887) called a 'unity of will' and what King (2004) has more recently labelled a 'stable culture' – provide a crucial bonding agent, turning what is otherwise an 'aggregation of disparate individuals' (Blumer, 1948, 546) into something with coherence and potential purpose. This 'potential purpose' is clearly critical for the discussion contained in this and later chapters, so is returned to below. One important caveat to this discussion so far, however, is that communities are dialectic in the sense that the views with which they become associated, or the agendas they pursue, will have been arrived at through discourse and debate (Bobbio, 2004). Panelli (2006) makes the important point that although social interactions will generate occasional agreement, and bring people together, the same interactions will also trigger division between competing groups and diverse interests. In the virtual world, it may be possible to 'unfriend' those with divergent views, or quickly leave one community and join another. In the live world, however, different interests and opinions necessarily co-exist in the 'same' socio-spatial community. We might point to fractures or the existence of sub-groups or cliques, but the lived reality is that communities seldom speak with a single voice, and that conflict is part and parcel of the make-up of dynamic social groups constituted on networks of social exchange. The regular fracturing of 'communities' has led some authors to doubt the concept's usefulness in sociological enquiry, with some arguing that it is used too readily in British and US literature (Schrecker, 2006). The view that social exchange eliminates difference, however, has been replaced today by an acceptance that communities remain heterogeneous (Panelli, 2006, 68), containing a mix of needs, values and beliefs, and may not always display outward signs of inward cohesion. The difference found in communities provides the basis of the governance challenge noted earlier and the rationale (that is, social complexity) for assigning communities a central role in planning and service delivery.

Despite increasing acceptance of community heterogeneity, it is important, however, to note that the cornerstone of Tönnies' thinking was a distinction between rural and urban communities, with the former viewed as homogenous and closed, and only the latter as heterogeneous and open. European cities, at the end of the nineteenth century, were social melting pots, subject to explosive growth and never static. Their social life, as far as Tönnies was concerned, comprised the 'being together of strangers' (Young, 1990, 345; or 'association' rather than 'community' in MacIver's 1924 translation) and this life was distinctly different from that built on the relatively static social configurations of many rural areas (Martin, 1962). But whatever truth existed in these past generalisations, fundamental shifts in the economic bases of rural and urban areas and consequent urban growth (and selective decline), counter-urbanisation and amenity-driven rural migration have since invalidated such claims. As early as the 1960s, Pahl was arguing that the terms 'rural' and 'urban' had lost all meaning in a sociological sense (Pahl, 1965) and, a few decades later, it was being argued that simple conceptions of 'community' repressed 'ontological difference' (Young, 1990, 339). Today, it is universally accepted (among researchers in this field) that 'community is a social construct to be variously and continuously negotiated' (Panelli and Welch, 2005, 1589), complicated in most places by a rich mosaic of values underpinned by patterns of gender, social class, ethnicity, disability or sexuality (Little and Austin, 1996; Cloke and Little, 1997; Delanty, 2003; Neal and Agyeman, 2006). These patterns shape the social interactions on which community is built, resulting in dynamic patterns of inclusion and exclusion. Yet much of this reality is ignored by policy makers who seek the 'quick fix' of connecting to communities in order to build legitimacy and assign vocal local actors a central role in the co-production of public policy. There is a real danger here of a convenient alliance between traditional public sector actors and a narrow section of acceptable community interest, which will clearly result in a missed opportunity to connect to different needs and plan with the social complexity that communities have come to represent (Innes and Booher, 2010).

Evolved thinking on the nature of community has occurred in tandem with the rise of the internet. Those who dismiss the significance of place communities often do so with reference to the preponderance of virtual lives: people finding stronger connections, and clearer purpose, on-line than off-line. Thinking on the nature of place-community has been greatly assisted by reflections on increased internet connectivity. This connectivity has underscored the significance of social interaction and network processes in building this thing we call community. In a significant body of work on this subject, Wellman (for example, 2001; 2002) has argued, like Delanty (2003), that contemporary communities are found in extended and stretched networks, and are personal rather than territorial, centring on identity rather than on residency: but at the same time, he has gone on to argue that new forms of social interaction (on-line) complement, rather than substitute for physical contact. New technologies, including the now ubiquitous smart phone, may diminish the spatial fixity of community, but they do not diminish sociability or weaken personal bonds.

There are two important foundational ideas to carry forward from this brief overview. First, communities comprise networks of social transaction, with either socio-spatial or virtual characteristics. They may be more or less cohesive, and often contain antagonistic elements. This book is primarily concerned with socio-spatial communities which, as Wellman points out, may well be strengthened rather than undermined by new technology. Second, communities are built on a common identity (notwithstanding internal fractures) which can rapidly become a shared purpose, in light of contextual drivers. For the socio-spatial communities examined in this book, that shared purpose may lead to a variety of community actions.

Communities, community action

The actions that communities (or sections of communities) take can be thought of as a 'product' of the interactive processes on which those communities are built and sustained. Through social exchange, and the strengthening of relationships, communities develop a capacity to act on belief and to respond to contextual challenges (Falk and Kilpatrick, 2000). This capacity to act (integral to 'community development'; see Gallent, Chapter 16, this volume) is dependent on a community's store of social capital, and this way of understanding the link between community and community action is explored at length in the next chapter. Chaskin and colleagues (2001, 7) argue that it is the social capital, or the resource potential of relationships, within a community that can be 'leveraged to solve collective problems and improve or maintain the wellbeing of that community'. It is the dialectic nature of communities that leads to a definition of 'collective problems' and agreement around actions needed to maintain wellbeing: although definitions may be contested and necessary actions disputed. Ultimately, however, actions may be taken that respond to context and reflect an interpretation of what needs to be done. Social exchange energises the community, delivers a consensus, and culminates in projects that are often taken forward by core or dominant groups, comprising individuals who feel most strongly about the need to act collectively.

It is through social networks that community action is realised, often resulting in its early stages in the emergence of community leaders and in the coalescence of groupings that go on to play a key role in catalysing further interest in the contextual challenges – challenges that are development and planning related in this book – that socio-spatial communities face. The nature of these contextual challenges was alluded to at the beginning of this chapter; they relate to a growing dissatisfaction with the way in which decisions are reached (which might be about new housing, new infrastructure, services or the design of places and physical things) and the consequences of those decisions for place communities. There is often a feeling that representative government is 'out of touch' with the needs of particular places or that public policy (shaping the way services are delivered), or indeed planning decisions, are insensitive to local context. These feelings may be rooted in a broader dissatisfaction with government or with the level at which key decisions are taken – nationally, regionally or even by the local state, which may still be considered too far removed from a community's or a neighbourhood's specific needs and concerns. Not all community action is triggered by dissatisfaction. It is often the case that community groups recognise intrinsic value in doing things for themselves – taking responsibility for key services, for example, as a means of building some of the capacities needed to take on bigger challenges in the future. Community projects, of various kinds but especially those that see local people running local services (see Moseley, 2000), may be viewed as a means of further strengthening social ties, or reaching out to hitherto inactive groups and expanding the networks across which communities are constituted. People may be motivated not by extraneous threats but by a desire to create a stronger community, or simply by the chance to enhance local wellbeing by voluntarily providing the community with goods or services that neither the state nor private enterprise are set up to deliver.

Community action may therefore be: a reaction to perceived threats or opportunities; a conscious effort to enhance social cohesion and 'community spirit'; or an exercise in self-help, augmenting service delivery by the state and therefore assisting, in particular, vulnerable groups. A fourth significant area of community action falls under the banner of 'taking control', responding to the insensitivity of the state, the social indifference of private enterprise, and the general 'democratic deficit' (Sturzaker, 2011) that many communities feel, by setting their own aspirations and goals, by challenging the priorities of government and by engaging in some form of community-based planning. Planning at the community scale comes in many shapes and forms. It was suggested at the beginning of this introduction that the plans which communities produce often have an internal and external face:

they are for the community itself and also for external consumption. These same characteristics are identified in Table 1.1, which attempts to link the four drivers of community action listed above with initial and secondary actions. In *reaction* to threats, communities may protest and lobby, ultimately drawing up statements or plans which express (internal) consensus and opposition (or support) to external decision-makers. In relation to *community building*, one-off projects or events or the setting up of interest groups may be augmented by plan-making, or community visioning, as a means of building interest in the community and its future. Regarding *self-help*, similarly one-off projects or initiatives may eventually be superseded by the setting of longer-term goals, with plans sometimes needed to secure external funding for various community projects. Finally, *taking control* through planning may initially mean expressing collective anger or opposition (that is, have a reactive quality), but may evolve into a more rounded articulation of aspiration, with proposals for future development that speak to higher authority.

There are many different experiences and models of planning by communities and at the community level. The case studies presented later in this book examine different experiences in a range of countries. What the planning undertaken by community groups in small rural towns or villages, or in urban neighbourhoods, looks like will depend very much on what planning means and looks like in different countries. There is one important distinction that can be made at this point, however: there is a critical difference between the *ad hoc* agenda-setting and visioning that communities do on their own, and the seeded community planning that is becoming increasingly prevalent across developed countries. In the latter case, communities are being told what they need to do and what community plan-making should involve if they wish to interface with, and influence, public policy. In England, for example, the past practice of communities simply bundling together local survey evidence with statements of aspiration has now been replaced with a formalised process of 'neighbourhood development planning' (see Parker, Chapter 10, this volume). The purpose, form, and also the cast of protagonists, of community-based planning has been transformed and this pattern of transformation is repeated across many parts of the world, as governments seek to connect to community initiative as a means of reconnecting to the citizenry and reclaiming authority.

Table 1.1: Drivers of Community Action

Drivers of community action	Initial response	Secondary response
Reaction (to context)	Protest Lobbying Funding bids	Build and express consensus within community appraisals, statements and plans
Community building	One-off projects/ events Forming local support groups Community infrastructure	Develop community vision as a focus for community building
Self-help	Running local services Community shops Local support groups Community buses	Secure funding through setting strategic priorities within a community plan
Taking control	Taking control of assets Developing plans which express opposition Developing plans which offer alternatives	Connect community plans to higher level strategies, find a community voice, seek influence over public policy and planning

...and planning

At whatever level planning takes place, however, it expresses a common (if not uncontested) purpose. Rydin (2011, 12) argues that planning is 'a means by which society collectively decides what urban change should be like and tries to achieve that vision by a mix of means'. Planning in many countries has, in the past, been dominated by the public sector (and often by a procedural view of planning as the technical regulation of land-use change). Direct public planning (beyond its regulatory function) frequently involved the local arm of the state taking control of land and acting as developer, sometimes planning and delivering entire new settlements and often building new homes. This model has generally given way to greater 'interaction between the public and private sectors', with planning adopting 'more indirect means of achieving desired urban change' (Rydin, 2011, 12). Today, this often means contributing through policies and projects to a 'vision of a sustainable future' (Rydin, 2011, 138), delivered through a planning process which brings together professional expertise with the aspirations, and the particular visions, of different communities and stakeholders. The shift towards an open, 'transparent, accountable and fair means' of engagement with these communities and stakeholders (Rydin, 2011, 138) has also been a shift away from the closed and professionalised model of governance – viewed essentially as administration (Foucault, 1982) – outlined earlier. It has also been a response to persistent and sustained popular attacks on professionals. In 1973, Rittel and Webber (p 155) observed that 'we've been hearing ever-louder public protests against the professions' diagnoses of the clients' problems, against professionally designed governmental programs, against professionally certified standards for the public services'. These protests have arisen because in 'a pluralistic society [see, again, Misztal, 1996] there is nothing like the undisputable public good' (Rittel and Webber, 1973, 155).

Public planning, however, has regularly attempted to define this 'public good', often in quite abstract terms: pursuing, for example, economic efficiencies that are disputable or welfare goals that are poorly defined. Recent notions of the public good have been aligned with the pursuit of very broad ideas of 'sustainability' or 'urban resilience'; ideas that are open to interpretation but which can be used to justify a range of different policies and projects. Such abstractions also signal the way in which planning is professionally produced by experts who may have limited contact with planning's user communities. Where planning seems closed, top-down and highly professionalised, the sector's defence and pursuit of the public good may appear to challenge the right of communities to set their own goals and pursue their own interests, resulting in development outcomes that appear to have been imposed on particular places and particular people. Hence, new housing, new industry and new infrastructure become contested, not only because of the form in which they are delivered, but also the manner of that delivery. Sitting in opposition to public planning and its underlying goals (to shape markets and deliver social welfare) is a liberal rejection of contributory actions:

> At its simplest, the liberal worldview holds that society consists, or should strive to consist, of an association of free individuals, detached from imposed duties and obligations and free to form their own aspirations and interpretation of the good life. (Sage, 2012, 267)

In this worldview, it is not the role of the state to 'impose a vision of the common good', but rather to protect individual rights. More strident 'neo-liberalism' in the 1980s onwards sought to emancipate markets from state interference, giving rise to a specific view on how planning processes should respond to (rather than try to adjust) the operation of those markets. A greater public good would be achieved though less planning and through an economic trickle-down (Jessop, 2002, 470). The advocacy of either strong public planning or liberalism/

neo-liberalism is necessarily underpinned by a particular understanding of society. The first sees society as coherent and possessing multiple and complex inter-connections; the second emphasises individuality over social cohesion, sometimes viewing notions of community as oppressive and as a threat to individual freedoms and personal intimacies (Schrecker, 2006).

A middle view, however, focuses on the importance of community and the value of particular 'social goods' that arise from the interactions that constitute community life:

> The starting point for communitarian theory is the basic tenet that the existence of strong community life – expressed as a state of affairs in which individuals *belong* to and participate in a wider group (or groups) of common interests and shared goals – is of inherent value in human society. (Sage, 2012, 267; emphasis added)

Belonging, according to Weber (1956), is central to communitarianism and to the reciprocities that deliver a sense of community. Planning rooted in communitarianism will (perhaps inevitably) relegate any abstract, politically motivated or professionally formed 'public good' behind community interest, believing that it is at the level of the community (or neighbourhood) that needs can be most clearly understood and solutions to social problems formulated. It might be argued, therefore, that planning at the community scale is rooted in a communitarian worldview, which rejects both the advocacy of strong public planning and neo-liberalism. This is a rather simple view, however, which ignores the reality of individual self-interest and necessary co-existence with higher authority. The experience of community-based planning to date is that it is not always driven by a communitarian spirit, but rather by a defence of narrow local interests (communities mobilising, for example, against development in order to protect private property values). Similarly, it does not always grow from a community, but may be implanted by the state as a means of steering (or rationalising) service delivery and gaining greater legitimacy for top-down government. In some instances at least, however, communitarianism is the space occupied by community action and embraced, for various reasons, by the existing structures of authority. 'Communitarian planning' – with its role in defining and extracting social goods – might be conceived as an ideal that is corrupted, on the one hand, by self-interest, and on the other, by state manipulation. A more generous view is that community planning, in whatever form it takes, must necessarily exist within 'the shadow of hierarchical authority' (Scharpf, 1999, 41). That authority plays a crucial leadership role, steering contributory actions (flowing from the duties and obligations that liberalism rejects) towards the achievement of a more clearly formed public good and acting as a counterbalance to the narrow self-interest that threatens the realisation of community and broader public goals. The legitimacy of its leadership, however, becomes increasingly dependent on its ability to articulate, and win support for, its own vision of the public good, which remains highly contested in a pluralistic society.

It is difficult to offer any definitive view, at this stage, as to what planning looks like at the community scale. This will become apparent through the case studies. But generally, community planning is a departure from the professionalised world of normative planning, meaning that there is great variety in the paths it follows, in its process, form and eventual content. The different motivations of community actors – and of national and local authorities – reinforces this variety, leading to many different outcomes. In its simplest form, community planning is disconnected from higher authority, aiming to deliver local, internal goals. Communities formulate plans that aim towards the maximum extraction of social goods. Plans which grow out of campaigns, however, often aim to connect to higher authority, adopting the norms and legalistic language of that authority and attempting to shape policy in its own terms. Likewise, community actions and plans that are seeded by the state will share these same traits, with communities pulled into the professional world of public policy. European 'spatial planning', for example, embraces communities as co-producers of that policy, drawing legitimacy from an assimilation of community action. All of this might suggest a distinction between communitarian planning as a by-product of community life (with its focus on social goods) and (implanted or hijacked) community planning as a product of the state's search for legitimacy – through extended interaction that delivers a less contentious vision of 'what urban change should be like'.

The book's structure

In order to understand the many alternative narratives of community action and planning, it is necessary to explore the different environments in which communities acquire the desire, and the competencies and capacities, to act. This book brings together a range of experiences with a view to analysing how local groups and communities mobilise, plan and seek to become – in some instances – part of the machinery of local and national governance. The approach taken in this book is to suggest a meta-narrative which moves from the local origins of community action, to engagement with ideas of planning and thereafter to the integration of local and normative ideas of planning at different scales. This is very much an ecological view of the social world, focused initially on spaces of proximity (examining contexts and actions at a community scale) shaped *directly* by community actors and then connectivity to an external macro-system in which those same actors seek *indirect* influence (Bronfenbrenner, 1979).

Some of the foundational issues emerging from this chapter are carried further in the first part of this book. In the next chapter, a more expansive focus on social capital as a basis for community action is offered. This is followed by an examination of the ways in which the dialectic community engages with the local state, seeking the indirect influence noted above. Three sets of case studies then follow, which collectively narrate the life-cycle of community action and planning. These focus sequentially on the rationales and contexts for local action, on expressions of community action and the development of a community planning focus, and on attempts to connect across different governance scales. The stories of community action and planning contained in this book all draw on recent local research. It is of course an incomplete set of stories and many other countries could have offered their own accounts of frustration with representative democracy, of the mobilisation of community actors, of different outcomes (including many different failures and successes) and of renegotiated relationships with political leaders and with the local and national state. We have drawn selectively and have done so in order to construct a sequencing of community action and planning, piecing together experiences from across Europe, North America and Australia and from contexts which are clearly urban to those that are suburban or deeply rural. Within the case studies, questions of governance, alongside challenges to the politics of planning, dominate. The cases are all drawn from countries at similar points on the development trajectory, with comparable and mature political traditions – and all with established models of representative government. Some of the countries have attempted, at various times, to seed community action. They have all been host to spontaneous community mobilisation, either as self-help, as a complement to established processes, or as a manifestation of urban counter-culture. Although it offers an incomplete cross-section of experience, it is hoped that it will nevertheless reveal some of the many ways in which planning is being owned and redefined at a community scale.

References

Allegretti, G, Herzberg C, 2004, *Participatory budgets in Europe: Between efficiency and growing local democracy*, TNI: Amsterdam

Bell, C, Newby, H, 1976, *Community studies: An introduction to the sociology of local community*, Allen and Unwin: London

Benedikter, T, 2008, *Democrazia Diretta, Più Potere ai Cittadini: Un Approccio Nuovo alla Riforma dei Diritti Referendari*, Alessandria: Sonda

Blumer, H, 1948, Public opinion and public opinion polling, *American Sociological Review* 13, 5, 542–54

Bobbio, L, 2004, *A Più Voci: Amministrazioni Pubbliche, Imprese, Associazioni e Cittadini nei Processi Decisionali Inclusivi*, Rome: Edizioni Scientifiche Italiane

Bookchin, M, 2005, *Democrazia Diretta*, Rome: Eleuthèra

Bronfenbrenner, U, 1979, *The ecology of human development: Experiments by nature and design*, Cambridge, MA: Harvard University Press

Chaskin, RJ, Brown, P, Venkatesh, S, Vidal, A, 2001, *Building community capacity*, New York: Aldine De Gruyter

Ciaffi, D, Mela, A, 2011, *Urbanistica Partecipata*, Rome: Carocci

Cloke, P, Little, J (eds), 1997, *Contested countryside cultures: Otherness, marginalisation and rurality*, London: Routledge

Cremaschi, M, 2008, *Tracce di Quartieri: Il Legame Sociale nella Città che Cambia*, Milan: FrancoAngeli

Delanty, G, 2003, *Community*, London: Routledge

Falk, I, Kilpatrick, S, 2000, What is social capital? A study of interaction in a rural community, *Sociologia Ruralis* 40, 1, 87–110

Foucault, M, 1982, The subject and power, *Critical Inquiry* 8, 4, 777–95

Habermas, J, 1984, *The theory of communicative action. Part 1: Reason and the rationalization of society*, Boston: Beacon

Innes, J, Booher, D, 2010, *Planning with complexity: An introduction to collaborative rationality for public policy*, Routledge: Abingdon and New York

Jessop, B, 2002, Liberalism, neo-liberalism, and urban governance: A state theoretical perspective, in *Antipode* 34, 3, 452–72

King, P, 2004, *Private dwelling: Contemplating the use of housing*, London: Routledge

Laville, JL, Gardin, L, 1999, *Le Iniziative Locali in Europa: Un Bilancio Economico e Sociale*, Turin: Bollati Boringhieri

Little, J, Austin, P, 1996, Women and the rural idyll, *Journal of Rural Studies* 12, 2, 101–11

MacIver, RM, 1924, *Community*, London: Macmillan

Martin, EW, 1962, *The Book Of The Village*, London: Phoenix House

Mathieu, L, 2010, *Les Années 70: Un âge d'or des Luttes?*, in *Encyclopédie Critique*, Paris: Textuel

Misztal, BA, 1996, *Trust in modern societies: The search for the bases of social order*, Cambridge: Polity Press

Moseley, M, 2000, England's village services in the late 1990s: Entrepreneurialism, community involvement and the state, *Town Planning Review* 71, 4, 415–33

Neal, S, Agyeman, J (eds), 2006, *The new countryside? Ethnicity, nation and exclusion in contemporary rural Britain*, Bristol: Policy Press

Pahl, RE, 1965, Urbs in Rure: The metropolitan fringe in Hertfordshire, *Geographical Papers 2*, London: London School of Economics and Political Science

Panelli, R, 2006, Rural society, in P Cloke, T Marsden, P Mooney (eds) *Handbook of rural studies*, pp 63–90, London: SAGE

Panelli, R, Welch, W, 2005, Why community? Reading difference and singularity with community, *Environment and Planning A: Environment and Planning* 37, 1589–611

Pasqui, G, 2011, Un ciclo politico al tramonto: perchè l'innovazione delle politiche urbane in Italia ha fallito, *Territorio* 57, 147–54

Revelli, M, 2006, *Oltre il Novecento*, Turin: Einaudi

Rittel, H, Webber, M, 1973, Dilemmas in a general theory of planning, *Policy Sciences* 4, 155–69

Rydin, Y, 2011, *The purpose of planning: Creating sustainable towns and cities*, Bristol: Policy Press

Sage, D, 2012, A challenge to liberalism? The communitarianism of the Big Society and Blue Labour, in *Critical Social Policy* 32, 3, 365–82

Scharpf, F, 1999, *Governing in Europe: Effective and democratic?*, Oxford: Oxford University Press

Schrecker, C, 2006, *La Communauté: Histoire Critique d'un Concept dans la Sociologie Anglo-Saxonne*, Paris: L'harmattan

Sturzaker, J, 2011, Can community empowerment reduce opposition to housing? Evidence from rural England, in *Planning Practice and Research* 26, 5, 555–70

Tönnies, F, 1887, *Gemeinschaft und Gesellschaft*, Leipzig: Fues's Verlag (translated as [1988] *Community and Society*, Washington, DC: Library of Congress Publications)

Weber, M, 1956, *Wirtschaft und Gesellschaft: Grundriß der Verstehenden Soziologie*, Tübingen: Mohr

Wellman, B, 2001, Physical place and cyberspace: The rise of personalised networking, *International Journal of Urban and Regional Research* 25, 227–52

—

Wellman, B, 2002, Little boxes, glocalisation and networked individualism, in M Tanabe, P Van den Basselaar, T Ishina (eds) *Digital Cities II: Computational and Sociological Approaches*, Berlin: Springer

Young, IM, 1990, *Justice and the politics of difference*, Princeton, NJ, Princeton University Press, selection republished in 2003 as *City life and difference*, in S Campbell, S Fainstein, S (eds) *Readings in Planning Theory*, 2nd edn, pp 336–55, Blackwell: Oxford

2

Communities, networks and social capital

Yvonne Rydin

Introduction

The last chapter explored the promise and challenges of community planning and made it clear that collective action to shape neighbourhoods cannot be taken for granted. There is a key issue involved: enabling the dynamics by which a group of people come together to develop and implement a vision for their locality. This chapter uses the concepts of networks and social capital to understand these dynamics more fully. It begins by building on the discussion of the previous chapter on the nature of communities. It then considers communities as networks and explores the concept of social capital. It looks at how to define the concept, the different ways in which social capital generates impacts (positive and negative) and, finally, the factors that can help shape social capital and those impacts.

Communities: definitions and assumptions

The idea of community action and planning presupposes the existence of communities. As the previous chapter explored, however, the question of what constitutes a community is a difficult one to tackle. The term 'community' is widely used these days. We talk of working- or middle-class communities, ethnic communities, online or virtual communities and business communities. There are, however, three notable features about the way the term is used, particularly within community planning debates.

First, there is often a strong normative dimension. Communities are generally seen as good things. The term suggests continuity, stability and possibly a degree of nostalgia. This is particularly evident in the media with television and radio soaps across the world built around self-described communities of people, organised into families and friends who know each other and each other's business. Certainly the community planning movement and localism agenda use the term positively to suggest that plan-making and decision-making based within communities will result in better outcomes.

Second, communities are often strongly identified with particular localities. This is certainly the case in those TV and radio soaps with their emphases on the historic 'East End' of London, mythical English Ambridge or sunny Australian Erinsborough. It is also apparent in planning debates, where there is a tendency to emphasise spatial communities, fixing them in specific geographical areas and giving them associated identities. There tends to be a conflation between labels for spatial mapping and for describing communities: the Moss-side community, the Chipping Campden community, and so on. We, therefore, see a locality or neighbourhood as containing a specific community. The spatial affiliation not only describes the community but limits it, setting borders on this community and separating it from another one.

Third, communities tend to be seen as unitary, because they are assumed to have common interests, values and identities at heart. For example, Taylor (1987) defines community as: 'a group of people who share beliefs and values, engage in relations that are direct and many-sided, and practice generalized as well as merely balanced reciprocity' (quoted in Orbán, 2012, 78). Often the perception of these common elements becomes so strong that members of a designated community are seen *only* in terms of these elements. There is a one-to-one mapping of the common set of interests, values and identity onto the members of a given community. Further, this is based on the spatial location; it is living in the same local area that is deemed to generate the common interests, values and identity.

So communities can all too readily be seen as desirable, spatially-located and spatially-contained groups of people who are defined by their common interests, values and identity, features which arise from their geographical co-location. It is important to recognise the limitations of such a definition and to open up instead a more flexible way of thinking about communities if realistic – as opposed to idealistic – notions of community planning are to be pursued. So let's consider these three aspects one by one.

If we see communities as groups of people who have something in common, such communities are not necessarily always a 'good' thing. This depends on what they have in common and how the community operates in relation to both its own members and others. Consider, for example, a community based on religion that has very restrictive notions of gender roles and enforces these strictly, perhaps even extending to violence against women. Consider, again, a political community with a strong sense of identity based in a right-wing ideology that justifies (to itself) hate campaigns against Jewish groups and individuals. Neither of these can (from my perspective) be seen as positive communities. Extreme as these examples may seem, an important general point arises. We need an approach to defining communities that does not see them through rose-tinted glasses.

We can also question the primacy of spatial location and boundaries in defining communities. In the next chapter, Matthews points to the nature of communities as constructed entities, constructed through identities, memories and a sense of place-belonging. He particularly identifies the selective nature of place-belonging that underpins the spatial labelling of communities. Campbell (2000), in the context of community health promotion, however, argues that communities exhibiting a common identity tend to be quite small and spatially localised. These are communities developed primarily through one-to-one, face-to-face contacts and the informal networks of kinship and friendship (see also Kilpatrick and colleagues, Chapter 5, this volume).

People these days are often very mobile, however. They do not necessarily stay in one location for any length of time and thus their affinity with a specific area may not be very deeply rooted. They are also often mobile on a daily or weekly basis, travelling to different localities from their main residence for work, leisure, shopping and a variety of other activities. They may, therefore, have multiple allegiances to different places. The immediate locality around their residence may or may not be their primary allegiance and they are certainly likely to connect in terms of interests, values and identity with people in several other areas. This issue may appear to be resolved by considering the area of relevance to a community at a higher spatial scale – the city rather than the neighbourhood, say. This may not actually represent the spatial pattern of allegiances of a given group, however; not all these allegiances may be contained within one urban area. Furthermore, this may result in identifying a large geographical scale to which people have only a weak allegiance. Rather, people may share a common affinity with the area around their co-located places of residence but then have a multitude of partially overlapping links to a variety of other places, near and far.

The same theme of fragmentation arises when considering if a community is necessarily unified by a set of common interests, values and identity. People today often have much more complex patterns of social affiliation than this suggests. Consider how different facets of people's lives – work, residence, children's schooling, leisure activities, religious attendance – all intersect resulting in fragmented social patterns. For example, the term 'the black community' provides only the most broad-brushed understanding of the experience of black Britons, emphasising the racism that they experience on a daily basis but oversimplifying many other aspects of their lives concerning employment, culture, religious practice, leisure preferences and so on. Clearly in all these ways, the experience of black Britons is that of many non-black Britons and they, therefore, are also members of communities defined by work, football club loyalty, and so on, rather than colour. A much more nuanced account of how people define themselves in relation to their lives and activities is required. This raises a question mark over whether a community will actually have common goals (as Szreter, 2000, for example assumes); it may be that any common goals can only be stated in very general terms, which all too readily descend into conflicts and tensions when examined in any more detail.

Communities as networks

This discussion suggests that we need a better way of analysing a community and understanding how it works. This approach needs to avoid seeing communities as overly stable, spatially contained and socially unified and to be flexible enough to understand the multiple ways that people inter-relate on the basis of common values, identities and activities. Furthermore it needs to be able to handle inevitable conflicts of interests and values. Networks provide such an approach.

Communities within a network approach are defined by the connections (and non-connections) between people. As Maloney et al (2000) put it, communities and networks are 'mechanisms for both inclusion *and* exclusion' (p 218). But within a network approach the boundaries of the community are not firmly fixed, like a hedge around a field. Rather, they occur where the density of connections decays to a point that they are no longer considered significant. It is more like the change between one kind of ground cover and another; where the grass of the dunes gives way to the sand of the beach occurs gradually and at some point the boundary between dune and beach emerges, even though some grasses are still apparent among the sand and there will be sand among the roots of the grass for some distance from the beach.

The relationships between members of a community may also take a wide variety of forms, from regular contact to sharing resources to having certain values and norms in common, or any mix of these and many other possibilities. There is, therefore, the potential for understanding connections between people in terms of multiple, partially overlapping networks, each formed by a focus on a different type of connection. A community does not have to be defined by just one set of relationships. Social Network Analysis, for example, can be used to map these multiple networks that together define community relations in a locality.

This network approach can seem almost too flexible, however. It can suggest that social relationships are only understood empirically, by studying the specific patterns of relationships within a given group of people. Is no other generalisation possible? This is where the concept of social capital can be helpful. It provides a network-based approach for analysing community relationships and, furthermore, understanding how these relationships enable a group to act collectively. The rest of this chapter explores this concept of social capital in more detail.

Defining social capital

'It is difficult to think of an academic notion that has entered the common vocabulary of social discourse more quickly than the idea of social capital' (Dasgupta and Serageldin, 2000, x). As with so many social science concepts, however, there are different definitions and contested terrain. Castiglione (2008) argues that there are so many disputes over the definition of social capital because it is a relatively new concept with a strong normative dimension. He notes that it is often unclear whether it refers to something concrete or is being used as a metaphor, the causal link can be uncertain to the point of whether social capital is an input or output, and it is not entirely apparent whether social capital is a 'capital' at all. He further makes the cautionary point that 'What is not uncommon, however, is the temptation among those who are enthusiastic about the concept to use it as a peg on which to hang all those informal engagements we like, care for, and approve of' (Castiglione, 2008). So we need to treat the definition of social capital with some care.

There are a variety of historical roots to the coinage of the concept. One can point to: Bourdieu's identification of social capital as one of many capitals; Coleman's empirical studies of education; and Putnam's work on regional government in Italy and social life in USA (see Baron et al, 2000). Since then, as Dasgupta and Serageldin above imply, there has been a veritable explosion in uses of the term, each with their own nuance. Sources such as Baron et al (2000), Halpern (2005) and Bartkus and Davis (2009) provide reviews of this variety but they also all point to some common threads. There is a focus on networks of relations that are imbued with trust and shared norms, values and expectancies. Among the shared norms, those of mutuality and reciprocity are particularly important. Mutuality refers to the sense of having a common purpose and may relate to a broad, general sense of the desired future or a more specific project or initiative. As suggested above, mutuality needs to overcome the fragmentation of and potential conflicts within a community. Reciprocity may be specific and between known members of a community (A will do something for B and vice versa) or generalised in that anyone in the community will offer that service in the expectation that someone else within the community will reciprocate at some other time. These norms have to be maintained and Halpern points to the availability and use of positive and negative sanctions to maintain norms within the network as a key aspect of social capital (2005, 10; discussed further below).

Within this general definition attempts have been made to identify different types of social capital. The most emphasised distinction has been between bonding and bridging social capital, a distinction that Putnam credits to Gittell and Vidal (1998; identified in Halpern, 2005, 21).

Bonding social capital involves relationships between similar people, between homogeneous actors. Such capital is typically strong and exclusionary. It links a certain group of people together with close ties but in doing so it creates a boundary between these and other people. Bonding social capital is generally used to describe (stereotypical) local communities that are close-knit, where everyone knows everyone else, trusts them and shares a way of looking at the world. The 'dark side' of social capital occurs where strong bonding capital is used for social coercion to maintain the community. Furthermore, such a community can be suspicious of 'outsiders' and it can be difficult for newcomers to become accepted and fully integrated.

Bonding social capital is contrasted with bridging social capital. If bonding social capital involves close, tight or strong ties, then bridging social capital involves more distant, loose or weak ties (Granovetter, 1973). Here heterogeneous actors are connected together and the demands on common norms are less stringent. There still needs to be a degree of trust and common purpose to enable the links within the network to be effective, but a network with considerable bridging social capital is more open and fluid. New actors can be more readily integrated and the nature of ties may change more readily. Actors will behave as if they have some trust in and expectation of reciprocation from other actors, but not the almost-certainty that is apparent in networks with high levels of bonding social capital. Granovetter argues that bridging social capital is important for creating political influence and employment opportunities (1973; Füzér and Monostori, 2012), while Halpern (2005, 194) sees bridging social capital as important in ensuring that the benefits of participatory governance are spread and not captured by a specific group.

Recent work has also looked at how bonding and bridging social capital can be combined. Bracing social capital refers to a selective combination of bonding and bracing social capital. Using the metaphor of scaffolding rather than glue or bridges, Rydin and Holman (2004) show how networks can be dense in some places, with many close linkages, and less dense in others with bridging links dominating. The suggestion is that some networks – particularly policy networks with a subset of dense connections, possibly organised around a key actor such as a planner, and with weaker connections out to organisations and actors on the periphery – will be more efficient in networking, avoiding the effort involved in creating an excessive number of close bonding links and enabling effective transmission of information and other resources without substantial transactions costs (Rydin and Falleth, 2006).

Another development is the idea of linking social capital. Woolcock (1998) uses linking social capital to discuss the extent to which an individual's or community's networks are characterised by linkages between those with power and resources, and those without. Halpern (2005, 25) describes this as 'a vertical bridge across asymmetrical power and resources'. This is particularly important in understanding connections across scales (see the Part 4, Chapters 14 to 16, this volume). Here a link from the local to the meso- or macro-scales can be helpful in accessing resources and making links to activate power relations.

In developing these various classifications of social capital, it is important to remember that this is a feature of social life that derives from the relationships between people and organisations. It is not a stock, a pile of community gold in the neighbourhood bank account. This relates to a point that Coleman makes (2000, 16), that social capital is not completely fungible: 'A given form of social capital that is valuable in facilitating certain actions may be useful or even harmful for others.' That is because social capital inheres in the structure of relations between actors and not the individual actors themselves.

Social capital as enabling collective action

The above section has unpacked the definition of the concept of social capital but not yet tackled the questions of what it does and why it works. Starting with the first question, the interest in social capital arises because it is seen as enabling collective action. The concept can help us understand how people, say in localities, relate to and work with each other with a view to achieving common goals. For example, Burton and Williams (2001) provide a useful case study of the effects of social capital. Comparing two similar redundant air force bases in the USA, they contrast one where all significant wildlife habitats were destroyed by real estate development with another where almost 25 per cent of the site was preserved as a wildlife refuge. The reason for the different outcome was based in the social capital inherent in the two communities, 'enabling one community to lobby and act much more effectively than the other' (2001, 171).

So how does creating networks of social capital make this possible? Clearly putting people in contact with one another is a first step towards such collaboration, and social capital measures the extent and density of such contacts. Contacts are not, in themselves, sufficient, however; it is always worth remembering that the baseline situation tends towards political apathy rather than demands for involvement in local planning activity (Clark, 2000). One of the key writers on social capital, Elinor Ostrom, emphasises the 'soft infrastructure' of social capital rather than the mere fact of being connected when understanding its effects. Her definition is as follows (2000, 176): 'It is the shared knowledge, understandings, norms, rules and expectations about patterns of interactions that groups of individuals bring to a recurrent activity.' She sees such social capital as helping to overcome short-term, perverse incentives and enable collective action to the mutual benefit of a group of people. Four different aspects of the operation of this soft infrastructure can be distinguished.

First there is the active creation of a common identity through the relationships between people and the way that they are maintained and reproduced in repeated interactions. The idea is that the existence of social capital, particularly bonding social capital helps to create this sense of a common identity and, further, generates feedback loops whereby strong network connections support a common identity and this common identity supports the bonding connections within local networks. Lelieveldt (2008) tells of how social capital was built in a Dutch street with the effect of reducing anti-social behaviour in public spaces. In Korenaardwarsstraat, Rotterdam, a greeting zone was inaugurated in January 2003 where it was advertised that 'greeting is allowed'. The result was an increase in social contacts and in social capital with positive results in terms of co-management of the street. Lelieveldt sees the attitudinal aspects of social capital as specifically helpful in affecting the perception of problems among local people.

In planning contexts, it has been suggested – using the concept of bracing social capital – that the combination of pockets of strong bonds with a set of weaker bonds can result in a strong sense of common purpose spreading across the network (Rydin and Holman, 2004). Key personnel (of the types that emerge in a number of the case studies in this book) can play an important role in ensuring that this sense of purpose permeates the network. These personnel are identified by being linked through bonding capital into the core group and also through bridging social capital into more peripheral organisations. This points to the way that local planners could help connect a group of people and, specifically, support a common identity and purpose through managing the weak links between strongly bonded sub-groups (see also the cases collected in Rydin and Falleth, 2006).

The second dynamic concerns the way that a group of people is encouraged and enabled to monitor each other and to exercise so-called 'soft sanctions'. The idea here is that people within the network will ensure that others behave so as to maintain network norms and fulfil the common purpose. They do this by using tactics of shaming and blaming. Coleman (2000) sees the operation of effective sanctions to support norms of obligations, expectations and general trustworthiness as one of the key ways that social relations within networks can constitute useful resources. Ostrom similarly stresses that the common understandings built up within a group can be readily eroded if a group expands or experiences rapid turnover in membership unless 'substantial efforts are devoted to transmission of the common understandings, monitoring behaviour in conformance with common understandings, and sanctioning behaviour not in conformance' (2000, 179). Looking at the micro scale of the 'traditional community', Halpern (2005, 12) discusses how social capital works within the network of neighbours through norms of reciprocity, due care of property and challenging strangers, and by the exercise of sanctions of recognition and honouring using gossip and social inclusion or exclusion.

Third, social capital within networks also raises the possibility of encounters between people being seen as a pleasure, rather than burdensome. Social capital is not called 'social' for nothing. Getting involved in activities to support the common purpose – whether attending a neighbourhood planning meeting or joining in a park clean-up weekend – can become a social activity with 'solidary benefits'. This means that people enjoy being involved and this positively encourages connections between people. Rydin and Pennington (2000) show how many local groups that form to protect and manage urban green spaces are sustained through the emphasis on sociability and enjoyable activities for members.

Fourth, networks with social capital can also be effective in spreading information and thereby enabling agreements because the density of linkages reduces transactions costs. Here the possibility of a network being (or coming close to being) a 'small world' is relevant; this means that most actors can be reached from all other actors in a small number of connections (Rydin, 2013). Being a small world potentially smooths the flow of information and makes commitments easier to negotiate. Coleman (2000) specifically identifies the relations of social capital as potential information channels. However, it is important to note that these are only potential channels. They have to be activated by people within the networks if the small world characteristics of a network are to be realised.

The hope of social capital is that through these means – of creating a common identity and purpose, social monitoring of the group, sociable enjoyment and easy transfer of information – communities will communicate more effectively, come to agreements more easily and take action to fulfil those agreements. Innes and Booher (2010) refer to this as 'network power'. They make a strong case that closely bonded networks enable members to communicate more openly and empathetically and thus create the conditions for agreement and subsequent action. This is a positive message for community planning.

The potential for negative outcomes

Positive outcomes may not always be so readily achieved by fostering social capital, however. Three negative possibilities are identified in the literature.

The first regards the nature of the agreement reached within a community. The idea that fostering networks with social capital of various kinds is likely to assist a community in delivering on a common purpose says nothing specific about that common purpose. It may be moral or immoral, sustainable or unsustainable, aimed at inclusion and justice or exclusion and maintaining inequalities. 'The existence of social capital does not necessarily entail just or democratic outcomes' (Maloney et al, 2000, 217).

Second, social capital is always about exclusion as well as inclusion. It cannot be assumed that strong local networks will involve all members (if that were possible) or even representatives of all sectors of a community. Clark (2000) reviews the research showing that the 'sizeable minority' (p 39) that do participate in local activism are dominated by people who are white, middle-class and middle-aged in 'self-perpetuating hierarchies' (p 176). He notes the 'widespread propensity for experienced and frequent participants to dominate proceedings within sites of political participation', acting as gatekeepers to the topics to be discussed and how they are to be discussed (pp 33–4). Batton and Ryfe found that (2005, 24):

> Over time, as participants shuffle in and out of self-selected groups initiated by voluntary associations, the groups risk being more exclusive and homogeneous. The bonding that takes place among the participants who return is bought at the price of cognitive diversity. One consequence may be that deliberation in such forums actually exacerbates group polarization, leaving participants with more extreme versions of the opinions with which they started.

The third point is particularly problematic for attempts at community planning. This refers to the way that the domination of community politics by a limited group adds to the professionalisation of public debate (Clark, 2000, 52) and how this can undermine the hopes of a more deliberative approach to planning. Procedures for participation can become a 'source of control and exclusion rather than an enabling forum in which the force of the better argument can hold sway' (p 177). Clark is pointing to the way that those who participate often are asked to do administrative work and that this affects the other types of political activity and debate in which they can engage (p 128). As a result, the involvement of civil society organisations and individuals in the 'business' of government can lead to political debate being curtailed. Eliasoph, in her study of participation, also found that people tend to avoid political discussion in favour of 'doing' things (1998, 6). Matthews' discussion in Chapter 3 of how planning timetables set by planners dictate the 'work' of communities is another example here. Interestingly, this is why Habermas argues that grassroots organisations should not cross the boundary into the administrative system because otherwise communicative rationality will be threatened (Outhwaite, 1996, 362).

The balance between positive collective action and these negative outcomes depends on the exact nature of the social capital generated. The final section explores the various factors that explain why social capital takes the form it does in specific situations.

Shaping social capital and influencing outcomes

The actual outcomes from the impact of social capital within community networks depend on the nature of that social capital. This section explores the factors that shape social capital and therefore determine those outcomes. It re-emphasises that social capital is not a static stock. Rather it is relational and has to be created and maintained.

Recognising inter-dependencies

The hope of network power is that the aggregation of social capital in terms of close relationships between people helps them achieve a common goal. The communicative conditions for this to happen are quite extreme, however, not only in procedural terms but also in terms of the expectations of the actors involved. Procedurally such movement towards agreement requires an emphasis on giving voice to all parties, listening as well as speaking and focusing on mutual understanding. This all takes considerable time and effort as well as expert facilitation to genuinely achieve deliberative encounters (Gastil and Levine, 2005; also discussed further below).

It also requires actors to see an advantage in coming together to work collectively. Innes and Booher (2010) identify this very clearly with their argument that network power can only work where actors recognise their inter-dependencies. Without this recognition, actors will not perceive the need to come together; and all actors have to recognise this, otherwise actors holding key resources for achieving a particular goal may withdraw from the collective effort. This is a demanding requirement. In many situations, some actors will not see themselves as dependent on others and rather seek to achieve their goals through independent action. Or they may only be interested in collective action to the extent that it meets their needs and refuse to accept that other actors' needs should also be considered.

Halpern (2005, 184) argues for members of communities to be tolerant of each other's views and wishes but this may not be easily achieved. To the extent that this is a matter of perceptions and framing, it might be managed by a key policy actor such as the local planner; but it also involves aspects of actors' roles and resources and the exercise of power within networks, as the rest of this section explores.

Actors' roles and resources

One danger of the social capital concept is that it can treat all members of a network as somehow equal and concentrates on the existence of connections between these members. Coleman (2000), for example, sees social capital as a public good available to all; however, Häkli and Minca query this public good characteristic of social capital, instead seeing social capital as an 'unevenly distributed resource that depends on the individual's ability to enact the power potentials that reside in their membership in social networks' (2009, 1). Indeed social capital is not a homogeneous resource: 'People are embedded in local networks in different degrees and in different ways' (Campbell, 2000, 193).

Different members of a community, therefore, bring different things to network relationships. This will shape the operation of the social capital existing within that community and have an impact on whose goals are being furthered by its development. So how do members of a community differ? Some may have particular institutional roles that give them greater influence within the network. This may give them control over the processes of collaboration and determine the outcomes of engagement between actors in terms of the consensus, compromise or agreement generated. For example, a prominent member of a local community may be given responsibility for setting up the forums through which discussion on a local plan or project may occur. How she exercises these responsibilities will affect which voices get heard, which issues seem most important to address and so on (Clark, 2000).

The discussions within local communities will be heavily affected by an appreciation of the resources that individual actors could bring to bear in their relationships with others. If it is known (or emerges during discussions) that a specific member of the community controls resources – finance, land and other property, media coverage, local standing and authority, personal connections outside the local area – which could be important for achieving a desired local goal, then that person will have the opportunity to influence the direction of discussions and the outcomes. The collective goal may even be reframed so that the interests of this actor are served. This does not necessarily mean that other members of the local community do not achieve their own individual and/or collective goals; but neither does it mean that they will. All that can be said is that the relationships of social capital provide the opportunity for actors with more resources to influence what happens as a result of community interactions.

Facing up to power

This discussion raises the issue of how power is manifested in a network (also discussed by Matthews, Chapter 3, this volume). Power can be understood in two ways in relation to networks. It can reside in the features and resources of individuals and organisations, so that an actor can be described as powerful and this power operates generally, in relation to everyone. For example, it is often assumed that ownership of financial resources gives an actor power in this general sense. Or, more in keeping with the relational ontology of network approaches, power can be seen as relational and a feature of the connections between people. This would put the emphasis onto how this actor is powerful in relation to other specific actors. So the holding of financial resources may be very influential in relation to some other actors, but resources of status, knowledge and forms of legitimate authority may be more important in relation to others.

However defined, the exercise of power within the networks is going to have an effect on the shape and impact of the associated social capital. It does not necessarily mean that the most central actor within a network will be the one with the greatest power. Powerful actors may actually be on the periphery of a network defined through frequent, dense and obvious connections. They may have a few select relationships through which power can be exercised. This power may influence the norms, patterns of trust, even the identity and apparently 'common' goals of the network as a whole.

Furthermore, power can spread from context to context. Coleman (2000) discusses the 'appropriable' nature of social organisations so that organisations established for one purpose can be used for another and, therefore, the social capital embedded in those organisations can be made available for a new purpose. Coleman sees this positively, arguing for the benefits of multiplex relationships where people are connected in several, different ways, compared to simplex relations which are singular; such multiplex relations allow the resources of one set of relationships to be used or 'appropriated' for another. They also, however, allow power relations in one context (say, local business connections) to have an effect in another context (say, a community planning initiative).

Shaping institutional structures

The above discussion of perceived inter-dependencies, actors' roles and resources and power relations within local networks all points to the importance of paying attention to the specific institutional arrangement in any context. Ostrom's work has particularly concerned the creation of institutional structures that facilitate the use and growth of social capital. She emphasises the potential role of the state in enabling rather than controlling decentralised collective action. For her, governments facilitate the creation of social capital when 'considerable space for self-organisation is authorized outside the realm of required government action' (2000, 182), although she recognises that social capital can also be destroyed (see also Maloney et al, 2000, 216). The term 'institutional structure' refers to the rules and routines that affect people's behaviour within organisational contexts. Such contexts can be a community setting such as a parish council or a volunteer-run community centre or local environmental NGO but also a neighbourhood planning effort where temporary institutional arrangements are put in place in order to prepare and implement the plan.

Behaviour in such contexts is shaped by formal and informal rules as to what is appropriate behaviour. Repeated appropriate behaviour results in routines that reinforce such rules. A strong 'logic of appropriateness' guides such behaviour (Rydin, 2003). As a result, a cycle can develop whereby appropriate behaviour reinforces routines that support the institutional rules. The opposite can happen whereby the 'failure' of people to adopt appropriate behaviour challenges the established routines and undermines the authority of prevailing rules. Furthermore, we have seen how social capital can support the maintenance and enforcement of such rules. What we have here is a complex interaction between individual behaviour, the rules and routines established by institutional structures and the exercise of social capital in encouraging positive behaviour for collective action and discouraging inappropriate behaviour. This suggests that the way that rules for interaction between people are set up and the way that routines are established and backed up by prevailing norms will have a significant impact on outcomes of network interactions. They may be able to help resist the influence of established roles, actors' resources and power relations. This puts considerable emphasis on the way that a community planning initiative is set up (Gastil and Levine, 2005).

The potential of social capital, therefore, needs to be seen in the context of these institutional structures of community planning, how they are drawn up and established over time. In their research into urban rehabilitation in Hungary, Füzér and Monostori (2012) recommend collaborative planning models because they create bridging social capital whereby local communities are linked to city managers, academics and urban planning experts. This is meant as an addition to established strong bonding social capital within urban communities, effectively arguing for the pattern of bracing social capital identified by Rydin and Holman (2004). Looking at the operation of various deliberative mechanisms such as citizens' juries, polls and forums, Carson and Hartz-Karp (2005) develop a model of a virtuous cycle of community engagement through deliberative democracy. In this, social capital drives community concerns and then community engagement. If this is deliberative, then issues become reframed and mutually acceptable solutions arise and are tested. This increases the local understanding of solutions and, at the same time, trust between decision-makers and the community. This, in turn, then builds more social capital.

One thing is clear: that building and using social capital in community planning is demanding. Potapchuk et al (2005) tell of attempts at neighbourhood planning in Hampton, Virginia which involved building leadership capacity through a neighbourhood college, creating new forums including a Neighbourhood Commission, reaching out to the wider community and specifically seeking to strengthen local citizenship and social capital. Throughout, they continually adapted and tried to learn. They conclude (p 262): 'Neighbourhood planning proved to be a slow, messy business demanding extensive creativity, flexibility, time and patience.' Furthermore 'planning is not a one-time event between the city staff and neighbourhoods but rather a long-term relationship of planning, doing, learning, and then planning some more' (p 265). Reviewing the role of social capital in underpinning effective local government, Halpern states: 'High social capital as manifested in high-trust, frequent meetings and freely flowing information among dense social networks can mean that the whole community is involved in decision-making, but it can also make the process time-consuming and extended' (2005, 173).

Community planning can, therefore, use embedded social capital to enable positive collective action but it is a challenge to make it work.

Conclusions for community planning

This chapter has reviewed the literature on community as networks and social capital, identifying how it works to enable collective action through: creating a common identity and purpose; social monitoring within the group to encourage participation and maintain common norms; making collective action sociable and enjoyable; and creating channels of communication for the easier flow of information flow and making of agreements. It has, however, also pointed to how these ambitions may be thwarted by agreement on a socially negative vision, exclusion of members of a community and the degeneration of

---

political deliberation into mundane governmental and organisational business. If the creation and maintenance of social capital within a community is to achieve positive outcomes, attention needs to be paid to the unequal distribution of resources between actors and the impact of power relations within networks. These often lie behind the failure to recognise mutual inter-dependencies within a community, a fundamental pre-requisite for network power to be effective. The key is to create institutional structures – within community planning exercises – that can resist the uneven distribution of power and resources across a community network. There are examples of such structures being effective within the collaborative and deliberative planning literature but it requires considerable time, effort and resources to make this work. The lessons for community planning are that building and fostered embedded social capital within local community networks can help but it is a challenging task. It is one that requires a clear-eyed look at the realities of community relations: the extent and nature of the network relationships; the character of the norms and how they are 'enforced'; the way that a mutual goal emerges and how it is framed; and the role of key gatekeepers in managing the weak and strong links across the network. If such clarity on existing community structures is achieved, then there is greater potential for community planning to use social capital to positive ends.

References

Baron, S, Field, J, Schuller, T, 2000, Social capital: A review and critique, in S Baron, J Field, T Schuller (eds) *Social capital: Critical perspectives*, pp 1–38, Oxford: Oxford University Press

Bartkus, VO, Davis, JH, (eds), 2009, *Social capital: Reaching out, reaching in Cheltenham*, Cheltenham: Edward Elgar

Batton, M, Ryfe, D, 2005, What can we learn from the practice of deliberative democracy?, in J Gastil, P Levine (eds) *The deliberative democracy handbook*, pp 20–33, San Francisco, CA: Jossey-Bass Books

Burton, L, Williams, T, 2001, This bird has flown: the uncertain fate of wildlife on closed military bases, *Natural Resources Journal*, 41, 4, 885–917

Campbell, C, 2000, Social capital and health: Contextualising health promotion with local community networks, in S Baron, J Field, T Schuller (eds) *Social capital: Critical perspectives*, pp 182–96, Oxford: Oxford University Press

Carson, L, Hartz-Karp, J, 2005, Adapting and combining deliberative designs: Juries, polls and forums, in J Gastil, P Levine (eds) *The deliberative democracy handbook*, pp 120–39, San Francisco, CA: Jossey-Bass Books

Castiglione, D, 2008, Introduction: Conceptual issues in social capital theory, in D Castiglione, J van Deth, G Wolleb (eds) *The handbook of social capital*, pp 13–21, Oxford: Oxford University Press

Castiglione, D, van Deth, J, Wolleb, G (eds), 2008, *The handbook of social capital*, Oxford: Oxford University Press

Clark, W, 2000, *Activism in the public sphere*, Aldershot: Ashgate

Coleman, J, 2000, Social capital in the creation of human capital, in P Dasgupta, I Serageldin (eds) *Social capital: A multi-faceted perspective*, pp 13–39, Washington, DC: The World Bank

Dasgupta, P, Serageldin, I (eds), 2000, *Social capital: A multi-faceted perspective*, Washington, DC: The World Bank

Eliasoph, N, 1998, *Avoiding politics: How Americans produce apathy in everyday life*, Cambridge: Cambridge University Press

Füzér, K, Monostori, J, 2012, Social capital, social exclusion and rehabilitation policy in the Hungarian urban context, in J Lewandowski, G Streich (eds) *Urban social capital: Civil society and city life*, pp 31–76, Aldershot: Ashgate

Gastil, J, Levine, P (eds), 2005, *The deliberative democracy handbook*, San Francisco, CA: Jossey-Bass Books

Gittell, R, Vidal, A, 1998, *Community organising: Building social capital as a development strategy*, Thousand Oaks, CA: SAGE

Granovetter, M, 1973, The strength of weak ties, *American Journal of Sociology* 78, 1360–80

Häkli, J, Minca, C (eds), 2009, *Social capital and urban networks of trust*, Aldershot: Ashgate

Halpern, D, 2005, *Social capital*, Cambridge: Polity Press

Innes, J, Booher, D, 2010, *Planning with complexity: An introduction to collaborative rationality for public policy*, London: Routledge

Lelieveldt, H, 2008, Neighbourhood politics, in D Castiglione, J van Deth, G Wolleb (eds) *The handbook of social capital*, pp 327–48, Oxford: Oxford University Press

Lewandowski, J, Streich, G (eds), 2012, *Urban social capital: Civil society and city life*, Aldershot: Ashgate

Maloney, W, Smith, G, Stoker, G, 2000, Social capital and associational life, in S Baron, J Field, T Schuller (eds) *Social capital: Critical perspectives*, pp 212–25, Oxford: Oxford University Press

Orbán, A, 2000, Cooperation and trust in urban residential communities, in J Lewandowski, G Streich (eds) *Urban social capital: Civil society and city life*, pp 77–113, Aldershot: Ashgate

Ostrom, E, 2000, Social capital: A fad or a fundamental concept?, in P Dasgupta, I Serageldin (eds), 2000, *Social capital: A multi-faceted perspective*, pp 172–82, Washington, DC: The World Bank

Outhwaite, W, 1996, *The Habermas reader*, Cambridge: Polity Press

Oxendine, A, 2012, City seclusion and social exclusion: How and why economic disparities harm social capital, in J Lewandowski, G Streich (eds) *Urban social capital: Civil society and city life*, pp 9–30, Aldershot: Ashgate

Potapchuk, W, Carlson, C, Kennedy, J, 2005, Growing governance deliberately: Lessons and inspirations from Hampton, Virginia, in J Gastil, P Levine (eds) *The deliberative democracy handbook*, pp 254–67, San Francisco, CA: Jossey-Bass Books

Rydin, Y, 2003, *Conflict, consensus and rationality in environmental planning: An institutional discourse approach*, Oxford: Oxford University Press

Rydin, Y, 2013, The issue network of zero carbon built environments: A quantitative and qualitative analysis, *Environmental Politics* 22, 3, 496–517

Rydin, Y, Falleth, E, 2006, *Networks and institutions in natural resource management*, Cheltenham: Edward Elgar

Rydin, Y, Holman, N, 2004, Re-evaluating the concept of social capital in achieving sustainable development, *Local Environment* 9, 2, 117–34

Rydin, Y, Pennington, M, 2000, Research social capital in local environmental policy contexts, *Policy and Politics* 28, 2, 33–49

Szreter, S, 2000, Social capital, the economy and education in historical perspective, in S Baron, J Field and T Schuller (eds) *Social Capital: Critical Perspectives*, pp 56–77, Oxford: OUP.

Taylor, M, 1987, *The possibility of cooperation*, Cambridge: Cambridge University Press

Woolcock, M, 1998, Social capital and economic development: Towards a theoretical synthesis and policy framework, *Theory and Society* 27, 151–208

3

Time, belonging and development: a challenge for participation and research

Peter Matthews

Introduction

Research accounts of collaborative events in development processes can appear oddly timeless. A focus on process can mean that if readers are not provided with dates, collaborative planning that may have occurred over many months or years can appear to have happened over a few meetings. Where no pre-existing history is acknowledged, accounts of conflict-ridden processes can make it seem that communities and developers were at loggerheads for only a brief period. This is not unique to planning research; because social science has more generally come to focus on the here and now, temporalities (as in the sense and construction of time as passed and passing) and histories have become increasingly side-lined (Pollitt, 2008; Savage, 2010b). Across a wide range of social science research 'the issue of time more generally, is one that is perpetually claimed to be overlooked by researchers' (Bastian, 2011, 6). In this chapter, I bring time to the fore, focusing on time as a factor in community-building and development. Furthermore, I highlight the varied temporalities – that is, experiences of time – that come together in planning and development processes creating conflict and the possibilities for consensus.

A good example of what this means in practice became apparent during the winter of 2013 when land-use planning became prime-time viewing in the UK with the BBC fly-on-the-wall documentary, *The Planners*. The dramatic voiceover at the start of the programme pitched it as a battle between the UK government prioritising new development for economic growth and concerned residents wanting to stop development – the NIMBYs. One particular segment got a great deal of attention. A volume housebuilder was proposing a large greenfield housing development on the edge of a rural town in the affluent county of Cheshire in the north of England. This met with fierce opposition and an organised campaign by concerned residents. Among these residents was a couple who were interviewed in their recently-built house that overlooked the site in question. Their house, of course, had been built on land that had very recently been greenfield itself. It was easy to dismiss this as typical NIMBYism – these people did not understand or acknowledge the strategic, long-term need for new housing and were resisting it even though they had benefited enormously from previous development. At play, however, were varied temporalities and experiences of time – the residents' modern homes had come to be understood as part of the 'historic' limits of the town; the immediacy of the recession and developer demands were rushing the planning process on; the longer-term vision of the planners in Cheshire was to deliver more affordable housing in a pressured location.

It is the contention of this chapter that gaining a richer appreciation of experiences such as this is crucial to understanding community engagement in planning processes and particularly whether collaborative planning can ever meet the ideals of collaborative rationality (Healey, 1997; Innes and Booher, 2010). Debates around collaborative planning and community engagement in planning processes have not fully interrogated time in all its forms – historic time; imagined time; developers' time; policy-makers' time; community time – in order to understand when and how consensus on development might occur. The result is a static concept of community as something that is simply there, ignoring that 'time has a major influence on the ways in which various community processes are interconnected' and that particularly 'the neglect of community time reproduces static typologies which fail to capture the dynamic nature of community formation and development' (Crow and Allan, 1995, 147). This means the development itself is often simplified – it is just controversial or something around which consensus develops through good practice.

In this chapter I will dissect these varied temporalities through a review of research in human geography and planning, focusing on place connectedness. Further, the meanings imbued in buildings over time are considered, in order to understand development and change as a trigger for conflict and consensus. Focusing on time and development outcomes – the buildings created and the meanings they assume – brings us to the heart of two questions this book seeks to answer: What is community?, and What does planning look like and what does it *mean* for communities? Specifically it produces subsets of these questions: How does community include the buildings and development within it?, and an important question: How do these meanings change over time? In order to deliver a more complete account of community empowerment, these questions need answering.

History, locality, narrative and belonging

It is easy to state that places have history which is (re)constructed by communities. That this history is contested and used in contemporary political debates about the future of places is less readily grasped, however. Indeed, planning policies and their outputs and outcomes are inherently part of a richer history. Planning has shaped our modern built environment, but this environment is then in turn subject to further development and planning. In case studies of community engagement, this *longue duree* of planning history is often invisible (Matthews, 2013). Places and communities that have been the subject of planning policies over an extended period are quite often presented as a *tabula rasa* experiencing planning and development for the first time, bringing their stories, meanings, grievances and experiences to a policy process afresh. Alternatively, communities are presented as already existing, undifferentiated, and largely opposed to new developments. Complexity and nuance is not fully explored and the dynamics of community change, and the relationship of these communities to their built environment over time is not interrogated.

Broader neighbourhood and community studies from human geography present a very different account of place-based communities. Here communities are rich in history and collective memories, much of it derived from previous political experiences of development and urban change. For example, Talja Blokland's detailed description of a neighbourhood in New Haven, Connecticut (Blokland, 2008; 2009), focuses on the collective memories and belonging among a diverse range of communities: incoming gentrifiers; Italian Americans, many of whom had moved away but retained a sense of belonging in the neighbourhood; and the poor, predominantly black residents of nearby housing projects. For Blokland:

> collective memories are not just memories shared when people interact. They can also be containers of stories that one personally has not lived through...With such containers, a community positions itself and sets boundaries, especially when what is cherished is related to a place that the group has lived with for a long time. (Blokland, 2009, 1595)

Subsequently:

> such memories are...forms of everyday politics...Such
> memories create symbolic representations that help to
> define who is and who is not part of 'the community'
> (although not necessarily willingly so) and what 'the
> community' needs. Such narratives thus contribute to place
> identities that in turn affect the distribution of resources in
> an urban system. (Blokland, 2009, 1609)

These collective memories also incorporate stories of development
and policy – such as a shared, but contested narrative of the gentrifiers
and the Italian American community who recognised that the
neighbourhood was historic when it was threatened by a major highway
development (Blokland, 2009). Alternatively, there was the stigmatised
sense of place negotiated by the African American residents who have
little choice but to live in the projects (Blokland, 2008).

That these collective memories are varied, complex and contested
also highlights how place belonging, and the political action that derives
from it, is very much elective and even selective.

In their research on place belonging, Mike Savage and his colleagues
interpret place attachment as part of a person's symbolic and cultural
capital that produces their social class position and identity (Bagnall et
al, 2003; Savage, 2010a). For middle class, more affluent households,
very much like the Cheshire households given voice in *The Planners*,
this is an elective belonging. This sense of belonging has an historic
temporality, and the 'culturally engaged' middle classes who share it:

> evince a sense of investment in place which links aesthetic
> and ethical values and an emphasis on 'choice'...The
> culturally engaged middle classes are highly vested in
> their place of residence, which they claim to have actively
> 'chosen', and which conveys great symbolic meaning,
> and a sense of their own self-worth, their identity, and a
> proclamation of who they are. (Savage, 2010a, 128)

When this sense of self-worth is challenged, the sense of belonging
becomes more selective. Watt's (2009) study of the residents of
'Woodlands' – a modern housing estate neighbouring an estate of
socially-rented housing outside London – demonstrates how residents
disaffiliate from many aspects of a neighbourhood which they do not
like. The limited economic resources of residents meant that many

who lived in the area aspired to housing in 'better' places. Even so, they had great attachment to their estate, to the quality of the homes and its 'faux-rurality', suburban character, but actively sought to distance themselves from the nearby social housing with its stigmatised image. They worked hard to ensure that their children did not have to attend the local schools; they avoided the local pubs; and went shopping in more affluent towns some distance away rather than in the local parade of shops. When this selective belonging was challenged by a planning application for a large new housing estate:

> the residents mobilised their social capital and economic capital resources by rapidly forming an action group and raising money in order to employ outside consultants. The action group and consultants produced a professional-looking document opposing the application and this, alongside several hundred protest letters, was sent to the local council. One of the main reasons for opposition to the development was that the [rural] 'character and layout' of the estate would be damaged. (Watt, 2009, 2885–6)

In the examples provided by Blokland and by Watt we can see that different histories and time are essential to a sense of belonging. An imagined history, a 'faux rurality', helped the residents of Woodland differentiate themselves. In both cases the sense of belonging evinced by these shared histories was a trigger to political action and engagement, to improve a neighbourhood and resist new development respectively.

As discussed in Chapter 1, the developing technologies of web 2.0 and social media are producing an online extension of this belonging (Wellman, 2001; Couclelis, 2004). Whereas early digital utopians saw the internet as transcending place and contributing to a sense of globalised distanciated propinquity, the banal reality is that the social and cultural capital owned and deployed by residents in the offline world is deployed in the online world as part of their socially-mediated public self (Baym and Boyd, 2012). This means that, increasingly, places are mirrored by a virtual place – a record of historic and current social connections and collective memory in the cloud. In my own research in the neighbourhood of Wester Hailes in Edinburgh, a deprived neighbourhood since it was first constructed in 1968, a Facebook page run by the local housing association – where historic photos of the neighbourhood are posted – is demonstrating similarly complex place belonging. In this case, belonging is expressed through the comments left by the more than 2,000 residents and former residents who 'like' the page. As with Blokland's Italian Americans, former residents of Wester Hailes use the nostalgia evoked by the images as part of their self-identity, and as a defence of where they grew up. Although many have moved away from the area, the images and positive stories associated with them instil a sense of pride in being from Wester Hailes. Others display the complex disaffiliation of Watt's Woodside residents, being happy to associate themselves with positive memories, but tempering these with the more difficult stories of growing up in a neighbourhood marked by very poor quality housing, high levels of unemployment and crime and anti-social behaviour (Matthews, submitted manuscript).

A plethora of community studies show clearly the complexity of communities and people's attachment to places. Although they tend to focus on the people within these communities, the built environment created by development and planning processes also plays a key role in generating a sense of place and belonging, giving broader and richer 'meaning' to the community.

Interpretive policy analysis and the built environment

Collaborative planning is heavily informed by interpretive approaches to policy making and policy analysis, indeed they share the same epistemological roots (Forester, 1993; Fischer, 2003; Healey, 2009; Innes and Booher, 2010). In planning research the focus of interpretive research has tended to be on dissecting planning processes; the approach has not been widely used to understand the built environment generated by those planning processes. Buildings, both homes and other structures, are also part of people's shared stories of belonging and these have political power in development processes. The built environment is rich with meanings for individuals within communities, and is part of what makes community for these individuals. These meanings are complex, interlaced and temporally varied, based on residence and the experience of lived time and historic time which individuals can evoke and selectively belong to. The research question then becomes: How can a development mean?

In her similarly titled book *How does a policy mean?* Dvora Yanow (1996) explored how the design of Israel's post-war community centres carried a number of meanings. First, the modern, open design carried the ambition of the policy of the Israeli Corporation of Community Centres to deliver this new kind of development in the socialist utopianism of the Israeli state. The concept of a community centre was so new to Hebrew culture that there was not a word or phrase that could be used to denote such a building. Therefore the buildings, with their modern, open design, had to carry the policy intention of creating a place where new migrants could meet and build community, engaging in a range of activities. By the 1990s, the symbolism and meaning of the new buildings had changed – now communities of new migrants, often from former Communist countries, saw the building of a new community centre as recognition of a need by the state and investment in the community.

In my own research in Scotland, particular buildings and the wider built environment is part of a complex narrative of policy intervention and community history dating back over 30 years. New, modern housing built during regeneration partnerships that ran from 1989 to 1999, and which replaced very poor quality housing, today testifies to the decades of fighting for improvements in the housing stock. Much of this housing was delivered by community-led housing associations, which grew from decades of activism. These developments therefore signify the way in which communities played a leading part in triggering a policy response and a subsequent development outcome (Matthews, 2012a). On the other hand, the same developments also say much about the way in which a focus on new housing failed to deliver against the wider needs of communities, leaving many in a state of concentrated deprivation, albeit with an improved physical fabric.

Most 'meaning-full' in this way was a community centre in one neighbourhood, Ferguslie Park. For activists, the centre that was supposed to have been for the community and run by the community was symbolic of how the community had been ignored. Ever since its completion in 1995 rents had been too high for community groups to use the facilities. Many of the rooms initially intended for these groups had been slowly taken over by other statutory organisations as they expanded. The building was regarded by the community as a 'white elephant' – it had technically gone bankrupt and ownership eventually passed from the local authority to the local housing association to make it sustainable. For community activists, many of whom had been fighting for improvements to the neighbourhood for 20 or 30 years, the building was emblematic of the way the community had been treated by statutory authorities and was tied to broader stigma towards the neighbourhood and how they were dismissed as 'feegies'[1] (Collins, 1999; Matthews, 2013). In the way development is interpreted and reinterpreted over time in communities, through social capital and discourse, its meaning for the community changes and can, occasionally, settle. Alternatively, it can remain as a symbol of conflict and tension, furthering political action in the present.

Time, meaning and the development process

From these two themes we can argue that, first, history and time are very important to communities and should be more important in research about communities. The social construction of time and the history of the neighbourhood are used in political action and in the future development of the community. Second, buildings and development are part of these histories, and their meanings are fluid. These meanings become less fluid and more fixed and settled over time. Bringing these arguments together we can put time and temporal dimensions centre stage in analyses of processes of community, development and place-making to produce more complex and nuanced accounts. In particular, these need to highlight how community is not an *a priori* category there for a planning system, or researchers, to engage with. There needs to be a greater sensitivity to time, history and temporalities both from planners carrying out community engagement and empowerment and researchers investigating these processes.

A sensitivity to time and the social construction of time means that we need to focus on the differing temporalities of actors and how they engage or clash. How the different temporalities of communities and policy-makers can rub up against each was apparent in the regeneration processes discussed in the previous section. It had taken over a decade for these communities, subject to regeneration and redevelopment, to reach a stage where some of the meanings ascribed to the built environment were stable. Bitterness over the broken promises and the way in which the communities had been treated in the regeneration partnership arrangements in the 1990s was still clearly apparent a decade later:

> NO THANK YOU [shouting]. I was looking forward to moving back into [street] where I'd raised my five kids. An' that's why everyone agreed to move at the time the land use strategy that was drafted up for the area quite clearly showed that new housing would be rebuilt on the site...but it never ever happened. So, if you like, we were given false information by the powers that be or else we would never've agreed to the demolition going ahead. (Community Activist, Ferguslie Park)

More positive experiences associated with, and made meaningful by, the built environment co-existed with this bitterness. All these meanings and shared stories helped the community activists understand

and make sense of policy changes that were occurring around them, empowering them to renew the activism of previous decades now that they found themselves in a world of strategic policy which they struggled to understand (Matthews, 2013).

For strategic planners, developing a forward vision, time was very different and this history burdensome. As one strategic officer leading community engagement expressed:

> '[neighbourhood] for example [has] got 12 neighbourhood councils that consist of a street next to another street which is a neighbourhood council next to another street which is another separate neighbourhood council and my head popped when I came here and I thought, 'What is all that?'

The neighbourhood councils were organisations that had a 20- or 30-year history of meaning and belonging for community activists and were closely tied to experiences of delivering improvement and the regeneration a decade previously. With a simple decision to cut funding, based on the view that they were overly-complex, this collective memory was destroyed to be replaced with a single organisation that suited the local authority's processes, structures and time. This is not unique to strategic decision-making without community collaboration; as Innes and Booher found in their research on collaborative processes, conflicting temporalities such as this 'surfaces a common dilemma in collaborative problem solving, where an emphasis on the future may neglect all that led up to the problem and interfere with building a sound foundation for a way forward' (2010, 58).

These differing temporalities are apparent in development processes and in our understanding of them. Developers, especially those looking for a rapid return on their investment, need the development processes to happen quickly, before the fluctuating and fracturing real estate markets undermines profitability (Adams and Tiesdell, 2010). They do not have the time for the lengthy engagement processes which the advocates of collaborative rationality argue will deliver greater consensus and reduced conflict (Healey, 1997; Innes and Booher, 2010). The result, particularly in a regulatory system like that of the UK, is that the trade-off between community engagement and 'efficiency' in decision-making regularly prioritises efficiency. The state is burdened with the duty to engage communities quickly, to achieve a quick fix in a limited time period – collaborative planning in an un-collaborative world (Brand and Gaffikin, 2007). Delays to planning processes – created by the need to engage and listen to communities, and even accept their grievances and perhaps halt or substantially change development proposals – can be ultimately overcome by Ministers[2] 'calling-in' decisions, forcing an outcome for the sake of 'sustainable economic growth' – most famously and controversially in Scotland with the case of Donald Trump's golf course resort at Menie on the north-east coast of Scotland (Jönsson, 2014).

With the burden for engagement placed on planning authorities, this raises the issue of which communities have the capacity to meet the statutory timescales set out by policy-makers. For example, the planning regime in Scotland sets a demanding target for plans to be updated every five years. This effectively means that once a plan has been adopted, the process of engaging on the next plan begins in earnest once again. Planners are now commenting on how communities are getting 'used' to this constant engagement process. The 'empowerment' of communities is not an outcome, but rather a never-ending process with little let-up. Policy is creating time and temporalities and expecting communities to fit in (Fitzpatrick, 2004). There is a widespread acknowledgement, although a much smaller research base, that it is the most able and affluent communities that can engage with planning processes effectively (Matthews and Hastings, 2013). As discussed in the previous chapter, they have the social capital, in terms of links to local politicians and policy makers, in their groups to gain influence and knowledge. They also have the cultural capital, in terms of knowledge of planning processes and what technical planning terms might mean. What is important, as Abram et al (1996) show, is that this cultural capital again has a temporal dimension – over time these affluent communities learn from previous unsuccessful engagements with the planning system to target their efforts at the best time in planning processes in order to have the biggest impact and the greatest chance of success, whatever that means. Time and temporalities are therefore also unjustly distributed in societies, and policy can often reinforce this injustice (Fitzpatrick, 2004).

Thus sensitivity to time is not just about the past, but also how this is projected into the future. A central tenet of collaborative planning is bringing the local and immediate concerns of communities into a strategic and longer-term realm of discourse within planning processes, a Habermasian coming together of interests (Innes and Booher, 2010). As stated, affluent, well connected, knowledgeable communities are more likely to find this process easier. Interpreting this behaviour as NIMBYist, like the attitudes of the Cheshire residents at the start of this chapter, however, we can critically see it as the alignment of these residents' immediate wishes to avoid the symbolic and economic diminution of the value of their property, with longer-term strategic issues of sustainable development (Sturzaker and Shucksmith, 2012). Arguably, these residents are no different in their outlook and inherent interests from residents of deprived neighbourhoods who prioritise immediate change through new housing and environmental projects over longer-term public health and education projects (Matthews, 2012a; Lawless, 2013). The main difference is the ability to articulate claims within the temporalities and cultural capital of planners.

That time is an expression of power, and that it produces agency, leads us to consider critical temporalities. As defined by Bastian (Bastian, 2013) 'a critical temporality is a time that is imagined, theorised or lived in order to make a better world'. The agonist critiques of actual existing collaborative planning processes suggest that the temporality of planning processes is producing a worse world – the pressure to engage in the timescales of developers and planners leads to conflict and processes of engagement cannot produce consensus (Huxley, 2000; Brand and Gaffikin, 2007). To bring a critical temporality into planning practice and research we need to fully understand and appreciate 'community time', a time that: 'is measured not only in terms of annual acts of symbolic renewal, it is also concerned with the rhythms of interaction in ordinary people's lives, the very essence of community' (Crow and Allan, 1995, 159).

Part of this interaction is with the built environment. Through intricate webs of meaning developments and new buildings can share this essence, and become symbolic parts of community memory and stories. Collaborative planning, as theorised and explored by Patsy Healey, is particularly sensitive to this. As she argued in her defence of collaborative planning, the aim of collaborative planning was to radically alter planning processes so that 'people can become aware that what they do in routine ways is not inherently "natural", but has become "natural" through a social history of acceptance and embedding' (Healey, 2003, 113–14) and this has to include both a sensitivity to, and awareness of, temporal dimensions of meaning-making and consensus-building, sharing and challenging social histories. The longevity of these processes of coming together are exemplified in many case studies of good collaborative planning and rationality, such as the case studies of Innes and Booher (2003; 2010, 41–88). A striking example of this is the experience of government-to-government planning with indigenous peoples in Canada. With the wounds of colonialism, these processes of collaborative planning involved extensive processes of capacity building on both sides to develop trust and understand grievances, injustices and very different relationships to land (Barry, 2012).

A sensitivity to the temporality of community enables us to understand different aspects of time: the deep time of history and shared stories; the imagined time of selectively or electively belonging to a projected history that aligns to cultural values; the shared experience and stories of broken promises, or distrust and broken relationships with planners and developers; the immediate past of the last partnership meeting where the selective amnesia of planners and developers has led to another broken promise. It also enables us to answer the criticism that: 'planning scholarship has become far too wrapped up in consensus politics and has, for the most part, turned its attention away from the political, and from conflict. A significant portion of scholarship effort in planning is orientated around what alarmingly often amounts to analyses of niceness and benevolence' (Porter, 2011, 478).

Research on place which is sensitive to the multiple dimensions of time demonstrates how shared memories are vital to producing conflict now and charging people with anger and emotion as they enter into political debates. Poor planning practice, which is insensitive to this, will be little more than 'niceness and benevolence'. Yet, as I have tried to demonstrate here and in my own research (Matthews, 2013), it is in this protracted, historic time, that we can see the vestiges of Habermasian-type consensus emerging. For those researching planning processes the question therefore is how do we bring this rich temporality and an understanding of community time to the fore in our research on community engagement and community planning? How do we account for the social construction of time and its relational nature, the 'struggles between collective actors over, and within, social time?' (Fitzpatrick, 2004, 211). If our scholarship is to move away from accounts of 'niceness and benevolence' we also have to demonstrate how we can make time in collaborative processes for temporalities to be explored, and for critical temporalities to be developed.

Notes

[1] A derogatory term used locally for people from Ferguslie Park.

[2] That is, law-makers in central government.

References

Abram, S, Murdoch, J, Marsden, T, 1996, The social construction of 'Middle England': The politics of participation in forward planning, *Journal of Rural Studies* 12, 4, 353–64

Adams, D, Tiesdell, S, 2010, Planners as market actors: Rethinking state–market relations in land and property, *Planning Theory & Practice* 11, 2, 187–207

Bagnall, G, Longhurst, BJ, Savage, M, 2003, Children, belonging and social capital: The PTA and middle class narratives of social involvement in the North-West of England, *Sociological Research Online* 8, 4, http://usir.salford.ac.uk/1487/

Barry, J, 2012, Indigenous state planning as inter-institutional capacity development: The evolution of government-to-government relations in coastal British Columbia, Canada, *Planning Theory and Practice*, 13, 2, 213–31

Bastian, M, 2011, *Temporal connectivities: A scoping study of the available research on time and community*, Swindon: Arts and Humanities Research Council (AHRC)

Bastian, M, 2013, *Power, time and agency: Exploring the role of critical temporalities – A collaborative multi-disciplinary workshop*, httpwww.temporalbelongings.org/power-time-and-agency.html

Baym, NK, Boyd, D, 2012, Socially mediated publicness: An introduction, *Journal of Broadcasting & Electronic Media* 56, 3, 320–29

Blokland, T, 2008, 'You got to remember you live in public housing': Place-making in an American housing project, *Housing, Theory and Society* 25, 1, 31–46

Blokland, T, 2009, Celebrating local histories and defining neighbourhood communities: Place-making in a gentrified neighbourhood, *Urban Studies* 46, 8, 1593–610

Brand, R, Gaffikin, F, 2007, Collaborative planning in an uncollaborative world, *Planning Theory* 6, 3, 282–313

Collins, C, 1999, Applying Bakhtin in urban studies: The failure of community participation in the Ferguslie Park Partnership, *Urban Studies* 36, 1, 73–90

Couclelis, H, 2004, The construction of the digital city, *Environment and Planning B: Planning and Design* 31, 1, 5–19

Crow, GP, Allan, G, 1995, Community types, community typologies and community time, *Time & Society* 4, 2, 147–66

Fischer, F, 2003, *Reframing public policy: Discursive politics and deliberative practices*, Oxford University Press: Oxford

Fitzpatrick, T, 2004, Social policy and time, *Time & Society* 13, 2–3, 197–219

Forester, J, 1993, *Critical theory, public policy, and planning practice: Towards a critical pragmatism*, State University of New York Press: New York City

Healey, P, 1997, *Collaborative planning: Shaping places in fragmented societies*, Macmillan: Basingstoke

Healey, P, 2003, Collaborative planning in perspective, *Planning Theory*, 2, 2, 101–23

Healey, P, 2009, The pragmatic tradition in planning thought, *Journal of Planning Education and Research* 28, 277–92

Huxley, M, 2000, The limits to communicative planning, *Journal of Planning Education and Research* 19, 4, 369–77

Innes, JE, Booher, DE, 2003, Collaborative policymaking: Governance through dialogue, in MA Hajer, H Wagenaar, H (eds) *Deliberative policy analysis: Understanding governance in the network society*, pp 33–59, Cambridge University Press: Cambridge

Innes, JE, Booher, DE, 2010, *Planning with complexity: An introduction to collaborative rationality for public policy*, Routledge: London

Jönsson, E, 2014), Contested expectations: Trump International Golf Links Scotland, polarised visions, and the making of the Menie Estate landscape as resource, *Geoforum*, 52, 0, 226–35

Lawless, P, 2013, Reconciling 'bottom-up' perspectives with 'top-down' change data in evaluating area regeneration schemes, *European Planning Studies*, 1–16

Matthews, P, 2012a, From area-based initiatives to strategic partnerships: Have we lost the meaning of regeneration?, *Environment and Planning C: Government and Policy* 30, 1, 147–61

Matthews, P, 2012b, Problem definition and re-evaluating a policy: The real successes of a regeneration scheme, *Critical Policy Studies* 63, 243–60

Matthews, P, 2013 , The longue durée of community engagement: New applications of critical theory in planning research, *Planning Theory* 12, 2, 139–57

Matthews, P, submitted manuscript, Neighbourhood belonging and social media: Providing ladders to the cloud, *Housing Studies*

Matthews, P, Hastings, A, 2013, Middle-class political activism and middle-class advantage in relation to public services: A realist synthesis of the evidence base, *Social Policy & Administration* 47, 1, 72–92

Pollitt, C, 2008, *Time, Policy, Management: Governing with the Past*, Oxford: Oxford University Press

Porter, L, 2011, The point is to change it, *Planning Theory & Practice* 12, 4, 477–80

Savage, M, 2010a, Class and elective belonging, *Housing, Theory and Society* 27, 2, 115–36

Savage, M, 2010b, *Identities and Social Change in Britain Since 1940: the Politics of Method*, Oxford: Oxford University Press

Sturzaker, J, Shucksmith, M, 2012, Planning for housing in rural England: Discursive power and spatial exclusion, *Town Planning Review* 82, 2, 169–94

Watt, P, 2009, Living in an oasis: Middle-class disaffiliation and selective belonging in an English suburb, *Environment and Planning A: Environment and Planning* 41, 12, 2874–92

Wellman, B, 2001, Physical place and cyberplace: The rise of personalized networking, *International Journal of Urban and Regional Research* 25, 2, 227–52

Yanow, D, 1996, *How does a policy mean? Interpreting policy and organizational actions*, Washington, DC: Georgetown University Press

Part 2
Contexts and drivers for community action

The first series of case-study based chapters focus on the contexts in which community action takes root, and the drivers which push it towards particular goals. These chapters explore four different contexts: the role of neighbourhood associations in Spain in negotiating the transition to democracy in the 1970s, and the way they subsequently played a major role in Spanish politics and the determination of public policy agendas; community support triggered by crisis in farming and fishing communities in rural Australia; the extremely challenging socio-economic environment for community 'empowerment' in Marseille; and an island community in Scotland using the acquisition of land as a platform for community development.

The emergence of community action from these very diverse contexts reveals that such action can be triggered in a number of ways. Vilà shows clearly, in Chapter 4, that a lack of national democracy provides a fertile context for the growth of local action as people seek to take greater control of their lives and their neighbourhoods. The Spanish example illustrates the effects of a very extreme form of democratic deficit and also the way in which local groups seek to counterbalance the power of the state even when representative government appears to have addressed that deficit. In a very different environment, Kilpatrick, Willis and Lewis focus on the self-help benefits of communities that 'pull together' in what they refer to as 'difficult times'. In the deeply rural context examined in Chapter 5, it was never likely that state services were going to be able to address the health challenges – physical and psychological – of remoter communities given their limited resources. Therefore, these communities were left to develop soft services through existing social networks, relying on their existing store of social capital, and on its expansion through the building of new links with private sector partners. The real context here is one of *socio-economic crisis*, leading to a clear community response. The case of Marseille shares some similarities with Barcelona 50 years ago. Messaoudène, Pinson and Berra show very vividly how local residents struggle to exert their rights in the context of a tradition of interventionist government, which arguably views communities – and the broader idea of 'community' – as a threat to statehood, attempting to iron out local difference rather than celebrating it. In Marseille, we see how some of the poorest communities in Europe engage in a daily battle against incredible challenges and how some win remarkable victories against the insensitivity of the local and national state, and this is despite a pattern of social and ethnic fragmentation which makes it difficult to identify clear communities. On the Isle of Gigha, on the other hand, an opportunity for an extremely different and 'closely-knit' community to take control of a key asset – that is, the island itself – was created through land reform in Scotland. The incentive to do so came from an indifferent experience of land ownership (a series of 'bad lairds' as Satsangi puts it in Chapter 7) which delivered few benefits for the community. Out of this context a desire for empowerment grew, with the community ultimately using the acquisition of land as a platform for further community development.

In the four chapters that follow, four very different contexts for community action and planning are laid bare. They deal with the desire of communities to win rights from an undemocratic state (in the case of Spain) and then retain those rights during the transition to democracy; with community action as a product of crises which the 'state' is incapable of resolving; with sustained action that evolves from more basic struggles against poverty and prejudice; and with key episodes in community development that lead to bigger, sustained actions.

4

From residents to citizens: the emergence of neighbourhood movements in Spain

Gemma Vilà

Introduction

This chapter analyses the emergence and development of community-based action in Spain. It focuses on its origins and the conditions making it possible, its development and characteristics, as well as its significance, not only in regard to urban planning, but also in the construction and consolidation of local democracy.

The emergence and development of community-based action was determined by a key factor that has differentiated Spain from other western European countries: its recent history of dictatorship and its subsequent transition to democracy. Despite the end of the dictatorship and the establishment of democratic institutions at all levels of government, this deeper history has had a marked impact on the development and mood of civil society in general, and that of community-based action regarding urban development, in particular. To analyse the origins and characteristics of community-based action it is necessary to understand the process of democratic construction that took place during the Francoist period, which was strongly rooted in the actions of politically active local communities that developed clandestinely during the dictatorship. This ultimately broad opposition movement brought together very heterogeneous people and organisations. The longing, however, for freedom, justice, participation and democracy permeated, from the very beginning, the objectives and forms of action and organisation of the civil society that was being forged and strengthened in the last years of the dictatorship.

In this context, there was one group of organisations that played a fundamental role and that specifically emerged from debates regarding urban space and development. These were the neighbourhood associations. Established during the Franco regime to demand improvements in neighbourhood living conditions, their actions went beyond this specific objective and the form of their actions and organisation generated a strong local democratic dynamic based on the local community. These neighbourhood associations were set up to be a reference for citizen participation and civic demands, especially in the major cities, and they contributed to empowering neighbourhood residents and constructing a critical and active citizenry. The democratic character that they acquired from their very beginnings as organisations, granted them significant legitimacy among the population. In this sense, these associations played a major role in the initial years of democracy, both in improving life in the cities, as well as in the creation and consolidation of a democratic logic.

Since their establishment, the neighbourhood associations have passed through various stages, some of greater glory, others more critical. In this process they have become spaces for reflection and debate over urban issues, and through their diverse activities they have had significant influence on the construction of the city. Today, they still play a fundamental part in the city through their participation, and by acting as a platform for a network that connects other social and urban movements. Of particular importance is the role they have played in urban planning: studying and analysing urban development projects, they have generated public debate, have participated in the design of interventions and have changed the direction of or even halted projects that have not had the support of the community. All this has been done based on a decentralised organisational model, articulated through a coordinator, and independent from the local government. Over time, the activity of neighbourhood associations has consolidated the existence of a stable and extensive neighbourhood movement that today provides a reference in urban debates and the construction of the city, and in defence of values such as justice and equity. This dual function, improvement of urban neighbourhoods and the creation and consolidation of democracy at the local level, makes Spain's neighbourhood associations both a particular and representative case that justifies in-depth analysis.

To achieve the aim of exploring the origins and characteristics of community-based action in Spain, this chapter focuses on neighbourhood movements as the main exponents of community-based action. Focus is placed on the analysis of the conditions that favoured the emergence of the neighbourhood movement, the key factors in its development, and its characteristics in terms of its organisation and forms of action. Its impact on urban planning and the significance it has had in the construction of the city and in shaping local democracy will also be analysed. The chapter explores the particular case of Barcelona, a city where the neighbourhood movement has had great presence and impact. The relationship between this movement and the local government is one of the key elements of the so-called Barcelona model. The characteristics of this model and the analysis of specific cases, especially linked to the transformation of the north east of the city, will serve as the backdrop for understanding the case we present. The ultimate aim of this chapter is to reveal the factors that contributed to favouring the development of community-based action, as well as those aspects of that action that have brought positive and negative results in the Spanish case. This permits us to provide some reflections on this case and compare it with other experiences to evaluate the extent to which these factors can guide the actions of other movements and local governments.

Community-based action through the neighbourhood movement: urban policies and the deepening of democracy

The intervention of the population in planning is explained, to a great extent, by a series of initiatives and the establishment of organisations that, arising directly from civil society, generated a structure of bottom-up participation. This participation took place, in some cases, within the legal framework for processes of participation.[1] In others, it defied laws and created spaces of representation and change where none had previously existed. In the Spanish case, community-based action had a key agent that acted as a reference and focal point for local actions: the neighbourhood movements.

A historical perspective is necessary to understand the significance of the neighbourhood movement and its role as a participant in urban policy. The process of formation of this movement in this historical, political and economic context and in the initial years of democracy, has marked the strategies and leitmotif of the movement up to the present time and given it a strong democratic character (Alabart, 2010). Thus, it has an importance that goes beyond strictly urban issues: the history of the neighbourhood movement is a synthesis of the construction of a democratic citizenry in Spain over the last 40 years (Pérez and Sánchez, 2008). Although neighbourhood associations exist across the country, the movement gathers together broad social representation that translates into a particularly strong presence in Spain's major cities, especially Madrid and Barcelona. The neighbourhood movements in both cities share a history, demands and objectives, but both also have their specificities resulting from their local context, and in the case of Barcelona, its regional context.

The analysis of the neighbourhood movement in this chapter covers a period of 40 years, a period of time that includes many economic, political and social transformations of great import. As a result, the neighbourhood movement has had to respond to changing contexts, resulting in diverse challenges and changes over time in its objectives, strategies, forms of action and, above all, in its relation to local government. Addressing these changes, in the specific case of Barcelona, three major stages can be identified: the first refers to the origin of the neighbourhood movement (1970–5), the second to its growth and subsequent crisis (1975–92), and the third to a change in the role of the movement in a new context (1992–2013). In what follows we analyse the characteristics of the neighbourhood movement in each of these stages, identifying the key factors that explain its role in community-based action.

The origin of the neighbourhood movement and the emergence of community-based action (1970–5)

The origin of the movement of neighbourhood associations is found in the final years of Francosim. Its roots are in the political repression and in the major structural deficits that the cities suffered as a result of their lack of infrastructure, services and facilities to cover the needs of their populations. At this time, Barcelona also faced the consequences of massive waves of migrants from the rest of Spain. These migrants increased the city's population and saturated its physical capacities. As a consequence of the structural problems of a lack of housing and a lack of resources, a significant proportion of the recently arrived population installed themselves in peripheral neighbourhoods with significant urban deficits and in housing they constructed themselves. These were Barcelona's 'shanty town' neighbourhoods.

In this period, citizens were recognised as subjects with rights, but their rights to intervene in the elaboration of laws were not recognised. Although, in the final years of the regime small openings were produced which permitted, among other things, a certain freedom of association, citizen action was strongly constrained within a very narrow legal framework (Pérez and Sánchez, 2008). In this context, local governments essentially exercised a normative-legal function according to which their actions were oriented toward regulating, in the specific case of the urban sphere, the conditions that shaped part of the urbanisation process (Pascual, 2011). In this context, the local government of the city responded to a vision of administration based on the rule of law in an undemocratic state (Pascual, 2011). Its task was to regulate the functioning of the city, but it did so far from the institutional values of transparency and representation.

In this context, an increasingly powerful and clear opposition to Francoism came into existence, led by diverse agents and developed clandestinely. The different grassroots movements were articulated around social–urban demands, cultural criticism of urban speculation, and local democratic demands regarding the rights of association and participation, the election of the municipal government and administrative decentralisation (Borja, 2009). This movement included neighbours, intellectuals, networks of clandestine parties and trade unions, representatives of professional sectors, and different media, among others. The Franco regime's 1964 Law on Associations permitted the existence of some organisations in defence of grassroots interests (neighbourhood councils, clandestine trade unions, youth associations, and so on) to acquire legal status by becoming neighbourhood associations. In addition, new neighbourhood associations were created that were legal from their very inception. This legalisation took place under the control of the regime, which approved the statutes of the associations and determined the rules of the game in a context of a lack of freedom (Andreu, 2009). Soon, these associations would make up a broad neighbourhood movement struggling to address the problems that the neighbourhoods and the city population were raising.

In Barcelona, the first associations were constituted in 1970 in three neighbourhoods with very precarious living conditions common to shanty town neighbourhoods (Torre Baró, Vallbona and Trinitat Nova). Residents initially got together to demand the services and infrastructure that were lacking. Soon, however, the movement extended to other neighbourhoods in the city, some with similar problems (the Zona Franca and Sant Antoni neighbourhoods, for example) and others that were comparatively better off (the Eixample, Sarrià and Sant Gervasi). All of these associations shared the same objective: to make neighbourhood residents aware of common problems and ready to take action to improve neighbourhood quality of life. All of them focused their actions on the same thing: involvement in public policy and urban planning as a way of actively participating in the transformation of their neighbourhoods (Alabart, 2010). From the beginning, therefore, the neighbourhood was constituted as the unit of reference for this movement. It acted as a place of reference that conferred identity on the community and was the space where relations of collaboration and solidarity took place. The neighbourhood became the setting for the identity of the associations, for the demands of neighbourhoods, but also a space for exercising citizenship.

It was during this stage that the structure, organisation and coordination of the movement was defined. At this time, a basic structure linking the different neighbourhood associations that had emerged in the city was consolidated, as the associations established two coordinating bodies, one of them the Federation of Neighbourhood Associations of Barcelona (FAVB). This model had important advantages for the movement: it permitted coordinated and organised work, overcoming the risk of disconnected local actions, and it contributed to defining a more inclusive model for the future of the city, that went beyond the specifics of each neighbourhood and posed an alternative to that of the local administration (Alabart, 2010). This meant that, at the same time as the movement raised and defended the specific demands of each neighbourhood, it elaborated and agreed on a common project for the city. Its origins led to a decentralised but coordinated movement independent of local government.

What is particularly significant is that since its beginning, the movement has had a strong democratic identity. It was consolidated as a space for the representation of the popular will. Through its efforts to achieve a better quality of life, the movement also demanded the right to freedom of expression, assembly and association. The associations were able to engage the neighbourhood population in their day to day work. The objective was clear: that neighbourhood residents would become active citizens. Hence, demands for democratic and direct participation guided movement objectives.

In short, in Barcelona the neighbourhood movement was initially a defensive movement that fought to keep speculative interests from ruining the neighbourhoods. At the same time, the movement organised for and fought to achieve a set of material demands (clean streets, adequate housing, traffic lights, public transport, health centres, and so on). The neighbourhood associations constituted a type of community-based action that first focused on making demands on local institutions and then subsequently organising protests in Spain's major cities. Soon, however, it went beyond material demands. The movement would end up constituting a form of organisation and purposeful local action, with an air of political protest. Its demands were also ideological: to construct a more egalitarian, participatory, democratically cohesive and united city. Thus, both demands for a better quality of life and the conquest of political and civic freedoms are two indissoluble objectives that have given shape to the movement since its inception.

The rise of community-based action in the construction of the democratic city: from the consolidation of the movement to crisis (1975–92)

This is perhaps the most intense stage the neighbourhood movement has gone through. It began with the political transition, which refers to the time from the death of Franco (20 November 1975) to the celebration of the first democratic local elections (3 April 1979), and it ended with the hosting of the 1992 Olympic Games in Barcelona. The number of changes and events that took place during this time was so intense that it makes it difficult to group them together in the same stage. Although, at the beginning of this period the movement was consolidated and spread across the city, the end of the stage was marked by crisis and internal debate.

The transition years were a period of significant politicisation of the neighbourhood movement. Although demands over urban planning continued to be the main aim of reflection and action, neighbourhood associations were involved in all actions that were aimed at the constitution of or deepening of democratic practices at the local level. At this time, there was one main slogan: *Salvem Barcelona per la democràcia* [Saving Barcelona for democracy]. Under this slogan, the demands were linked by three ideas: democracy, freedom and autonomy. In this stage, the movement was committed more than ever to the project of constructing a grassroots base that would be capable of intervening in the city; in short, its efforts focused on converting neighbours into citizens. It did this through actions focused on training and education, not only on matters related to urban planning, but also in the cultural, political and civic spheres.

With regards specifically to urban planning, the neighbourhood movement was structured around two tasks: on the one hand, campaigns in opposition to the diverse sectoral plans that were developed as part of the former planning approved during the dictatorship,[2] and against speculation and in demand of services and facilities; and on the other hand, campaigns to educate the neighbourhood population about the new plan that was being approved.[3] To do this, the associations collaborated with experts who provided advice and helped in the task of educating neighbourhood residents regarding the implications of the plan. Professional associations (mainly comprising architects and economists) played a central role in this. This sector had initiated, along with other actors such as intellectuals, journalists, clandestine party militants, and so on, a cultural and political critique of urban development during Francoism. The union between the movement, neighbourhoods and the intellectual critique took an almost organic form, to the extent that there were countless collaborations. In this period, a line of critical opposition was agreed on and alternative plans were elaborated. They were guided by a democratic urban perspective that had been developing during the previous stage (Borja, 2009). In all cases, the neighbourhood population was highly involved, consolidating an active community-based opposition, but one which also proposed alternatives. In a period in which dialogue with the administration was still not possible, the neighbourhood movement was a reference in the struggle for democracy.

By the end of the transition, the neighbourhood movement had spread throughout the city and included 80 associations. The movement had significant influence in the neighbourhoods and contributed to creating a sense of belonging and identity. At this time, the neighbourhood associations were highly thought of: public awareness was very high, as was trust, making the neighbourhood movement highly valued and providing the associations with significant public legitimacy. From an organisational perspective, this stage is characterised by increased coordination that went beyond the borders of the city. The FAVB was consolidated as a platform providing leadership and the movement collaborated with other social movements.

The first democratic municipal elections and the constitution of the first democratically elected municipal governments were a turning point for the movement. In almost all of Catalonia the presence of left-wing parties in municipal governments was consolidated, and Barcelona was no exception. The left-wing government had the support of the city's social movements, its economic and professional sectors and the intellectual and cultural spheres. The neighbourhood movement celebrated this victory for several reasons: first, because many of the members of neighbourhood associations were also activists in these parties; second, because many of the movement's own proposals had been included in their programmes, and last, because the movement saw an opportunity to carry out a real transformation in local government and achieve the democratic values it had been demanding.

The first democratic governments faced two tasks: first, to reform and modernise local administration, converting it into a democratic institution with public legitimacy. Second, to develop those projects for change that had been forged and agreed on by civil society earlier. At this time, the municipal government was committed to participation. This was a period of maximum rapport and consensus between local government and civil society. Community-based action found continuity in the institution of local democracy. Urban and social demands found support among city politicians and technical experts, in part because these groups had emerged from representatives of the city's social and neighbourhood movements. The cultural and political ideas and values that were forged in the previous stage were the main legitimators of and guide for the city's government (Borja, 2009). Stable channels for dialogue and citizen participation were opened and a model of territorial decentralisation in the decision-making process was proposed to bring the administration to the city's neighbourhoods and citizens. In this context, the neighbourhood movement was a reference for addressing citizen demands. Its demands were listened to and addressed and it was invited to form part of the process of defining the city's new territorial organisation.

From an urban planning perspective, a stage of participatory urbanism began (Borja, 2009). There was broad agreement around the direction of urban change and the types of project needed to deliver that change. These projects had been thought about, debated and developed within the city's social movements and neighbourhoods. At this time, it was accepted that the agent of urban transformation was the local government, but with the collaboration of the citizenry. The municipal agenda would emerge and be collectively agreed on between the administration and neighbourhood movement.

Initially, urban policies were aimed at covering the city's deficits and, in particular, those of its peripheral neighbourhoods with the most needs. This was a period focused on the physical improvement and rehabilitation of the neighbourhoods and the provision of facilities and services. The rapid intervention of the administration was possible thanks to the existing consensus regarding the main objectives of urban policy and which projects should be prioritised. The fact that social demands were addressed reinforced public trust in local government. In addition, at this stage, urban policy was not only focused on what was urgently needed, but other major projects were also undertaken. The model was also consensual in this regard: the population demanded a compact, diverse and egalitarian city. The best example of this was following the concession of the Olympic Games to Barcelona in 1986.

The celebration of the games was seen as an opportunity to give a boost to the major transformations that the city was facing, especially regarding urban redevelopment and major infrastructures. The city's funds also had to be used for pending projects in the neighbourhoods. The good rapport at this time between the citizenry and the local government is common knowledge; the population was excited, involved and participated in the construction of the city. This, in combination with public–private collaboration in city development, referred to as concerted urban development, established what has come to be called the Barcelona Model and explains why the project had so much support. In contrast, the role of the neighbourhood movement was different. Neighbourhood associations were involved, but from a critical perspective. They focused much of their activity on defending the projects pending in their neighbourhoods, preventing them from being neglected in favour of other projects. Citizen based action managed to block certain schemes but was unable to introduce a number of local and community concerns into the overall Olympic project (Naya and Recio, 2010). The neighbourhood associations monitored public works, debated projects and protested over public–private partnerships, which they saw as giving greater weight to private rather than public interests. They also defended the model of a balanced city that had been previously agreed.

This was a period of change in the direction of municipal policy and the relationship between the citizenry and local government. This was the beginning of a time of major urban development projects that represented a leap in scale (Nel·lo, 1992), and the trust between the city's social movements and the government suffered a setback that generated distance between them. After a stage of close collaboration, difficulties in the relationship between movement and government would soon emerge and conflicts would become frequent. There seemed to be fewer opportunities for participation and local government became more authoritarian. A dynamic of distrust was established between the two forms of political action (representative and grassroots). Paradoxically, it was specifically the arrival of left-wing parties in the government that would mark the beginning of a deep crisis in the neighbourhood movement. Along with this situation, other factors need to be considered: the economic crisis became a preoccupation for much of the population, which put less effort and energy into the movement; in addition, the loss of clear objectives, feelings of disappointment and, above all, the professionalisation of the main representatives of the movement, many of whom left for positions within the government, left the movement without leadership for a time. To all this must also be added the lack of experience in political action within a democratic setting. The rules of the game had changed and the logic, objectives and strategies of the movement had to be modified. In short, a stage characterised by distrust, lack of leadership and indecision began. This translated into a decline in the movement, resulting in a loss of members, a decline in activities and an unravelling of the coordinating network. Some associations even disappeared, and a great number of others came close to doing so.

Neighbourhood action in the context of the new urban model: a new stage (1992–2013)

The Olympic Games initiated a new stage in urban development in Barcelona. The city was increasingly oriented toward the development of services and tourism and laying the foundation for becoming a cultural reference and centre for the knowledge economy (Busquets, 2006). This stage was based, in part, on major urban projects that were considered to be a strategic element in the future development of the city, and in part on a new type of governance based on a relationship between public and private agents different from that at the beginning of the democratic period.

Many projects were developed throughout the city. The greatest effort, however, was the reform of the north east of the city, especially the neighbourhood of Poblenou, in the Sant Martí district. This neighbourhood, was originally designated to be part of Cerdà's *Pla de l'Eixample* (expansion plan) in 1860. It developed in a different manner from the rest of the Eixample and was consolidated as an industrial area, in continuity with its past.[4] In the 1980s the neighbourhood declined and was abandoned by many residents. At the end of the 1990s a comprehensive renewal of Poblenou was planned, considered a continuation of the project that had developed the Olympic Village. The plan was aimed at integrating this peripheral area into the city, developing it as a strategic zone: new commercial and residential areas were designed, with new cultural facilities and new transport nodes, and above all, a new business district was planned. There were two mega-projects that were part of the overall project: the construction of infrastructure and facilities to host the Forum of Cultures in 2004, and the construction of a business district, referred to as 22@Barcelona, which would offer the infrastructure and conditions necessary for the area to become a reference in the development of the knowledge economy in the city.

The Barcelona municipal government faced all these challenges and others in other parts of the city with fewer resources than in the previous stage. This led the administration to look for support from the private sector, which meant designing projects that would be sufficiently profitable to attract private investment (Pascual, 2011). In addition, this is the stage in which public managerialism was consolidated. In this period, the city adopted techniques to encourage and measure the productivity and efficiency of the administration. The predominant values were those of the private sector: economy, efficiency and productivity. The municipal government continues to present itself as a provider of services and projects, but, from this perspective, the neighbourhood resident and the citizen are seen as customers who must be satisfied (Pascual, 2011).

This change in direction provoked significant opposition from broad sectors of the population, who saw, in the different urban projects, a model of urban development that prioritised commercial and competitive factors above the public interest. In this stage, the neighbourhood movement had little weight in setting the city's urban policy agenda (Alabart, 2010). In addition, with the turn of the century, the new urban policy coincided with a real estate boom characterised by intense speculation, processes of gentrification and rapid increases in house prices. This was a period of not only distance between the population and city hall but also of confrontation. Despite the city opening new channels for participation (basically of a consultative or, at times, propositional nature), direct popular opposition to urban development projects was constant. The most paradigmatic example of this was the process of design and construction of the reforms associated with the Forum of Cultures.

The Forum was posited as a mega project, which, as with the Olympic Games, would permit, on the one hand, the celebration of an event that would bring worldwide recognition to the city, and on the other hand, urban development. The project included the renewal of a degraded area in Sant Martí, converting it into an area of services and infrastructures for the city and bordering with the new high-end residential area, Diagonal Mar. The objectives were similar but there was a significant difference between the Olympic Games and the Forum of Cultures, the latter lacking public involvement. The project that was developed had no support from the neighbourhoods, or from the FAVB, which presented a manifesto criticising the Forum and demanding citizen participation and the need for a space to debate its content. In addition, the manifesto denounced the unwillingness of the government to incorporate public debate into the process, as well as the powerful role of private actors in the related urban reforms and the disproportionate investment involved in comparison to other projects (FAVB, 2004). The neighbourhood movement felt excluded from this major event. The Forum became a symbol of the feeling of dispossession felt by many citizens during this period; the direction of urban development no longer seemed to be along an agreed path (Pascual, 2011). This was not only evident with the Forum; the experience with the referendum over the Diagonal was another example,[5] as was the construction of 22@Barcelona. The notion of constructing a smart city, which would be a crucial node in the knowledge economy, became an abstract idea far removed from the interests and, even, the understanding of the majority of city residents (Gavaldà and Ribera-Fumaz, 2012).

In this period, community-based action took diverse forms (demonstrations, platforms, associations and so on) in protesting against the development of various projects, the majority of which involved the reclassification of land use and were seen by neighbourhood residents as having only speculative ends.[6] The neighbourhood movement again played a central role. The neighbourhood associations continued to play an educational and deliberative role among the population regarding the projects affecting their neighbourhoods, while also leading protest actions, and the movement again prospered. Providing services to neighbourhood residents came to occupy a privileged place in the activities of the associations, although the main objectives continued to be focused on political participation and demands (urban renewal, transport, housing, the environment and so on). Despite this, during this stage new spaces for participation and collaboration opened up that offered examples of a different way of making a city, one that would be more democratic and participatory. One example of this is the Trinitat Nova Community Plan, a plan that was initiated with a participatory diagnosis of the problems and opportunities in the neighbourhood. Under the leadership of the neighbourhood association other groups were also involved, as well as experts and professionals with the support of the administration.

In this context, the FAVB played a central role. While the neighbourhood associations acted like small lobbying groups, defending the interests of their neighbourhoods, the FAVB was the defender of a model of a balanced city. The Federation, supported by expert advice, continued its efforts educating the population regarding development projects, and criticisms were again heard from professional associations (Borja, 2009). The FAVB continued proposing measures to be incorporated in urban plans, and organised and led protest actions while denouncing the lack of opportunities for participation. Its pressure in some cases led to its demands being heard and incorporated, although only partially (this was the case with the plans for 22@Barcelona). The FAVB also became a connection point for different social movements, adopting many of their demands. Today it plays a role as a transversal socio-political reference (Andreu, 2009).

Community-based action and planning: the significance of the neighbourhood movement in Spain

The aim of this chapter has been to analyse the emergence and development of community-based action and its role in urban planning in Spain. To do this, we have focused on Barcelona's neighbourhood movement as a primary actor in the grassroots community. Up until now, we have looked at the origins of this movement emphasising the factors that fostered and explain its creation and subsequent development until today. In this section, we address the significance this movement has had on community-based action and its participation in urban politics. We ask what explains the central role that the neighbourhood movement played in community-based action in Barcelona, and what contribution it made to creating the civic base of the city and, in short, in the construction of the city. There are various factors that are important.

First, and foremost, is the role of the neighbourhood associations as generators of social capital. The actual approach of the neighbourhood movement since its beginnings explains the central role it has had in the generation of social capital, understood both from a structural as well as a cultural perspective. According to Bourdieu and Wacquant, social capital is the sum of current and virtual resources available to an individual or group because they possess a more or less institutionalised network of lasting relationships of mutual knowledge and recognition (Bourdieu and Wacquant, 1992). If we analyse social capital from a cultural perspective, and, therefore, place emphasis on values and attitudes, the neighbourhood movement has clearly been a generator of social capital. Beyond the concrete demand to improve living conditions in the neighbourhoods and the city as a whole, the movement has had a more autotelic approach: aimed at creating a sense of belonging in the neighbourhoods, constructing a collective identity, getting the neighbourhood population to act as citizens, generating community service and relationships between neighbours, and fostering democracy and citizen participation. Essentially, the neighbourhood associations have had a clear effect in generating trust among persons participating in the associations, within the movement, in the general population, and, at certain times, in city institutions as well.

If social capital is analysed from a structural perspective, we understand it as a series of factors that facilitate the relationships and the actions of persons belonging to a particular organisation. If we follow the approach of Esmans and Uphoff, in which they suggest which factors tend to favour the success of an organisation as a shaper of social capital

(Esman and Uphoff, 1984), it is easy to see the key elements of the neighbourhood movement that have contributed to this social capital. Here, we highlight two of them. First, is the informal nature of the organisation. This informality has allowed the movement to increase the number of member associations and increase the participation of broad sectors of the population, whether members or not. It has also allowed the movement to avoid a bureaucratised structure. Second, is the fact that local organisations function better when they are initiated by the local population. This is essentially an organic characteristic of the neighbourhood associations, which, from their very beginning, were a creation of the residents of each neighbourhood, who joined together to respond to the specific problems of their neighbourhood. In addition, the other organisations that emerged, such as the coordinators, also followed a bottom-up sequence and in no case were any proposed or imposed by local government.

There are other elements that were important factors in explaining the origin and subsequent development of the movement and its significance. We will analyse these in what follows.

First, is the relationship of the movement with the municipal government. This aspect has been widely addressed throughout this chapter. Here we emphasize the fact that the neighbourhood movement was established clandestinely and based on a structure completely independent from the local government; it emerged as a grassroots movement specifically to fight against the undemocratic structures of the government. The neighbourhood movement emerged organically and directly out of civil society as a force of social protest and mobilisation. As we have already seen, its relationship with local government became more complex once democracy was established and has passed through different stages. What has remained stable over these years is that the movement continues to act as an intermediary between the population and the administration. Today, although the movement continues to have a high degree of independence in its relationship to local government, many of the neighbourhood associations have become dependent on municipal funds. In any case, the form in which the movement developed and, especially its relationship with the local government in the initial years of democracy, were an important innovation. Gallent and Robinson argue that

> the collaborative approach is underpinned by (and also advocates) the principles of participation, empowerment, partnership working and network action. It relies on innovative forms of consultation or dialogue as a way of

transforming adversarial relationships into more cooperative ones. This differentiates it from traditional forms of government as it requires 'communities of interest' to be directly included in the decision-making processes, rather than decisions being made unilaterally, based solely on the input of advice from experts. (Gallent and Robinson, 2013, 13)

The Spanish situation is unique as this collaborative process was generated during the construction of democracy, not as a way of improving democracy. This was the context in which the movement had the greatest impact on urban policy.

Second, is its organisational structure. One of the keys to the success of the movement has been, since its beginning, its form of organisation, based on a decentralised geographic structure, articulated through the neighbourhood and the community but coordinated by federations at the second or third level. This structure is based on horizontal, not hierarchical, internal relations and a dual form for external relations: horizontal relationships with associations of the same nature, and vertical relationships with second and third level organisations, such as federations or confederations. This structure allowed them to defend specifically local neighbourhood interests, which led to a close relationship between the movement and its popular base. At the same time, it was able to develop common strategies for action across neighbourhoods and define an overall model for the city. Of equal significance was the networking that characterised the movement. At its start, the neighbourhood movement sheltered and promoted a wide variety of social initiatives and forms of community-based action. Some were tied to urban issues, others to more social issues. At the same time, the movement supported diverse mobilisations and the activities of other entities, offering a way of working in networks. The neighbourhood movement has been characterised by its open structure, looking for relationships not only with neighbourhood residents, but also with other entities, organisations and movements that have shared the objective of improving life in the city and defending social rights. The FAVB in particular, plays a role as a node in a system of citizen action whose connecting thread is found in the demands of the movement.

Third, an element to emphasise is the legitimacy that the movement has acquired over its history among the population and local powers. The demands for the construction of a democratic government and city, and actions based on the democratic ideals of participation, freedom and representativeness, gave the movement great recognition and social legitimacy. In this sense, the movement became a reference for city projects and an opinion leader.

Fourth, is the movement's form of collective action and impact on public policy, particularly urban planning. At its inception, the neighbourhood movement defined a model of the city it wanted to achieve, but also acted and intervened in numerous urban projects. In some, it participated directly, contributing to their development, in others it proposed alternative plans, and in yet others, it oriented its activity toward protesting against plans it considered to be an attack on the city model it defended. The movement referred to these actions as 'neighbourhood struggles'.[7] Its role in planning also developed through its efforts as go-between with different agents and, especially, through the creation of educative and deliberative spaces for the local community to learn about and discuss different urban development projects. This work, concrete and based on the needs of the neighbourhoods, made the neighbourhood movement a reference for community-based action with a significant impact on the city.

Fifth, is the movement's defence of the public interest. Since its beginning, the neighbourhood movement's top priority has been the physical improvement of the city's neighbourhoods. Its concerns, however, have also included issues related to quality of life and the attainment of democracy, and have led to the movement's spheres of action and types of actions going beyond merely urban issues. The associations have developed services aimed at improving the quality of life of neighbourhood residents (providing training and educational courses, legal services, and so on), while at the same time broadening their types of demands (focusing on women's rights, support for youth and the elderly, the environment, sustainability and so on). In addition, the movement's actions have also gone beyond the interests of association members and those directly affected by specific issues, its structure permitting the participation in discussion and deliberation over urban projects of anyone interested, not only members. Although it is true that many actions have been aimed at defending sectoral interests, particularly in regard to urban policy, these have always been framed within a model of a city that has had broad support.

And last, is the movement's defence of the values of a democratic city and the task of achieving a civically active population. The effort of the associations in terms of generating identity and converting neighbourhood residents into citizens has made them real schools of citizenship in defence of the public good.

Notes

[1] In this respect, a change took place between the legislation established in pre-democratic periods and that which has been established in the democratic period, in particular with the gradual incorporation of instruments for citizen participation. The relationship between local administration and citizen actors went from being based on public information, to a process of citizen participation based on new legislation that has established the obligation that each new urban development plan be accompanied by a participatory process (Fernández et al, 2010).

[2] 1953 County Plan. This plan generated significant neighbourhood opposition as it was seen as a plan for speculation and social injustice (Alabart, 2010).

[3] 1976 General Metropolitan Plan.

[4] The Poblenou neighbourhood is part of the Sant Martí district. Before its annexation by Barcelona in 1897, it was a municipality called Sant Martí de Povençals, known as the Catalan Manchester because of the high level of industry concentrated there.

[5] In 2010, the Barcelona Municipal Government, in an attempt to demonstrate its openness to citizen participation, planned a referendum so that city residents could choose the future they wanted for Barcelona's Diagonal Avenue. The referendum included three options: a) approval of reform project A, b) approval of reform project B, and c) no reform of the Diagonal. In this consultation, the local government invested effort and economic resources to present the two projects and to carry out the referendum, developing an infrastructure based on new technologies that had never been used before. The cost of the process was widely criticised by opposition groups and the public. The result of the process was very low participation in the referendum (12.7 per cent of a total of 1,414,783 eligible voters participated) and a victory for option C: leaving things as they were. The experience was considered a failure and provoked the dismissal of the city's first deputy mayor.

[6] For example, the case of the Barça 2000 project, which was based on reclassifying the land around the Camp Nou stadium. Neighbourhood opposition even managed to stop the plan.

[7] The FAVB published a collection commemorating the 100 main neighbourhood victories of the movement in Barcelona that included actions aimed at defending neighbourhood heritage, attaining facilities and green spaces for the city, and blocking and revising development projects considered

to advantage speculation and undermine the achievement of social goals (FAVB, 2010).

References

Alabart, A, 2009, El moviment associatiu veïnal, quaranta anys després: un balanç, In *Revista Nous Horitzons*, 195, 34–42

Alabart, A, 2010, Polítiques urbanístiques i moviment associatiu veïnal, *Barcelona societat* 19, 87–98

Andreu, M, 2009, Els veïns i la ciutat democràtica, In *La veu del carrer*, 114, 4–6

Blanco, I, 2009, Does a 'Barcelona Model' really exist? Periods, territories and actors in the process of urban transformation, *Local Government Studies* 35, 355–69

Bonet, J, 2012, Quin és el sentit del moviment veïnal avui?, in Federació d'Associacions de Veïns i Veïnes de Barcelona (FAVB) (eds) *Moviment veïnal, reptes de futur*, Barcelona: Editorial Mediterrània

Borja, J, 2009, *Luces y sombras del urbanismo de Barcelona*, Barcelona: Editorial UOC (Universitat Oberta de Catalunya)

Bourdieu, P, Wacquant, LJD, 1992, *An invitation to reflexive sociology*, Chicago, IL: University of Chicago Press

Brownill, S, Carpenter, J, 2009, Governance and 'integrated' planning: The case of sustainable communities in the Thames Gateway, England, *Urban Studies* 46, 2, 251–74

Busquets, J, 2006, *Barcelona: The urban evolution of a compact city*, Cambridge, MA: Nicolodi and Harvard University Graduate School of Design

Capel, H, 1981, *Capitalismo y morfología urbana en España*, Barcelona: Libros de la Frontera

Capel, H, 2005, *El modelo Barcelona: un examen crítico*, Barcelona: Ediciones del Serbal

Esman, M, Uphoff, N, 1984, *Local organizations: Intermediaries in local government*, Ithaca, NY: Cornell University Press

FAVB (Federació d'Associacions de Veïns i Veïnes de Barcelona), 2004, *Resolució de la 32 Assemblea de la Favb sobre el Fòrum 2004*, Document electrònic del 27 de març de 2004, www.favb.cat/node/131

FAVB (Federació d'Associacions de Veïns i Veïnes de Barcelona), 2010, *1970–2010: 40 anys d'acció veïnal*, Barcelona: Editorial Mediterrània

Fernández Plé, C, Rabaud, GS, Roig, CS, 2010, *Cap a una estratègia participativa en urbanisme: Reflexions sobre un urbanisme participatiu de qualitat*, Barcelona: Fundació Catalunya, Segle XXI

Forester, J, 1987, Planning in the face of conflict: Negotiation and mediation strategies in local land use regulation, *Journal of the American Planning Association* 53, 3, 433–46

Gallent, N, Robinson, S, 2013, *Neighbourhood planning: Communities, networks and governance*, Bristol: Policy Press

Gavaldà, J, Ribera-Fumaz, R, 2012, Barcelona 5.0: From Knowledge to Smartness?, *Working Papers Series: Internet Interdisciplinary Institute WP12-002*, Barcelona: Universitat Oberta de Catalunya

Martí-Costa, M, Arias, A, 2012, Apunts sobre les relacions entre les AV i l'Administració, in Federació d'Associacions de Veïns i Veïnes de Barcelona (FAVB) (eds) *Moviment veïnal, reptes de futur*, Barcelona: Editorial Mediterrània

Naya, A, Recio, A, 2010, El moviment veïnal de Barcelona davant els Jocs Olímpics, *La veu del carrer* 117, 19

Nel·lo, O, 2009, *Les repercussions urbanístiques dels Jocs Olímpics de Barcelona'92*, Barcelona: Centre d'Estudis Olímpics UAB (Universitat Autònoma de Barcelona)

Parés, M, Bonet-Martí, J, Martí-Costa, M, 2011, Does participation really matter in urban regeneration policies? Exploring governance networks in Catalonia (Spain), *Urban Affairs Review* 42, 2, 238–71

Pascual, JM, 2011, *El papel de la ciudadanía en el auge y decadencia de las ciudades*, Valencia: Tirant lo blanc

Parker, S, 2004, The contested city: Politics, people and power, chapter 7 in *Urban theory and the urban experience: Encountering the city*, London: Routledge

Pérez, V, Sánchez, P, 2008, *Memoria ciudadana y movimiento vecinal*, Madrid: Catarata

5

Community action in Australian farming and fishing communities

Sue Kilpatrick, Karen Willis and Sophie Lewis

Introduction

This chapter is concerned with the contexts and drivers of community action: it explores how communities come together in the face of externally imposed challenges, and the social processes and resources that shape community action in response to these challenges. Collectively labelled 'difficult times', prolonged drought, floods, increasing financial and occupational stress, labour intensification, government regulations and a widening division between rural and urban communities in Australia, have had a serious and detrimental impact on the physical and mental health of farmers and fishers in recent times (Albrecht et al, 2007; Alston and Kent, 2008; Hossain et al, 2008). The responses of five farming and fishing communities in Australia to the challenge of maintaining physical and mental wellbeing while facing various environmental, economic and regulatory pressures on their industries reveal the key role of industry organisations and social processes, including people we term 'boundary crossers', in the incubation of community action.

The small rural communities, each with populations of between 1,000 and 5,000 people, were located between 100 and 1,500 kilometres from their nearest large regional service centre. While local health services were used for emergencies and minor ailments, the presence of a service did not necessarily mean that farmers and fishers used it in their health maintenance strategy. Preferred formal and informal services, programmes, social supports and information sources were those initiated and/or maintained through the agency of community social capital and local leadership. Local people who were able to work across the boundary between the farmers or fishers and health services were key drivers of community action for health and wellbeing, and links to health and wellbeing resources outside their communities. Communities which had experienced more severe pressures over longer periods (associated with prolonged drought in particular) tended to have embedded mechanisms to support mental wellbeing into community life, suggesting that external pressures can trigger effective community responses.

Although farmers and fishers have always been vulnerable to the unpredictability of climate and global economic forces, in recent years there has been an accumulation of factors including the global financial crisis, severe climatic and natural disaster events, and long-term drought, that have had particularly severe effects on farmers and fishers in rural Australia. Staying healthy in the context of difficult times is challenging. There are limited health services and human and physical infrastructure to promote health and wellbeing in rural communities. This is due to a range of factors including lack of availability of services, higher costs, health workforce shortages, and high turnover of healthcare providers (King at al, 2006). Farmers may also have difficulties in accessing services due to remoteness and reduced income in difficult times (Birchip Cropping Group, 2008). Social and geographical isolation places farmers and fishers at greater risk from poor health and declining wellbeing. The stress incurred from working in isolation, combined with less social cohesion and connectedness with their communities are associated with poorer health outcomes in rural communities (Caldwell and Boyd, 2009; Lower et al, 2011).

Identification, connectedness and involvement with a farming community are related to improved health outcomes (Alston and Kent, 2008; Caldwell and Boyd, 2009). Research reveals that strong social networks (Hegney et al, 2007; Humphreys, 2000; Alston and Kent, 2008; Caldwell and Boyd, 2009), and involvement in organised community activities, including sporting groups, are important in promoting positive health and wellbeing in rural communities (Alston and Kent, 2008; Townsend et al, 2002). As such, provision of social activities may help farmers to cope with the pressure of difficult times by reducing isolation and increasing social connectedness with others in the community (Birchip Cropping Group, 2008).

Social capital is the '[networks,] shared norms, values and understandings that facilitate cooperation within or among groups' (OECD, 2001, 41). Different forms of social capital operate within (bonding), between (bridging) and outside (linking) communities (Woolcock, 1998; see also Rydin, Chapter 2, this volume). Rural communities that are cohesive and have strong networks, or bonding social capital are better able to harness and manage their own resources (Falk and Kilpatrick, 2000). Farming industry associations contribute to the social capital of communities (King et al, 2009). Interactional infrastructure is the visible face of social capital, represented by networks, events and meetings, communication sites, procedures, rules and precedents and leadership (Kilpatrick and Falk, 2003). It includes formal and informal community/industry interactions (Alston and Kent, 2008; Kilpatrick and Loechel, 2004). Crucially, the quantity and quality of places and opportunities for community members to come together, that is, community interactional infrastructure, are determinants of the quantity and quality of social capital a community builds, and how effectively that social capital is used for the benefit of community members.

Social capital and interactional infrastructure in farming and fishing communities, through the relationships mobilised through community and industry organisations, can influence health decision-making and create opportunities for access to health information, programmes and services to achieve good health and wellbeing (King et al, 2009). For example, industry association networks, which have high trustworthiness and credibility with farmers and fishers, are part of bonding and linking social capital. Their networks extend outside the communities through state and national bodies to source external resources to build capacity in agricultural communities (Haslam McKenzie, 2003; Healy et al, 2004). As such, the actions of industry organisations can have a positive impact on farmers' health.

Community and industry organisations are most effective when they have leaders that are able to draw on bonding, bridging and linking social capital. 'Boundary crossers' are key mobilisers of social capital for community outcomes such as health. They are people who live in a rural community, may be employed in the health system, but have other roles within the community. Boundary crossers understand and have relationships with people in both industry and health domains, and are trusted in both. They provide leadership and cross the boundaries between the community and outside, through their relationships. Boundary crossers understand existing community capacities and can lead actions to build and use these capacities for health development. They understand, and thus can negotiate differences in, the perspectives of both healthcare providers and community members, help align expectations and achieve outcomes that benefit both these groups, thus increasing the effectiveness of health industry and rural community collaborative action (Kilpatrick et al, 2009).

Our research illustrates an internally driven community development approach to rural health by providing examples of how communities develop health actions during difficult times. This is important in providing more information about how communities in diverse locations use existing community capacities to mobilise and enhance community health action. Exploring the responses of five farming and fishing communities allows the examination of community action between contexts in different places, but also allows examination of community action as a function of place.

About the research and sites

Our research used a multi-site case study and a strengths-based approach to investigate how farmers and fishers stay healthy during difficult times. Five sites were purposively selected for inclusion in the study by a project steering committee of rural industry and health sector stakeholders. Sites were diverse in size, location, remoteness, and industry-base. They represented five different rural industry areas: sugar cane, cotton, fishing, grains and mixed farming, were of different degrees of remoteness from regional service centres, and were spread across four Australian states. The selection of different industries with different circumstances, allowed for exploration of variations in people's resource use, information-seeking and health behaviours, as well as different health service provision settings. Cane and cotton growers reported that they were emerging from difficult times while the mixed farming and grains site had been severely affected by drought. Fishers reported considerable concerns in terms of reduced income and future uncertainty because of increased industry regulation and declines in population and services in their communities of place. In contrast to other sites where farmers live in the community, some fishers do not live permanently within the site where they work

Participants were owners and managers of farming/fishing businesses within an hour's drive of a focal town and were recruited with the assistance of on-site informants from local health services and industry organisations. Data were collected from three sources: in-depth, face-to-face interviews with farmers and fishers; completion of health journals by a subset of interviewees; and mapping of health information, services and resources in the sites. Interviews were conducted in 2010, were approximately 45 minutes in duration, digitally recorded and transcribed verbatim. Open-ended questions explored information seeking; service access; wellbeing behaviours; perceptions of effectiveness of current behaviours or actions; and perceptions of gaps in accessible information, services and infrastructure to support health. A sub-sample of interviewees kept fortnightly health journals for three months after completing the interview. Journals were in survey format and asked questions about general health, diet and exercise; health services, advice or information accessed in the past fortnight; and additional comments. Analysis was both deductive and inductive. Each site was analysed separately, and then comparisons were made across the sites.

A total of 110 farmers and fishers (15 to 30 per site) were interviewed. Most were over 36 years old and about one-third were female. Roughly one-third also had paid work outside their farming or fishing business and most had been farming or fishing for more than 20 years. Most had a partner and one or more dependent children. Nearly all cane growers and fishers were male reflecting the gendered nature of those industries, and there were roughly equal numbers of males and females from other industry areas. Cane growers were older, while fishers and grain growers were younger. Cotton growers were the most highly educated, followed by grain growers.

Use of services

The array of formal services and programmes and informal mechanisms to support health and wellbeing varied between sites, with the grains site having the most limited range, which were mostly visiting services. In contrast, the mixed farming, cane and cotton sites were well serviced with on-site GPs, allied health, community health and hospital services and alternative therapy practitioners. All sites had a local emergency and GP service, a pharmacy and aged care, although not all towns within the sites had these services. All sites had local or visiting mental health services.

Although there was awareness of a wide range of services that were available in their local communities or within accessible travel distance, many services were not used by farmers. Local services were used for emergencies, minor ailments and to obtain prescriptions for ongoing medication. Health check-ups for most fishers, mixed farmers and grain growers, however, were 'incidental' as their GP was opportunistic in screening patients and providing general health information when farmers presented for other reasons. In contrast, cane and cotton growers described regular health check-ups. While very few farmers reported using local mental health services, they were more likely to use nonprofessional mental health support strategies such as local group programmes.

Social capital in the form of community networks were important sites of health service advice and information with many farmers seeking health information from friends and family members who lived in the community. Mixed farmers reported higher use of information from groups, rather than individuals. This perhaps reflected the relative richness of interactional infrastructure in the form of community and industry groups in that site in terms of number and diversity of groups, and their level of community action. For example, one male mixed farmer received information about a variety of health issues through emails and programmes delivered by the Landcare environmental group:

> The Landcare group sends emails...it does send a fair bit, a reasonable amount of information in with some things... they've run health things, you know, they have their male health things in [town name]. (Male mixed farmer)

Group-related activities such as mental health first aid were the most common sources of information about mental health. These were typically sponsored by, and delivered through community interactional infrastructure: industry groups, peak bodies, and community groups, such as the local football team, County Fire Authority or Landcare:

> We had a three-hour [community programme] directed at farmers a couple of years ago that...a lot of men came to, and older people came which was also very good. And because we've run them, people are willing to talk about mental health in our area, and depression. (Female grain grower)

Limited health service provision in some sites triggered community-based initiatives. Industry and community groups, clubs and organisations facilitated local access to health services and programmes that were not available in the community, filling a gap in health programme provision. These community action initiatives complemented formal services by providing additional opportunities for farmers to maintain their health. This raises concerns, however, that there may not be a minimal level of formal services to meet community needs at some sites:

> It's not only playing tennis, it's the going there and it's your barbecue after it...by closing [the tennis club] that down it wasn't just the sport, it was the interaction of going to things you know...over here there's no Shire [local government] support. (Male mixed farmer)

The role of boundary crossers and community and industry organisations acting as soft entry points

Two key sources of community action for health initiatives were evident in the sites. Both were internal to the communities. First, local people who acted as boundary crossers between health services and the farming community; and second, industry and community organisations that established soft entry points for people to participate in health programmes. While evident in all sites (except fishing), the role of boundary crossers and community and industry organisations were most pronounced in the mixed farming and cane sites.

Local people who were able to work across the boundary between the farmers or fishers and health services were key drivers of community action for health and wellbeing, and the link to health and wellbeing resources from outside their communities. Some farmers reported that they participated in programmes because they were legitimised by community or industry leaders, or they were personally invited to attend by an individual acting as a boundary crosser. A female mixed farmer highlighted the importance of boundary crossers in her community by describing how she did 'a lot of farm gate visiting' to provide information to farmers whom she said would be unlikely to actively seek out health information and programmes 'just off their own bat'. In the mixed farming site, a holistic health programme called Sustainable Farm Families used a nurse who was credible in the health field and well known in the community and industry, who acted as a boundary crosser to encourage people to participate:

> It was done through Landcare and [Name] rang up and said you better go...And she's someone that we grew up with... she's a nurse and she was the secretary of the Landcare group...and was organising that and probably when a group like that is trying to do something, I probably think well you probably should go. (Male mixed farmer)

The tennis club drew on the social capital of club leaders to run community dinners from the Drought Support group with a range of health and welfare support organisations in attendance. Again, direct contact from someone acting as a boundary crosser, well known in the community and industry was effective in getting farmers to come:

> Being in a very public place [was] very difficult for a lot of people. It was one-on-one invitations. We went out,

each one of four or five of us went out to everybody individually and sat with them, had a cuppa tea and said, 'You are personally invited, there's your invitation'. They didn't have to pick it out of the mailbox and think, 'Ooh, I wonder who will be there?' or 'What's going on?' (Female mixed farmer)

In an example of boundary crossing in the grains site, a primary health nurse who was part of community social networks that included farmers accessed external funding to implement a mental health programme after this need was identified by farmers living in that site.

It was just something I saw on the Internet, on the Farmers' website, and said to [name], 'Can we do this?' And anything we've sort of seen or suggest that we thought was good, [name] has found funding…I said, 'We will get them in [name of town].' And we did…And that started women in our community saying, 'I've been having problems.' (Female grains grower)

Local leadership was important in influencing farmer awareness of health and wellbeing related behaviours, and in planning and provision or sponsorship of programmes and services to support wellbeing. In the cane and mixed farming sites, the local industry organisation and local health service respectively supported and delivered farmer health education programmes and encouraged farmer participation through industry leaders. A feature of the cane site was an industry leader who was particularly active in promoting health in the community. This person, credible and trusted in both the health and cane sectors, acted as a boundary crosser, and influenced the planning of the community's health and wellbeing programme as well as encouraging cane growers to participate:

I have been going to a morning breakfast with community health coordinators. And they talk about all sorts of things, from bereavement health for people that have had a death in the family to suicide health, to mental health […name] is the coordinator here in town. I could show you probably ten emails here now that she has sent me in the last two days of the different projects that they are doing, you know? (Male cane grower)

Industry and community groups played a crucial role by acting as effective soft entry points to health services and information, particularly information and services about mental health

> New South Wales Farmers will provide money for a barbeque at the hall down here. And it's just a social event where there might be six or seven workers from Beyondblue [a national mental health initiative] or a support, Centrelink [national government welfare agency] and stuff, and they'll only have five minutes to chat – they'll just do a five-minute very informal thing but have tables of handouts and stuff. And I think – like they're good nights aren't they? And they're good; people pick up a lot of stuff. (Female grain grower)

Community group leaders used their credibility and good standing with the community to encourage community members to participate in health programmes and activities that are incorporated into other, industry related functions. For example, in the mixed farming site, a Landcare group was the access point for the Sustainable Farm Families programme, while the Country Fire Authority (CFA) (a local group made up primarily of volunteers) was an access point for health checks:

> Through the Land Care group, we did it as a group. I think it was a really good thing. We've been doing it three years. We've been back each year for follow-up checkups to see how people have lost weight or their blood pressure or their cholesterol and those sort of things; just checkups. And that was a really good thing and I think doing it in a group made you aware and it sort of put a bit of pressure on you to achieve something at the end of it. (Male mixed farmer)

> They [the Country Fire Authority] sent a little team of people around and we all had our cholesterol and blood pressure and weight and all that sort of stuff checked...it was actually done at someone's house. There was about, sort of about 25 of us in the brigade and we all got checked over. (Male mixed farmer)

Soft entry points to health services resulted from leadership actions of community members. At the mixed farming site, a female farmer had applied for funding to provide a new gym for the community;

to provide a space for community members for both physical activity and social connection:

> I've applied for a grant for $5,000 to update a gym in [name of town], and my purpose of that is to get, not only [a] discussion group of farmer people, they're on an exercise bike having a chat but also to get the arthritis group there and get the footy club there...a community gym, that people can come and go. Not everyone's going to use it but hopefully [after the upgrade] more in the community can use it. (Female mixed farmer)

Groups that were associated with each industry were especially effective in attracting farmers and fishers to health programmes and events. Industry associations in the cotton and cane sites, and community groups in the mixed farming site assisted farmers to develop and act on strategies to support their health and wellbeing during difficult times.

Industry organisations were also important in advocating for services for communities where their members lived and worked. They also drew on bridging and linking social capital in connecting farmers with external health services and resources that fitted with farmers' needs and used their shared identity and trustworthiness with farmers to encourage farmers to make the best use of services. In the cane site, the local branch of the industry association was very proactive in keeping in regular contact with cane growers, and in supporting and brokering health programmes for the benefit of members. Industry organisations were also highly valued in the cotton site because of their provision of activities and programmes that facilitated social connectedness and social support among community members:

> To me health and wellbeing is not just physical; it's mentally as well. And because they're [Cotton Australia] so supportive and they do organise different workshops and different social things as well, that's obviously getting us all out of our comfort zone and being able to interact with so many things. (Female cotton grower)

Several health-related programmes in the cane site including the Community Response to Eliminating Suicide program (CORES) used the Cane Growers Association to contact potential participants. As well as ease of access to their target audience, health programme providers were able to use the credibility and trust the farmers have in their industry organisations to promote their programmes to potential participants:

> Cane growers aren't running them, but they are involved with the people running it, and using our organisation to help them get in contact with more people. (Male cane grower)

Interactional infrastructure

Communities are a primary source of interactional infrastructure and are places to maintain and build social connectedness. In all communities except fishing, there was a perception that people 'look out' for one another: 'when you're all in it together you can just sort of jolly each other up' (Female mixed farmer). While farmers in all sites used physical infrastructure for health and wellbeing such as gyms, yoga classes and sports clubs, sports clubs were also a key piece of interactional infrastructure in communities and provided valuable opportunities for social connection. Most farmers were involved in community groups and said the main benefit of being a part of community groups was mental wellbeing:

> It's been very important to have mental health information in the community and where we can get people to talk about it in a non-threatening environment. An informal gathering. The one we had was at the pub at [name], a dinner. (Female grain grower)

Community interactional infrastructure was especially important in mobilising community action for health during difficult times. More vulnerable communities, in particular at the grains and mixed farming sites, which had been experiencing drought for over ten years, developed interaction to encourage community connectedness. For example, one female grain grower described how the drought had brought the community together and there was a stronger emphasis on supporting the community as a whole to 'get through' the drought in good health and wellbeing: 'but if anything the drought has brought the community together...things will turn around as long as we can all get through this in good health. And that's been our emphasis.'

These communities developed informal opportunities to get together to help cope with the stress of difficult times. For example, in the mixed farming site, a mixed farmer and friends organised community dinners, a women's friendship group and a mystery bus tour for men to get them away from their farms. This is another example of where community members were the initiators and drivers of the social connectedness initiative and sourced sponsorship from local industry groups to supply goods for these events:

> I organised the friendship days for the women, [and] I organised for a coach load of farming men to go into town on a mystery tour...I thought [it] was really important that we go and pick them up rather than the other way around, because you'd never get them there otherwise...they went into [town name] and I had a motivational speaker ... that's known across Australia just about – and they had lunch provided for them and they played ten pin bowling. (Female mixed farmer)

In the grains site which was suffering from ten years of severe drought, one person's house became a drop-in centre and a mechanic business had formed an informal men's support group for farmers. This informal support group that had developed spontaneously and provided a social connection opportunity for local farmers provides a good example of community responsiveness during difficult times in developing interactional infrastructure that could provide protection from poor mental health:

> The garage is good because we go there for morning *smoko* [colloquial term for a tea or coffee break] or afternoon *smoko*, like half past ten or something and have morning *smoko*. And you know we'll sit down and have a cup of coffee and have a yack about the footy or whatever...it's not official, it's just everyone goes there for *smoko*. (Male grain grower)

> The garage, [name]...I think that's been a saving feature for a lot of the farmers. They just go in there, and it's just been somewhere to talk – not judgemental...It's very informal...there are some people who go there every day, they come in to town just to go. And it's been a wonderful thing. They won the Community Group of the Year last year. (Female grain grower)

While some farmers valued community activities because they provided opportunities to talk to others in similar difficult circumstances, others valued social interactions with people not involved in farming:

> We belong to the [name] cropping group and they are a fantastic supporting group. They were very helpful in the depths of the worst droughts that we've had...They weren't having troubles but they were, they were really sympathetic, you know, and warm and welcoming and things. (Female mixed farmer)

Some identified how participation in locally run farmer health education programmes during difficult times was beneficial because they raised awareness of mental health needs and developed skills and capacity to allow them to better identify potential issues and manage difficult times. Younger farmers were more likely to report having participated in these sorts of programmes. For example, one younger male farmer described how programmes provided them with tools and strategies to help cope with stress and anxiety:

> I was asked to go along and I thought that was a good thing to do...I thought it was really useful, yeah, I mean changing you mentally, changing your mind around actually taking it in, you think you know everything but actually changing about the importance of certain things got you, really. (Male mixed farmer)

Communities which had experienced more severe pressures over longer periods of time, associated with prolonged drought in particular, tended to have embedded mechanisms to support mental wellbeing into community life, suggesting that external pressures can prompt effective community responses. Industry associations had been active in sponsoring mental health programmes in the grains site:

> The New South Wales Farmers put on a few meetings that I went to about mental health, depression and things like that. I went to a few of those just to confirm in my mind that, yeah, that it was probably I had to watch what I was doing. (Male grain grower)

The community-initiated mental health programme, CORES was also offered in the grains sites and was one of several health-related programmes that used industry organisations to persuade people to take part in the programme. In the mixed farming site, community dinners were run by the Tennis Club for the Drought Support group and organisations such as Centrelink, Rural Financial Counselling, Rural Finance and a family care organisation were in attendance to provide support to farmers:

> Our Tennis Club actually instigated [the community dinners] and through our Drought Support and we had all the, that was one of the very early ones. All the Centrelink, Rural Financial Counselling, Rural Finance, all the bodies, ah, [name of district] Family Care, everything invited to there. They set up their stands and they had, were able to have people interviewed and so forth. That was fantastic support...and it was fantastic the people that turned up that I thought would never, ever, but I think that everybody got to that stage where we've got to have something for ourselves but we've also gotta stick together. And that way, you're stronger! (Female mixed farmer)

Farmers in the grains sites who reported that they were under more stress from difficult times than people in other sites, commented that services need to be appropriate to community needs. Within this site there had been a number of mental health initiatives and it is possible that as a result grain growers were more likely than other groups to describe social connectedness actions as part of their strategy for staying healthy. They were critical that the same programmes were repeated over and over, however, and there was no coordinated strategy. This may be attributable to the lack of focused local industry leadership and coordination to facilitate health planning at the grains site, unlike at the cotton and cane sites.

When community members are under pressure, small communities became resource stretched. Farmers talked about the need for those outside of their community to recognise the costs of providing additional services.

> I think the community does have a responsibility, and... there are some of us within the community that have looked into the provision of mental health service. But I don't know that the community has to bear the cost of it, I think that's too high an expectation for a little town like this. (Male cotton grower)

Some communities do not become energised, however. Within the fishing site there was limited interactional infrastructure or leadership roles undertaken by boundary crossers. While cane, cotton, grains and mixed farming communities were cohesive and supportive, there was not the same sense of community identity and cohesion in the fishing community:

> Looking at this town, it's dying. And from what I'm hearing up and down the coast all the little towns are dying...there's a lot of greedy fishermen left, don't care about their fellow fishermen, all it's just 'me, me, me'. (Male fisher)

Exclusion from benefits of community action

All four farming sites appeared to be inclusive, and leaders' actions intended for the good of their community generally rather than some individuals within it. In contrast, fishers discussed feeling isolated within their geographic community and excluded from the benefits of community action and social capital observed in the other sites. While farmers in other sites lived and worked in their communities, reflecting a collective sense of geographical community, some fishers travelled into the site for work and lived external to the community where they worked. As a consequence, fishers faced more challenges which affected their ability and willingness to access an appropriate range of health and wellbeing supports:

> I haven't, I don't get involved. Things changed from, you know, I don't, 'cause I don't sort of base myself like we used to, you know this was home eight years ago. You knew everything that was going on, but really I'm not up with it. (Male fisher)

Fishers were less likely to mention attention to mental wellbeing and social connectedness as part of their efforts to stay healthy, were likely to use alcohol to relieve stress and were less likely to access mental health services because of social stigma.

> I'm wrecking it [my health] by smoking and drinking. I like me drink. Always have. You know, in this environment of fishing, always been a drinking environment. (Male fisher)

You could employ ten people, psychologists, and I don't believe you would get ten fishermen to go and see them. Personally that's what I think. Well I know none of our family would. (Male fisher)

These behaviour patterns were less observed in other sites. Fishers were also less likely to draw on industry organisations for broader health and wellbeing support, particularly mental health support. There was no active industry organisation in the site with the capacity to cross the boundary between industry and health services and broker appropriate support.

Conclusions

Difficult times can exacerbate the negative impacts of isolation and limited health service provision in rural communities, although they can also bring communities together. The difference in the resources and capacity of community and industry groups and organisations influenced the decisions and behaviours of farmers, as did the level of community and industry social capital. Internal community and industry resources incubated community action through boundary crossers and interactional infrastructure in particular.

Boundary crossers are key actors who provide their communities with bridging and linking social capital resources. Farmers preferred services and programmes that were initiated and maintained through the agency of community social capital and local leadership. They engaged with information and programmes that were endorsed by credible and trusted individuals and organisations. Boundary crossers and local leaders possess these important characteristics.

Community action in farming communities is supported from private as well as public sources. Private resources in the form of community and industry groups acted to provide effective soft entry points for farmers to access publicly funded health services and programmes. These groups can provide spaces for physical activity and social interaction in small rural communities where there is limited interactional infrastructure. Community action responds to difficult times by building and drawing on interactional infrastructure.

The fishing site provides an example of a community that was not energised, and highlights key factors that may be important in mobilising community action, such as a sense of identity and a sense of place, which appear to be lacking in communities within the fishing site. As a result, many fishers were excluded from support; they 'slipped between' communities.

A clear implication of this research is the desirability of a collaborative approach to planning for community benefit. Much of the interactional infrastructure in small rural communities is in private hands, typically community and farming industry groups, while many key services are publicly funded. Boundary crossers are a mechanism for harnessing resources both internal and external to communities to generate programmes and services that align with community needs.

References

Albrecht, G, Sartore, G-M, Connor, L, Higginbotham, N, Freeman, S, Kelly, B et al, 2007, Solastalgia: The distress caused by environmental change, *Australasian Psychiatry* 15, S1, S95–S98

Alston, M, Kent, J, 2008, The Big Dry: The link between rural masculinities and poor health outcomes for farming men, *Journal of Sociology* 44, 2, 133–47

Birchip Cropping Group, 2008, *'Critical breaking point?' The effcts of drought and other pressures on farming families*, Final report, Victoria: Birchip Cropping Group

Caldwell, K, Boyd, C, 2009, Coping and resilience in farming families affected by drought, *Rural and Remote Health* 9, 2, 1088–8

Falk, I, Kilpatrick, S, 2000, What is social capital? A study of interaction in a rural community, *Sociologia Ruralis* 40, 1, 87–110

Haslam McKenzie, F, 2003, The challenges of achieving community self-determination and capacity building in a neo-liberal political environment, *Australian Journal of Primary Health* 9, 1, 39–49

Healy, K, Hampshire, A, Ayres, L, 2004, Beyond the local: Extending the social capital discourse, *Australian Journal of Social Issues* 39, 3, 329–42

Hegney, DG, Buikstra, E, Baker, P, Rogers-Clark, C, Pearce, S, Ross, H et al, 2007, Individual resilience in rural people: A Queensland study, Australia, *Rural and Remote Health* 7, 4, 1–13

Hossain, D, Eley, R, Coutts, J, Gorman, D, 2008, Mental health of farmers in Southern Queensland: Issues and support, *Australian Journal of Rural Health* 16, 6, 343–8

Humphreys, JS, 2000, Rural families and rural health, *Journal of Family Studies* 6, 2, 167–81

Kilpatrick, S, Falk, I, 2003, Learning in agriculture: Building social capital in island communities, *Local environment* 8, 5, 501–12

Kilpatrick, S, Loechel, B, 2004, Interactional infrastructure in rural communities: matching training needs and provision, *Rural Society* 14, 1, 4–21

Kilpatrick, S, Cheers, B, Gilles, M, Taylor, J, 2009, Boundary crossers, communities, and health: Exploring the role of rural health professionals, *Health & Place* 15, 1, 284–90

King, D, Lane, A, MacDougall, C, Greenhill, J, 2009, *The resilience and mental health and wellbeing of farm families experiencing climate variation in South Australia*, Adelaide: National Institute of Labour Studies Incorporated

King, KM, Thomlinson, E, Sanguins, J, LeBlanc, P, 2006, Men and women managing coronary artery disease risk: Urban–rural contrasts, *Social Science & Medicine* 62, 5, 1091–2

Lower, T, Fragar, L, Temperley, J, 2011, *Health and safety on Australian farms*, Barton, ACT: Collaborative partnership for farming and fishing health and safety, Rural industries research and development corporation

OECD (Organisation for Economic Co-operation and Development), 2001, *The well-being of nations: The role of human and social capital*, Paris: OECD

Townsend, M, Moore, J, Mahoney, M, 2002, Playing their part: The role of physical activity and sport in sustaining the health and wellbeing of small rural communities, *Rural and Remote Health* 2, 109, 1–7

Woolcock, M, 1998, Social capital and economic development: Toward a theoretical synthesis and policy framework, *Theory and Society* 27, 2, 151–208

6

Associative action in urban planning: case studies from Marseille, France

Maha Messaoudène, Daniel Pinson, Mustapha Berra

Introduction

'Community planning' (as an instrumental action, pursuing a positive public good) may initially appear inappropriate to the French situation with regards to urban planning. Although associations founded on a platform of voluntary action – like the *Fondation de l'Abbé Pierre* or militant groups like the DAL (*Droit au Logement* – the right to housing) and the action of collective movements meeting irregularly on a regional or city-wide basis – are accepted and sanctioned by the state, these associations are often regarded, both by those who initiated them and by those who have been confronted by them, less as vehicles for self-help and more as expressions of opposition to authorities which are seen as abusing their powers or failing to address the concerns and needs of minority or dominated groups. They are viewed as militant, often mobilising in the face of perceived threats from urban development or the practice of urban planning. It is from this viewpoint of general consideration that we shall examine the relationship between basic urbanist actions and the authorities in power, in France and in the region of Marseille, and several specific cases. Our concern in this chapter is with the challenging context for 'community' action, and the struggle to secure basic rights and representation, in some of Europe's poorest and most disadvantaged neighbourhoods.

Let us assimilate those entering the country (to the tune of 'Allons Enfants de la Patrie...', La Marseillaise, Rouget de L'Isle, 1792)

The republican conception of French society

In the French understanding of society, the notion of 'community' generally refers to a group distinguished by ethnic or religious origin, and which may possibly be part of a well-defined region. Alternatively, the idea of community may simply be associated with the 'commune' (the lowest level of territorial governance), in which case there is no allusion to religious, ideological or ethnic basis. The community merely comprises the residents, French citizens, of a particular place. So conceptions of community divide into two types: the first looks for particular traits that bind people together; the second is 'socio-spatial' but does not assume any particular bonds between individuals: they are merely co-located. The community discourse in France has been dominated not by the positive interactions between community actors (which is the focus throughout much of this book), but by a fear of the introverted nature of some communities and by the social tensions that arise from a lack of cultural integration.

Thus the term 'community' is viewed differently in France than in many Anglo-Saxon countries. Its meaning is ambiguous and even suspect, being associated with a pejorative form of 'communitarianism' which threatens national unity. The existence of minorities – sometimes with their secessional ambitions (for example, Corsicans, Bretons or Basques) or displaying a tendency to retreat into ghettos (for example, those from the former North African colonies) – fuels irrational fears among Republicans, leading both national government and local authorities to deny these regions and groups the means to do more for themselves, for fear that it will accelerate social disintegration. This is clearly a very different context for community action: one in which that action, if undertaken in areas of severe social need or political ambition, is viewed with suspicion and as a force for undermining the state. There is a tradition of interventionism in France, exercised by and in support of a strong state, and this colours attitudes towards the idea of community and perceptions of what rights and responsibilities should, or should not, be assigned.

Assimilation as a model, and social mix as an approach in the field of housing

Assimilation has been a key goal of the French immigration model. After the Second World War, immigrants arriving in the country to assist with reconstruction (especially from the former colonies) and who helped achieve the 'Trente Glorieuses' – the 30 years of economic growth after the war – were repatriated once their periods of employment had ended. This approach was slowly phased out and immigrants exercised their right to stay in France. The state then set about housing immigrants and their families in the large public estates of the 1960s, moving to a policy of integration (Kepel, 2012) which aimed to achieve social mixing. The goal of this strategy was to realise the republican vision of social assimilation, and it initially yielded some positive results with French and immigrant families integrating well. Evaluations at the time pointed to the many benefits achieved: upward social mobility through a sharing of contacts; effective integration of children within the school system; and clear socio-economic advantage for the longest-standing immigrant families, who enjoyed many social benefits over the previous generation.

The strategy was particularly effective for the first waves of immigrants from the Maghreb immediately after the war. It seemed to work less well, however, for immigrants from more distant cultures (those from Vietnam, China or 'black' Africa). The growing economic crisis of the 1970s, combined with the departure of the now more affluent immigrant (and non-immigrant) families from the great housing estates during the same period, triggered the socio-economic decline of these places. They became 'sink' estates from which the previous social mix of residents disappeared, to be replaced by an ethnic mix whose common denominator was extreme poverty.

From suppressing local co-operation...

Co-operative action has ancient origins in France, but its development in the twentieth century was hampered by the strong intervention, noted above, that has orientated the structuring of French society. There has been a concern to steer social development in a particular direction: policy-makers have not celebrated difference, and nor have they promoted different approaches to development in different places. At the beginning of the twentieth century, public bureaus were established, under the Bonnevay Law 1912, to fund public housing. As in other parts of Europe, the rate of public housing production accelerated in the 1950s as part of wider reconstruction efforts and in response to economic growth. That growth followed on from a period of acute shortage of housing just after the war, which was highlighted by Abbé Pierre (founder of the Emmaus movement, which helped homeless people and refugees) and to which the state responded with an authoritarian policy of property requisition and industrial construction, based predominantly on the model set out by the Modern Movement. An enormous 'public housing enterprise' (Raymond, 1984) was set in motion which was mainly concerned with building and management, relegating social programmes behind this primary mission. Other initiatives were suppressed, including the self-build schemes being promoted at the time by trade unionists (Pinson, 2012).

...to resident mobilisation

Requisition became a catalyst, however, for unrest. After 1968, many inner-city neighbourhoods became stages for popular struggles against evictions, and these struggles gave residents the opportunity to unite and collectively organise the defence of their homes. The immediate impact was often non-eviction; but the longer-lasting legacy was a changed vision of the city and new forms of social organisation within these neighbourhoods. The struggles also prompted a reappraisal of public housing policy and a softening of what had previously been a very centralised approach to housing delivery and management. Suddenly, there were calls to focus on the 'social development of neighbourhoods' (Blancherie et al, 1972) and the subsequent 'Public Housing White Book' of 1975 asserted for the first time that the mobilisation of residents and their active participation in neighbourhood affairs should be a key goal of future public policy. It added that the mere maintenance or physical renovation of housing could no longer be the sole occupation of that policy, but that it should extend its reach into the social, economic, cultural and educational life of neighbourhoods. Very soon, a raft of initiatives were launched that aimed to address these concerns.

During the years that followed, however, the attention given to 'problem neighbourhoods' tended to have a stigmatising effect. For that reason, the focus switched – by 1990 – to whole town policies which avoided targeting particular areas. These tried to create a level playing field of social and economic opportunity without advertising any 'priority geography' or setting any particular 'urban boundaries' for intervention. This meant that much of the targeted funding for social programmes, created after 1975, started to dry up and the organisations that had formed in the early 1970s began to look for direct funding from the state. This was subject to strict conditions and proved difficult to access. It did little, therefore, to promote social development.

This brief narrative says much about the French resistance to supporting community development and initiative and the preference for strictly controlled interventions. Early promotion, 40 years ago, of social development at a neighbourhood level was quickly reined back and straitjacketed by funding restrictions, which had the aim of restricting activities according to particular central policy objectives. Neighbourhood organisations found themselves corralled into specific areas of activity, seeking support from the ANRU (*Agence Nationale de la Rénovation urbaine* – National Agency for Urban Renovation) for physical regeneration, or the ACSE (*Agence nationale pour la cohésion sociale et l'égalité des chances* – National Agency for social cohesion and equal opportunities). Neighbourhood activities became tightly 'administered' from Paris. Local groups needed the support, but it came with many strings attached, as government sought to steer the types of projects and activities of those organisations emerging from the protests of the late 1960s.

Challenging representative democracy

The crisis in representative democracy – felt throughout Europe and beyond – has, however, given further impetus to local activism (see Chapter 1, this volume). Since the 1980s, the rate of abstention in most local, regional and national elections has been increasing. In response, new opportunities have been created for citizens to express their views on changes or developments affecting their environment or daily lives. A series of laws – beginning with the Bouchardeau Law 1983 (requiring that all projects likely to have an impact on the environment be subject to public inquiry) (European Conference of Ministers of Transport, 2003, 83) and then moving through the Solidarity and Urban Renewal (SRU) Law 2000 and Local Democracy Law 2002 – have gradually strengthened the requirement to consult and involve residents in transport and development decisions. The 2002 law, for example, created *Comités de Quartier* (neighbourhood committees) in cities with more than 80,000 inhabitants. This followed on from the creation of a National Commission for Public Debate (CNDP) in 1997, with responsibility for facilitating engagement around large-scale developments.

These legislative changes have given rise to an important debate within the political and research communities. This has focused on the motives behind the move to a more open democracy in which there seem to be greater opportunities for input and discourse. Is the aim to genuinely compensate for the limits and failings of representative democracy, delivering real empowerment, or is the actual goal simply to diffuse local conflict, with minimum impact on top-down interventions, and in order to protect government from the accusation that its mandate is increasingly fragile?

A number of research networks in France are now focused on this critical question, including the 'Democracy and Participation' (GIS) group, formed in 2010. More broadly, the '*Collectif Pouvoir d'agir*' –

comprising individuals, local associations and national research groups concerned with the political responses to social exclusion – was created in the same year. *Pouvoir d'agir* or the 'power to act' is taken to have the same meaning as the English term 'empowerment'. The collective published a key report in 2013, advocating a 'democracy of involvement' (Bacqué and Mechmache, 2013) though it is too early to say whether such mobilisation will have any effect on urban policy.

So far in this chapter, we have drawn a picture of neighbourhood action in France growing from the urban protests of the 1960s, but in a broader context of official resistance and an overarching philosophy of centrism and interventionism: ideas that support the republican conception of statehood and national unity. The crisis of democracy and the risk of a weakened electoral mandate for central intervention has, however, provided an added impetus for more open democracy in France over the last 20 or so years. In the remainder of this chapter, we examine how participation and the *pouvoir d'agir* is able to express itself in the region of Marseille and in the working-class areas to the north of the city in particular.

The city of Marseille

Marseille has always been considered a 'special case' among French cities. It is a city of pronounced segregation, with the historic line of the *Canebière* running from the Vieux Port separating the very poor north from the wealthy south. In recent years, this line has become perforated as the middle classes flee the city, bringing a penetration of poorer households into the south. Marseille is now the most impoverished large city (with a population of more than a million inhabitants) in France. A third of the population live beneath the poverty line and within the working-class areas, more than half of all young people are unemployed. At the time of writing, a long and slow journey towards socio-economic recovery (assisted by the *Euromediterranée* project focused on the rejuvenation of the city's port area) which seemed to be given momentum by Marseille's designation as European Capital of Culture in 2013, appears to have been brought to an abrupt end by a fresh outbreak of violence and gangland killings linked to drug trafficking. An almost apocalyptic picture has been painted of the city, within the media and by a number of politicians. In that climate, it is difficult to detach oneself from the everyday drama and to think critically about what has been achieved through experimental participative urbanism in Marseille's working-class neighbourhoods. In the sections that follow, we examine the story of the 'MOS', a housing renewal intervention with the attendant aim of promoting and co-ordinating social development and community organising, first in Marseille and then in other French inner-cities.

The Petit Seminaire experiment and the repowering of neighbourhoods

The MOS (which later became MOUS) was born in Marseille; it grew out of the work of the *Centre d'Etudes, de Recherches et de Formation Institutionnelle du Sud-Est* (CERFISE), a research unit founded in 1975 by the sociologist Michel Anselme. The unit's focus was on bringing about a transformation of social housing areas in the city. Anselme was influenced by Michel Foucault's work on the 'equipment of power', and the struggles that individuals engage in against exploitation, undertaken during the 1970s (later published in 'The subject and power', Foucault, 1983). CERFISE and Anselme worked, in the early to mid-1980s, on the '*Petit Seminaire*', an area of social housing built in 1959 which had become blighted by a range of problems. In that project, focus was put on understanding the lives and the values of inhabitants. Anselme began by inventing a fictional city in which people could express opinion freely without fear of ridicule or repression. He offered that vision to the bureaucrats in charge of Marseille's public housing, challenging their view that residents articulate only confused and contradictory opinions and therefore that the role of bureaucrats, as public landlord, should be to replace lay 'irrationality' with an informed and expert vision of a 'good neighbourhood'. CERFISE eventually acted as an intermediary between the landlord and the tenants. It tried to convince these groups that residents are not always irrational, and intervention is not always negative, eventually proposing to create a 'public space' (or 'public sphere' in the sense used by Habermas to describe an area that promotes social life, where individuals can congregate to work through their problems) which would be a place of ritual and drama and with great 'power attached to it' (Anselme, 2000). The aim was to establish the interactional infrastructure (akin to that in Kilpatrick and colleagues' study) of the city, which was hitherto lacking, and which could be used to draw out shared values and, in the long term, assist in 'community development'.

Specificities of the Marseille social world

Social unity (and therefore the potential for community development, as understood elsewhere in the world) is, however, perhaps more difficult to achieve in Marseille than in many other cities. Anselme believed that family networks, underpinning criminality, had become an 'inescapable reality for those wishing to understand...the dynamics and specific management problems facing authorities', adding that Marseille was witnessing a 'reappearance or perpetuation of a type of Mediterranean sociability' (Anselme, 2000), based around the family and fuelled by poverty. The more recent consequences of this have been the creation of a volatile and violent 'gangland' in which families compete for monopoly control of various criminal activities. There is great solidarity within the gangs, which could be said to possess an abundance of 'social capital', but not always wielded with positive ends in sight (see Rydin, Chapter 2, this volume).

It is not only the criminality which poses a significant challenge in Marseille, but also the reality of spatially diffuse family and ethnic networks being stronger than local bonds. This means that the sense of belonging, locally, to a place is weaker in these poorer neighbourhoods: the reality is of a city comprising a complex mosaic of affinity with sometimes dozens of different ethnic groups living in close proximity but displaying limited sociability with one another. This weakens any sense of a 'socio-spatial community', making it difficult to achieve the dialectic goals of an open democracy or Anselme's fiction of the ideal city.

Obstacles to democracy in Marseille: the economy of drugs and corruption

Marseille is a city of multiple unofficial economies, from the makeshift economy of repair services (Tarrius, 2002) to the international trade of people trafficking. These activities can be highly profitable for their participants (Péraldi, 1999) but, alongside the drug economy, they have a hugely detrimental effect on the urban society (Duport, 2012). These activities come to dominate economic life and come to be seen as 'normal' by many young people. Rather than having school, apprenticeships and career aspirations as their reference points, those growing up in these areas can quickly become drawn into the unofficial economies and this acts as a brake on open dialogue as people become locked into crime and increasingly fearful, as a result, of engagement with authorities. There seems to be little point, in this context, of investing in the interactional infrastructure called for by Michel Anselme. The interactions that do occur have not always been positive: the structures of local power have occasionally been drawn into some of the criminal activity that festers in Marseille's working-class neighbourhoods. The president of the *Conseil General des Bouches du*

Rhône was found to have given out a procurement contract for waste treatment in return for bribes; members of a specialist unit of the national police (the BAC Nord), since disbanded, were found to be guilty of protecting some drug gangs in return for a percentage of the profit from trafficking. Such episodes do little to build trust between the neighbourhoods and the local state and create an obviously challenging environment for positive community development.

Self-development in the Marseille region

Despite this sombre picture, however, there have been a number of localised community development initiatives. Some of these started with very modest ambitions but have been assisted by national agencies. The '*Compagnons Bâtisseurs*' (or 'building companions') came together to assist new immigrants (principally Comorians) develop the skills needed to improve the very poor and neglected private accommodation in which they found themselves when arriving in France. They provided not only the technical skills for undertaking immediate repairs, but also skills that might be of use in the labour market. In some instances the building companions have been called on to assist middle-class households, residing elsewhere in the city or even further afield, in group build projects. In recent years, small complexes of typically 10 to 12 apartments, built by their occupants, have sprung up all over France.

Back in Marseille, however, there have also been more broadly focused 'self-help' initiatives aimed at improving the social, economic and physical circumstances in which immigrants find themselves. The success of these initiatives has been circumscribed by a number of factors, as we shall see in the two examples that are now presented.

Participation and choice in two Marseille estates (Bellevue and Bassens)

The illustrative cases used in this section draw from research into participative processes in the Bellevue and Bassens areas of the city (Messaoudène, 2010; 2012). Both look at the way in which the *pouvoir d'agir* is expressed, its outcomes and the limits to this form or power and action. The cases also say something about the degree of acceptance of difference and different needs within French society and by the state.

Bellevue is in the third *arrondissement* of Marseille, in the Saint-Mauront district. The example of participation concerns engagement around a top-down intervention leading to the demolition and rebuilding of part of the existing public housing in a very rundown area with what is a diverse population, but dominated by settled North African immigrants who have been joined by an influx of Comorians since the 1990s. Bassens is in the fifteenth *arrondissement* close to the Arnavaux industrial estate. The example here is of a small housing estate with a 'transitory' population. It was built in the 1960s and has since become home to an Algerian population with very dense social networks which have had a strong impact on the form and outcome of residents' initiatives. Like the Bellevue case, this example also involved mobilisation and participation around housing renewal.

Figure 6.1: Bellevue and Bassens

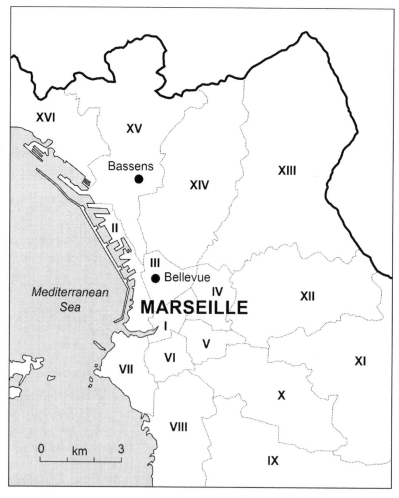

The Bellevue and Bassens interventions

Bellevue in the late 1990s was subject to the *Plan de Sauvegarde* (1999–2004) which aimed to reduce housing density in the area by removing 132 apartments from a total of 814, and thereafter renovating and improving the remaining stock. This was a top-down intervention, but one that sought to engage with an existing residents' association – the *Amicale des Locataires* (Tenants' Friendly Society) – which, however, was largely inactive and seemed to represent very few of the area's residents. From the point of view of the local authorities, the objective in Bellevue was to generate trust in the process, by spreading information about the project and by being receptive to local concerns. It was generally felt that dialogue between residents and the institutional stakeholders would quicken the pace of development and reduce friction and potential conflict. To that end, a total of 54 meetings took place. Yet attendance at those meetings was not always high and it proved difficult to connect to some groups: the established North African community was easier to mobilise, but the newer Comorian migrants tended to distance themselves from the orchestrated participation. A particular issue in Bellevue was the 'cultural distance' (and trust) between more settled immigrants and the public authorities and between the newer arrivals and those same authorities.

In Bassens, participation was again prompted by proposed housing renewal in the form of a MOUS intervention. Originally built in 1964 to replace what had been a 'shanty town', it was decided in 1991 that the complex of apartments on the site should be demolished and that residents should be decanted to homes outside of Bassens. The 1964 development had comprised 110 apartments each of less than 40 square metres. This number was reduced to 56 by an earlier intervention in 1975. In some ways, the story of Bassens is more complex than that of Bellevue. Some of the Algerian residents, incensed by the plan to demolish their homes, refused to move, which prompted prolonged engagement and more spontaneous forms of local action. It also led to a further project by the Marseille–Habitat public housing body between 1998 and 2004 aimed at allowing the remaining 31 families on the site to be rehoused in situ, in 40 apartments (built in two phases) in a low-rise 'maisonette' style (see Figure 6.2).

Image 6.1: Bellevue (Messaoudène, 2005)

Image 6.2: Bassens (Messaoudène, 2005)

Processes

In this section we wish to focus briefly on the experience of participation in the two study areas, drawing on observations from meetings between representatives of the local authorities and resident groups. It is sometimes said that participation is an opportunity for those who have already taken key decisions to merely persuade 'community actors' of the wisdom of those decisions: to convince them at an early stage of the 'right' decision (that is, to 'educate') and therefore avoid later conflict. Meetings in both areas were sometimes confrontational. In one instance, a resident objected to the replacement of communal windows in the apartment blocks (in Bellevue) with metal bars. Irritated by the criticism, the local authority representative said that the replacement had become necessary as many residents elected to throw rubbish out of the communal windows, often breaking them, and displayed absolutely no respect for their homes or the communal spaces. There was no focus on working with residents to change behaviour (perhaps by installing new means of disposing of rubbish quickly from upper floors), but rather the imposition of what appeared to be punitive (and cheap) measures that might well have resulted in rubbish piling up in corridors.

It was clear in the meetings that residents were concerned about their living environment. Many wished to see the installation of automatic watering systems for flower beds and green areas, rather than infrequent manual watering. This was dismissed as too expensive and 'technically difficult'. The Bellevue residents appeared to have little capacity to understand costs and lacked the knowledge needed to rebut what were clearly flawed technical arguments from the local authority. The clear intention was to drive the project through, making only minor tactical concessions to the residents. The only 'victory' won by the *Amicale des Locataires* was the naming of a new access road to the site.

The entire engagement at Bellevue appeared tokenistic: the local authority provided basic information on the operations underway, and displayed little concern for promoting genuine involvement. The core problems, however, lay with the residents themselves. Their *pouvoir d'agir* was critically constrained by their own internal divisions. The North Africans were tentatively engaged with the *Amicale des Locataires* but the Comorians were entirely absent from this organisation. This might simply be explained by the short period of time they had spent in the area, relative to their North African neighbours. Detailed research with Comorians in Marseille (Direche-Slimani and Le Houerou, 2002) has, however, shown that patterns of sociability are shaped by 'dense, complex associative organisation' sometimes expressed in extremely closed social and cultural events. In other words, these recent immigrants keep themselves to themselves and may be suspicious of broader social engagement, not being familiar with its rules and rituals. They expend their energy, instead, on internalised activity and a 'veil of invisibility' has therefore hung over Marseille's Comorian 'community' for a number of years. For reasons of protection, it is closely knit and difficult to penetrate. In Bellevue, the particular division between the North Africans and the Comorians may appear odd as both groups are Muslim, but they participate in different Islamic practices and are not therefore joined in common worship.

The Bassens area displayed no such divisions, and the Algerian population was accustomed to fighting for its rights. Since the Beurs' March for equality and against racism in October 1983 ('Beur' being French slang for people with North African roots) the attitudes of many North Africans against the 'host' population had changed. A belief developed that protest offered a real means of changing attitudes and outcomes, and from the 1980s onwards, immigrants from this part of the world became much faster to mobilise and to voice opposition to unwanted interference, or claim particular rights. The right to better housing had become a regular battle cry, which was quickly heard in Bassens. From the very first meeting organised by the newly-formed residents' committee in Servières, it was clear that there would be conflict. The local authority's aim was to demolish Bassens and relocate its residents away from the nearby industrial estate. In the face of stiff opposition – galvanised behind a local man who emerged to lead the committee and mobilise the area's residents – the authority offered a range of incentives, none of which were accepted by the Algerian community.

The contrast with Bellevue could not have been more striking. Faced with an articulate, well-organised community (which knew its rights and had a single, clear, goal), the local authority was quickly forced onto the back foot. By the time the authority came round to the view that it needed to work *with* the community towards a compromise, the latter's goals had been much refined. It no longer wished merely to stay put, but had a very specific set of requirements. The local authority returned to Bassens in 1998; this time with a proposal to replace the existing apartments with new homes, and to move residents away from the industrial estate and bring them closer to an adjacent railway line. The tenants' committee was unconvinced by the plan and therefore asked the City of Marseille to intervene and require further physical protection from the railway. Once this was agreed, the works commenced according to a plan that had been approved by the local community.

What became clear during these second phase negotiations was that the community was technically adept at interpreting plans, weighing up their implications, and responding with clear counter-arguments and requiring specific alterations. There was a capacity in the tenants' association to communicate beyond the area (on the part of the leader of the committee) and to understand the technical arguments and realities presented by the authority. In Bellevue, these resources were entirely absent. In Bassens, they were in ample supply, with the community endowed with a great deal of social capital. One good example of this is what happened after the authority had completed the first phase of the project on-site. Many of the residents of Bassens worked in the building trade and were familiar with 'plans of works' and building quality standards. After the first homes were built, they were inspected by these residents, who drew attention to poor workmanship, problems with sound insulation and instances of kitchen layouts not adhering to the original plans.

Once again the residents mobilised, using a cultural festival organised by a young artist from the neighbourhood as a platform for their concerns. Following a lengthy protest, during which the community was unable to persuade the local authority to respond to the problems, the two parties took their grievance to court. A subsequent ruling in favour of the residents led to the appointment of an independent inspector of works. The inspector instructed the authority to rectify a number of problems with the completed homes. These works commenced in April 2000 and the residents were finally rehoused in 2004.

Outcomes

In contrast to Bellevue, there was no pre-existing tenants' group in Bassens. Rather, a tenants' committee was established in response to the MOUS intervention. Its president, a charismatic personality in whom the residents had great faith, was to play a determining role in the way in which the project was carried out and in realising the final outcomes for tenants. He proved to be a pragmatist and networker, someone able to communicate effectively with public officials. He was very much the 'everyday fixer' described by Van der Pennen and Schreuders (Chapter 8, this volume) and the 'boundary-crosser' described by Kilpatrick and colleagues (Chapter 5, this volume). With his leadership, there was a proactive mobilisation of residents through a number of associations and staged events. The public authorities were confronted by a vocal group, able to articulate their concerns on their own terms. They could not be merely 'persuaded' of the logic of the intervention and the planned decant through staged participation, as the public authority had wished; instead, they sought a compromise with their landlord and what they saw as a better overall deal for the 'community'. Indeed, the manner of their mobilisation (home-grown rather than externally engineered) gave the tenants' committee a strong hand in negotiations; and because of their evident competency and knowledge in all matters technical (Deboulet, 2013), they were eventually able to confront the landlord in court and win a compromise involving the demolition of their existing homes and the building of the Marseille–Habitat apartments.

Although not perhaps an entirely positive experience for the local authority, the Bassens case says a great deal about the latent potential, in Marseille, for sudden eruptions of highly effective 'community action', in spite of all the contextual challenges noted above. The ingredients were all there: a small neighbourhood with close social bonds based on common ethnicity; a charismatic leader with the skills needed to bring people together; and an external threat to individual wellbeing, that became 'up-scaled' through the mobilisation into a clear 'community' issue. None of these ingredients were present in Bellevue. No leader emerged; the community was heavily divided along ethnic lines, and its mobilisation was forced, with poorly-attended meetings becoming merely an opportunity for the local authority to tell residents what was about to happen to them. Hence, the more numerous but less mobilised residents of Bellevue were not able to shape the outcome of the intervention in any way. Indeed, they were subject to a very obvious form of authoritarianism, hidden behind a façade of good intention and made possible by the incapacity of the community to come together behind any defined goals.

Conclusion

In this chapter, we have examined the manifestation of 'community planning' (a term that is not widely recognised or used in France) in a very specific context: one of large-scale immigration, poverty and social and ethnic segregation. Besides the struggles documented in this chapter, other forms of community action exist in France. These include the collective group build projects dotted around the country, fuelled by the appetite of middle-class households to take more direct control over their housing situations and, where possible, to lighten their ecological footprint by promoting greener forms of development. The origin of these projects can be traced back to the self-build promoted by trade unionists in the 1950s, which crumpled under the weight of the modernist housing project, but which is now emerging in a new, privatised form.

In the working-class neighbourhoods of Marseille, some examples of community action have emerged from the recent renewal and reconsideration of the large social housing projects of the 1960s. From the 1980s onwards, lip-service was paid to the '*développement social des quartiers*' (DSQ – social development of neighbourhoods). This later transformed into a broader '*politique de la ville*' and a wider concern for urban governance, centred on large-scale programmes and projects and given added impetus by early signs of a crisis of electoral involvement during those years. Major housing interventions, however, continue to be dominated by large public bureaucracies whose primary focus is physical renewal. They concentrate their efforts on persuading the residents of target neighbourhoods of the logic of their interventions and rarely encounter significant resistance. This is because 'communities' tend to be diffuse, divided and often disconnected from the immediate neighbourhood. They have other priorities, are blighted by crime, or lack trust in public authority. Residents often struggle to find common focus. Where they do, such as in Bassens, the conditions for effective community action are just right – the neighbourhoods are relatively closed, they share an ethnicity, and they possess the skills, knowledge and leadership needed to confront what might be described as bureaucratic indifference. These conditions are rare, however. The Bellevue example is more typical of the interactions between 'community' and the 'state' in Marseille and in France more generally.

The interventionist tradition, originating in the welfare state, is a powerful force in French politics. It finds expression in many areas of public policy and also in urban planning. Power is not easily relinquished and even when confronted by what appear to be quite reasonable community concerns (as in the example of Bassens), the state will choose to fight rather than bow to local action. Even in instances where it is funding (from *Caisse des Dépôts et Consignations* or CDC) local initiatives, associations or foundations, it is clear that it is doing so in order to exert influence rather than to 'empower'. It is possible that – in the years ahead – a greater proportion of funding for voluntary initiatives will start to come from non-state sources (as seems increasingly likely given the level of government debt). This might provide the impetus for a transition away from 'participative' forms of urban planning aimed at legitimising state action to more 'communitarian' forms of planning with communities in control. Such a transition, hoever, would be dependent on a willingness of the state to accept and support different 'communities', while those communities would need to develop the capacities needed to lead and deliver projects. The situation in France serves as a reminder, if one is needed, of the very different and sometimes difficult contexts in which community action gestates. Many of the chapters in this book deal with the aspirations and consequent mobilisation of middle-class communities, which face few, if any, of the challenges encountered in Marseille's working-class neighbourhoods. Here, the capacity to act is a rare commodity, but one that sometimes shines through adversity to bring vital gains for some of France's most disadvantaged citizens.

References

Anselme, M, 2000, *Du bruit à la parole: La scène politique des cités*, La Tour-d'Aigues: Éditions de l'Aube.

Bacqué, M-H, Gauthier, M, 2011, *Participation, urbanisme et* études *urbaines, Participations*, 1, pp 36–66, Bruxelles: De Boeck

Bacqué, M-H, Mechmache, M, 2013, *Citoyenneté et pouvoir d'agir dans les quartiers populaires*, Paris: Ministre délégué à la ville

Berra, M, Pinson, D, 2006, L'Autoréhabilitation comme reconstruction de l'habitat, de l'habitant et des métiers, in J-Y Toussaint (ed) *Concevoir pour l'existant*, pp 63–79, Lausanne: PPUR (Presses Polytechniques et Universitaires Romandes)

Blancherie J-M, Bernard, J-P, Lecomte, P, 1972, Les groupes d'action municipale dans le système politique local: Grenoble, Valence, Chambéry, *Revue Française de Science Politique* 22, 2, 296–318

Deboulet, A, Nez, H (eds), 2013, *Savoirs citoyens et démocratie urbaine*, Rennes: PUR (Presses Universitaires de Rennes)

Denèfle, S, 2012, *Réponses institutionnelles aux projets d'habitat participatif en France* (VIIe Congreso Rulescoop), UMR CITERES Université F Rabelais: Tours

Direche-Slimani, K, Le Houerou, F, 2002, Les Comoriens à Marseille, d'une mémoire à l'autre, *Collection Monde/Français d'ailleurs* 133, Paris: Les Editions Autrement

Douzet, F, 2012, Oakland au cœur de la tourmente: Bouleversements démographiques, rivalités de pouvoir et crise de gouvernance dans les villes californiennes, in L-N Tellier, C Vainer (eds) *Métropoles des Amériques en mutation*, Montréal: PUQ (Presses de l'Université du Québec)

Duport, C, 2012, Trafics de drogue à Marseille: Un bilan des recherches, in *Etudes et Travaux de l'ORDCS* 4, Aix-en-Provence: MMSH (Maison Méditerranéennes des Sciences de l'Homme)

European Conference of Ministers of Transport, 2003, *Implementing Sustainable Urban Transport Policies: National Reviews*, Paris: OECD Publications

Foucault, M, 1983, The subject and power, in H Dreyfuss, P Rabinow (eds) *Michel Foucault: Beyond structuralism and hermeneutics* (2nd edn), pp 208–26, Chicago: University of Chicago Press

Kepel, G, 2012, *Banlieues de la République: Société, politique et religion à Clichy-sous-Bois et Montfermeil*, Paris: Gallimard

Messaoudène, M, 2010, Logiques habitantes et offre résidentielle dans le processus de renouvellement urbain à Marseille, *Articulo: Journal of Urban Research*, Briefings, 16 Juin, *http://articulo.revues.org/1491*; DOI: 10.4000/articulo.1491

Messaoudène, M, 2012, Une cité de Marseille sur la scène de la participation, *La Pensée*, 372, October–December

Péraldi, M, 1999, Marseille: Réseaux migrants transfrontaliers, place marchande et économie de bazar, *Cultures and Conflits*, 33–4, Spring–Summer

Pinson, D, 2000, L' "usager" de la ville, in Th Paquot, M Lussault, S Body-Gendrot (eds) *La ville et l'urbain, l'état des savoirs*, pp 233–43, Paris: La Découverte

Pinson, D, 2004, Urban Planning: An 'undisciplined' discipline?, *Futures* 36, 4, 503–13

Pinson, D, 2012, Les monuments domestiques pour le plus grand nombre: Une autre histoire…, in C Compain-Gajac (ed) *Conservation: Restauration de l'architecture du Mouvement Moderne*, pp 87–99, Perpignan: Presses Universitaires

Raymond, H, 1984, *L'Architecture, les aventures spatiales de la raison*, Paris: CCI-Centre G Pompidou

Tarrius, A, 2002, *La mondialisation par le bas: Les nouveaux nomades de l'économie souterraine*, Paris: Balland

7

Communities, land-ownership, housing and planning: reflections from the Scottish experience

Madhu Satsangi

Introduction

This book's aims include positioning community-based action in different planning and local government contexts, enquiring into the conducive conditions for community-based action and asking how different systems are harnessing communities' energies and with what effect. To contribute towards these aims, this chapter examines the traditions of activism and empowerment embodied in Scotland's community land trust movement. The movement is particularly significant as it provides a clear alternative to the country's dominant form of individual rural land ownership. Furthermore, the movement is seen as an important means of finding an answer to the 'land question', of diversifying ownership of the key resource that underpins rural development. The chapter looks at the Isle of Gigha Heritage Trust as an example of a community land trust, and comments on how it has developed its model of community governance and the forces of power at play. The circumstances that fostered the genesis of the movement are explored and factors behind the success of the movement are examined, looking at both structural issues and fortuitous combinations of circumstance and individual actors. The chapter brings out the reasons why community land trusts have significance in both debates in the literature and debates on the direction of policy.

The focus in this chapter is on rural places, the locus in the pioneering work of Tönnies (1887) for the existence of *gemeinschaft* or community, which he characterised as a grouping based on feelings of togetherness and mutual bonds. Since this conception, as alluded to in the introductory chapter of this book, there has been and continues to be persistent interest in its (re-)definition. Thus, a concern of the Chicago school of sociology was seeing community as a specific model of social organisation and searching for its structural features. Cohen's (1985) work takes a somewhat different perspective, arguing that in themselves structures do not give meaning (such as togetherness) to people. Rather, he argued that community is better understood as a system of values, norms and moral codes that provides a sense of identity. As such, community is symbolically constructed.

Cohen's work has been highly influential across sociology and social anthropology (Rapport and Overing, 2013) and geography, where Silk (1999) argues that 'community' might be characterised by one or more of a set of features: 'common needs and goals, a sense of the common good, shared lives, culture and views of the world, and collective action' (p 8). He goes on to note that 'the chances for development of community are maximised when there is unmediated face-to-face contact between people, as when they share a restricted territory' (Silk, 1999, 8). Similarly, Smith (1999) argues that 'spatial as well as social relations are widely regarded as crucial to the development of moral values...some may be more conducive than others to those human encounters and experiences which can encourage such virtues as care and justice' (p 33).

Harking back to Tönnies' (1887) notion of association (*gesellschaft*), Young (1990) was highly critical of the ideal of community:

> Whether expressed as shared subjectivity or common consciousness, on the one hand, or as relations of mutuality and reciprocity, the ideal of community denies, devalues, or represses the ontological difference of subjects [p 339], [favouring instead] 'city life'...a form of social relations which I define as the being together of strangers. (p 345)

Panelli and Welch (2005) are also concerned with the dynamics of relations. They start from the recognition that 'community is a social construct to be variously and continuously negotiated' (p 1589) and identify a number of themes that are important for studying these processes: the importance of context, the need to acknowledge the diversity of people, the articulation of meanings and the possibility of social relations being spatially constituted (Panelli and Welch, 2005, 1592–3). Mackenzie et al (2004) discuss four cases of community land purchase in the Highlands and Western Isles. In this work, the weighting given to the individual arguably seen in Young (1990) and Panelli and Welch (2005) is reduced in favour of an emphasis on collectivity. One of the characteristics of all of these views of community is their focus on the centrality of relations between people;

relations that are likely to shift in nature over time: the meaning of community conceived as a social construct cannot be fixed but must be subject to processes of change.

We saw earlier how 'rurality' and 'community' were elided in Tönnies' (1887) work: this has been seen as a marker of the 'idyll-isation' of rurality (Satsangi et al, 2010) and is problematic in a number of ways. First, it tends to ignore or underplay the existence of different interests and purposes found in any grouping of people. In place, it ascribes a 'unity of will' and thus universal subscription to a fixed set of interests. As noted in Rydin's and Matthews' chapters, unity of will (and of purpose) may temporarily bring a group together but that does not necessarily equate to longer-lasting bonds between individuals. Second, if there is adoption or prioritisation of a particular set of interests (implying agreement, consent or veiling dissent between individuals) this may indicate a particular power dynamic at play within a group. A third issue is the danger of ignoring heterogeneity: while we might not need to go far as Young (1990) in conceiving of a group as necessarily a set of strangers, we do need to recognise individuality. The composition of a spatially-defined group must change as people are born and die, and move in and out (see also Moore and McKee, 2013).

The land question and community land trusts

> Contemporary interest in community ownership is... nothing new – it's a reawakening of a notion that's been around for a very long time. (Wightman, 2004, 13)

In 2001, the Edinburgh University sociologist David McCrone wrote that the 'land question' was central to Scottish national identity, reflecting the fact that the pattern of land ownership in Scotland has long been a significant political issue. Why so? One reason is the concentration of ownership, 50 per cent of Scotland's privately owned land is owned by just 432 people (0.008 per cent of the national population), a ratio chosen by Hunter et al (2013) as an emblematic title for a particularly significant paper.[1] The simple statistic indicates a profound inequality in the ownership of a vital asset.

The second reason follows directly from the first: this economic inequality inevitably brings an inequality in political power. As analysed by Lukes (1974), this means an inequality in decision-making relating to land. It also means the concentration of control over local political agendas through explicit or hidden mechanisms and the concealment of people's 'real' interests. In using this term, Lukes follows neo-Marxian lines of analysis to refer to a person's interests by virtue of their class status. The inequality in power has for centuries been legitimated via feudal tenure.

Third, the country has witnessed the abuse of land owning power: most clearly in the enforced clearances of tenants from their land and homes in both Highland and Lowland Scotland in the eighteenth and early nineteenth centuries. In the early years of the last century, Tom Johnston (1909), a Scottish Member of Parliament,[2] had written that feudal power relations were an anachronism: they were to survive this indictment, however, for another century. Indeed, while feudal tenure per se was abolished by legislation in 2000,[3] its power imbalance endures.

Power may of course be exercised in a benign or malign manner. It is both the malign exercise of power and the existence of imbalance in itself which have motivated land reform campaigns in Scotland; campaigns that led eventually to legislation at the beginning of the twenty-first century.[4] Under that legislation, crofting communities[5] became entitled to purchase land from a landowner, whether or not that owner was willing to sell. Further, non-crofting communities, once recognised and their interest registered by Government, could bid to acquire land when an owner put it up for sale.

A decade after that legislation, the Scottish government established a land reform review group. Overcoming some fears that the terms of this would be limited to a fairly narrow inspection of the minutiae of the land reform legislation, the group was remitted to identify how land reform could:

- enable more people in rural and urban Scotland to have a stake in the ownership, governance, management and use of land, which will lead to a greater diversity of land ownership, and ownership types, in Scotland;
- assist with the acquisition and management of land (and also land assets) by communities, to make stronger, more resilient, and independent communities which have an even greater stake in their development;
- generate, support, promote and deliver new relationships between land, people, economy and environment in Scotland. (Scottish Government, 2013)

The review terms thus invoked a re-visioning of the purpose of land reform. In its second objective, the review signalled, in part, some discontent with the lack of progress in community land acquisition post-2003. Indeed in addressing the annual conference of Community Land Scotland in 2013, the First Minister set a target of doubling the amount of land (to 1 million acres) in community ownership by 2020.

Community land ownership in Scotland had not been created by the 2003 legislation. The first community land acquisition, in 1908 in Glendale on the Isle of Skye, followed a highly-charged struggle, assessed in the leading history to have marked the beginnings of the Highland land wars (Hunter, 2000). The country's longest-established but scarcely-heralded community land trust – the Stornoway Trust (on the Isle of Lewis, the most populous of the Western Isles) – dates from 1923, covers almost 65,000 acres and has a total population of 13,500 (Boyd, 1999). It was gifted to the community by the laird (Lord Leverhulme) but other trusts have relied on public support from the (UK) National Land Fund, set up soon after the end of the Second World War. Figure 7.1 below shows a timeline of community land purchases, significant policy events and funding streams. Wilson (1994) documents some of its acquisitions but notes that from the mid-1950s, it changed its name to the National Heritage Memorial Fund and its focus to art and buildings. Bryden and Geisler (2007) refer to the dilution of feudal powers in the 1970s and Boyd (1999) comments on the resurgence of interest in community land ownership in the 1990s. The purchase of land by crofting communities in Assynt, Borve and Melness (all 1993) were widely heralded (Bryden and Geisler, 2007; Chenevix-Trench and Philip, 2000). From 2001 to 2006, the Scottish Land Fund took over the vestiges of previous public funding to support community land acquisition. From 2006 to 2010, the Scottish Land Fund responsibilities were discharged by a lottery-funded body alone, its second programme of work was joined in 2011 by a reborn Scottish Land Fund.

To look at evidence on how community land acquisition has been initiated and actioned and what its initial impacts were, this section documents events in, and subsequent to, the community purchase of the isle of Gigha. Primary data are drawn from in-depth interviews with key stakeholders, including around ten members of the community, undertaken in Spring 2005. These interviews took the form of semi-structured discussions between the author and individuals alone and groups of residents. The course of discussion was guided by questions from the author, though their sequence varied according to what flowed in conversation. These data are supplemented by data from two community housing studies, one assessing need, one looking at means of meeting need (Rural Housing Service, 2001 and 2002) with some corroborative evidence from a case study of the Community Land Trust

(McKinney et al, 2004). The section draws on my previously published work (Satsangi, 2005, 2007, 2009; Satsangi et al, 2010).

Figure 7.1: Timeline of community land purchases, significant policy events and funding streams

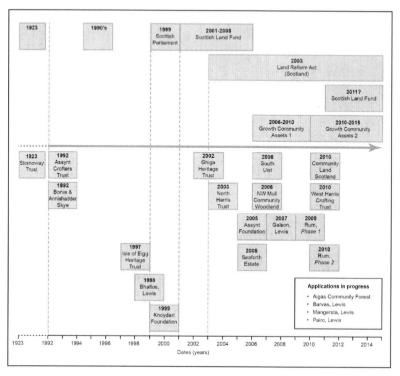

Community land ownership on the Isle of Gigha

Gigha is a small (7 square miles) island off Scotland's west coast, linked by a half-hour journey by ferry to the mainland. From the late eighteenth century until the middle of the twentieth, it had a succession of family owners, who built at various times their own house (in vernacular terms, the 'big house'), named Achamore and cottages for estate workers. Parcels of land were let to tenant farmers, their housing being on agricultural tenancy. From 1944 to 1972, Gigha was owned by the Horlicks family. Its head, James Horlicks, was acknowledged by older residents to have been a 'good laird', that is, a benevolent paternalist owner. He invested in the creation of the fifty-acre Achamore Gardens, home to rhododendrons and exotic shrubs (the gardens are now one of the island's main tourist attractions). He also sold small land parcels for housing (the last being for a council house in 1971) and invested in the upkeep of estate housing. James Horlicks died in 1972, and bequeathed Achamore Gardens to the National Trust for Scotland. The island was bought and sold successively by the Lansdale and Poitier families, the latter being forced to sell in 1993 because of bankruptcy to the Holt family.

No owner after the Horlicks family, according to interviews, did anything more than make minimal investment to the big house. They built no new housing, made token investment in estate houses and sold no land. The Lansdales oversaw the closure of the Gigha cheese factory. One interviewee recalled how she had been given a 'flat refusal' when she sought to buy a small parcel of land for housing, despite her being the Gigha primary school teacher and her husband being in employment. Unsurprisingly, Poitier, Lansdale and Holt were seen as 'bad lairds'. As an older life-long resident of Gigha expressed, however, there was another issue associated with monopoly ownership: 'It's bad enough having a bad laird, but when you come home and find yourself taken over by someone, that's another thing all together.' Thus, despite living and working on the island and contributing to an owner's income and wealth, residents were clearly not in control of their own lives. The same interviewee went on to say that 'looking back, people's recollection of this was important in them saying that we should go forward with buy-out.'

For all of the residents of Gigha interviewed, there were clear symptoms of the absence of concern on behalf of the laird for employment, for housing and for the fate of the island, summarised as 'an island in decline'. Most commonly, reference was made to population loss – from 180 and a school roll of 28 in 1981 to 110 and a school roll of seven in 2001 – and deterioration in housing quality. Housing tenure was, in 2001, dominated by the laird. This was in a very direct sense as the estate owned 48 of Gigha's 67 houses (the big house and 47 others). Furthermore, land for the others (13 owner-occupied houses, four council houses and two houses tied to employment) would also have been part of the estate. At that time, only one of the 47 estate houses met the national 'tolerable housing standard', the majority being damp, with inadequate heating/insulation and dry rot being some of the problems experienced by their tenants (Rural Housing Service, 2001). Survey evidence suggested that nine households were 'hidden homeless' (with no home of their own) and ten others were in unsuitable (overcrowded, too small or too poor condition) housing (Rural Housing Service, 2002). The island's population at the start of this century divided roughly equally between those who had lived on the island all their lives (or who had been born there, left and returned), and those who had moved there (McKinney et al, 2004).

When Holt put Gigha up for sale in August 2001, seven long-term residents of the island formed a group that organised public meetings about the sale and to discuss the possibility of community purchase. It is important to note, as recollected in interviews in 2005, that there was not unanimity behind the idea of purchase. Opposition was marshalled by some estate employees and Holt's children, who were working on the estate. Looking into the feasibility of community purchase was supported by a grant from the Scottish Land Fund. The person who was to become chair of the Gigha Community Land Steering Group (and subsequently a director of the Community Land Trust, 'The Isle of Gigha Heritage Trust', hereafter simply the Trust) stated that 'the grant was extremely helpful to us...four people went to the Isle of Eigg (purchased by its community in 1997) including two people who were opposed to it (buy-out). When we got back, everyone was for it...if they (on Eigg) could do it, so could we!' From there to taking possession (March 2002), discussants referred to 'hard work and long negotiations', both with external agencies and among residents of Gigha: 'there were people who were opposed to us buying the island and others who thought we couldn't do it'. Nevertheless, there was majority support and the Trust bought the island for £4 million. That sum was provided by public sector grants and loans, with £165,000 to be repaid within a year and a further £1 million to be repaid within two years.

As noted above, reaction to the past, and particularly the recent experiences of living under absolute ownership, gave impetus to the idea and aspiration of community purchase. A minority of elderly residents, however, suggested that 'we might be better off with a good laird', reflecting a perception that with rights come responsibilities and that these may not be easy to discharge. For the majority of residents, however, the lack of self-confidence seen in this remark and some tendency to be quiet at public meetings was felt to be 'what people are used to'. In other words, there are cultural and behavioural markers of a legacy of paternalism in acquiescence or obedience to decisions made by another.

This dynamic of power also has reflection in other motivations. Among both younger and older residents, there was a strong view that buy-out and the actions that followed should yield long-term benefits. Many older residents shared the view expressed by one Trust member that 'It's not going to benefit a lot of people like me in the Trust who are 60 or so, but it's the next generation that are going to see the benefits.'

Housing and other development was seen in this vein. During the three years following community acquisition, six building plots were sold to individuals/families to build their own houses along with two land parcels to a housing association (Fyne Homes, a social housing developer eligible for capital subsidy from the government) to build 18 low cost houses. It also saw the start of the Trust's rehabilitation of the estate houses it purchased. Land was also sold to allow two small workspaces to be developed.

The scale of the housing development is important in three respects. First, it provides a dramatic contrast to the previous 35 years that had seen only one low-cost house being built. Second, it is rather greater than the level of current or anticipated future need among the resident population of Gigha. Estimates of the number of houses that would be allocated to current non-residents ranged from four to eight. For the majority of residents, Trust directors or otherwise, this was positive and appropriate: 'we've got to get new people in, with different skills, with children for the school', 'we can't just keep it (the island) as it is now'. For a minority of older residents, there were, however, concerns about 'how are you going to sort out who gets the "extra" houses...are they going to go to people who know what it's really like to live in a small island community?' Third, resident involvement in the planning and design of the development was extremely high. Meetings at which competing architects presented their ideas, for example, were attended by over 70 residents.

These remarks lead on to a discussion of governance and decision-making in the Trust. Its constitution results partly from local context and partly from conditions of funding from the Scottish Land Fund. It has a membership comprising all residents of the island and a board of eight directors (the majority of whom had been the members of the Community Land Steering Group). The board of directors is selected by the membership and all decisions (save minor matters) are taken by the members at Trust meetings, accepting or overturning directors' recommendations. Thus decisions on whether to sell or let land or any other asset, how to maintain and improve the estate and its houses, what rent should be charged for Trust houses and how to attempt to grow the island's economy are exercised by the Trust rather than by a laird.

Trust directors were keen to emphasise that it was the membership as a whole that made decisions. In part, this showed sensitivity to some perception that the board of directors might be 'in control'; in part, it reflected a desire to avoid any establishment of a 'them' and an 'us'. Meetings are recognised to be well-attended and, in the words of a Trust director 'there'll always be different views...you don't always get 100 per cent support, but you need a good majority to carry on.' Another director observed that dissent commonly started with those who had been less enthusiastic (or hostile) to community purchase. In order to hear views from people reticent about speaking in public, a Trust director has regular surgeries for individuals to put across their point of view or raise concerns.

There is a strong symbolism that can be seen in decisions made by the Trust. It has chosen a motif of 'a new dawn' and has sold the big house. A key physical marker of the past, individual monopolisation of benefits has therefore been transformed into a sharing of benefits. A Trust director pointed out that there had been opposition to the sale, that it might be better to hold on to the asset but, 'looked at another way, it was just bricks and mortar and what good had it done us in the past? How many islanders had actually been inside? [New owner] created a business and some employment.' At the same time, future land sales are likely to be restricted: 'We bought Gigha for its future, not just to sell most of it off and keep a wee bit.' The consensus aspiration too was that 'we should support ourselves: we can't rely on whatever government agent...', suggesting an ethos of self-reliance.

These data on the purchase and subsequent development of governance of the island suggest that what was happening in the first three years after buy-out were a continuous process of redefinition of identity and renegotiation of community. There were visible signs of a 'common good' in aspiration for the future, but fractured and differentiated views as to how that good should be produced. There was a recognition that if the island community had ever indeed been closely-bounded geographically, such a spatial definition was inappropriate for its survival.

Conclusions

The success of the Isle of Gigha Development Trust can be attributed to the strength of commitment to purchase resultant from the island's history and the islanders' experiences of different landowners' behaviour. It can be attributed to considerable amounts of voluntary work by a small group of islanders and their ability to gain support, legal, technical and financial, via a state agency. It can be attributed also to the establishment of a mode of governance post purchase that has been able to maintain legitimacy in the minds of islanders. To what extent is Gigha typical of community land acquisitions? Leaving aside the particular circumstances that engendered community interest in purchase, it is clear that its scale makes it unique. At the same time, there is some evidence that the processes and outcomes observed here are to some degree generalisable. Mackenzie et al (2004) look at four community land purchases and note that although the purchases' histories, starting points and processes were different from area to area, the claim to land and the identity and constitution of community are in each case very strongly interlinked: 'the boundaries of collective identities, of community, are re-worked through the processes of re-claiming collective rights to the land' (Mackenzie et al, 2004, 178). Skerratt (2011) presents evidence from a review of 17 community land trusts, concluding *inter alia* that:

1. Communities are motivated to buy land as they see land as the foundation on which all other developments rest, a foundation that has been used to secure a variety of housing, economic and community development assets.
2. Community land trusts rely on a significant amount of voluntary input, some but not all had development staff.
3. Community land trusts face challenges that relate to their age and status: the long pre-purchase phase necessitates confidence and perseverance, the five-year period from purchase needs financial, legal, organisational management and governance skills, success thereafter depends on the ability to innovate and maintain community buy-in, as well as external networking.

How can the Gigha experience be understood with reference to the meaning of community? The purchase and subsequent decision making by islanders have clearly been motivated by a clear purpose: to realise future growth and self-determination. This would mean replacing an historically-derived 'norm' (Cohen, 1985) of being subject to the will of a disinterested or neglectful owner with one of collective control and responsibility. Islanders' hopes were that the facilitation of development would allow the fulfilling of a value of all sharing the benefits of growth.

While recognition of a common value was forged through memory and through taking an opportunity, it is clear that this did not mean universal subscription to the idea of purchase. Dissent from the view that buy-out was desirable and likely to yield benefits for Gigha can be seen as a concern about whether islanders had sufficient know-how and resources to manage the island. It reflects an unease about entering an unfamiliar context. It is also suggestive of Lukes' (1974) third dimension of power: instead of explicitly claiming the right of self-determination, those opposed to purchase appeared to choose subservience.

Notes

[1] The paper's significance rises when it is noted that it is a briefing paper for an inquiry conducted by the House of Commons Scottish Affairs Committee. Its interim report of March 2014 suggested that significant recommendations would be forthcoming on mitigating abuses of tax reliefs and exemptions (House of Commons Scottish Affairs Committee, 2014).

[2] Johnston later became Secretary of State for Scotland during the Second World War.

[3] In The Abolition of Feudal Tenure etc. (Scotland) Act 2000.

[4] In addition to the Act noted above, the Land Reform (Scotland) Act, 2003 and the Title Conditions (Scotland) Act, 2003.

[5] Crofts are small agricultural landholdings, subject to special legislation beginning with the Crofters' Act 1886. This legislation was largely a response to the complaints and demands of tenant families who were victims of the Highland Clearances. The tenure is restricted to Scotland's seven crofting counties: Inverness-shire, Ross and Cromarty, Argyll-shire, Sutherland, Caithness, Orkney and Shetland.

References

Boyd, G, 1999, To restore the land to the people and the people to the land: The emergence of the not-for-private-profit landownership sector in the Highlands and Islands of Scotland, in *Social land ownership: Case studies from the not for profit landowners project group in the Highlands and Islands of Scotland*, Inverness: Not-For-Profit Landowners Project Group and the Scottish Community Education Council

Bryden, J, Geisler, C, 2007, Community-based land reform: Lessons from Scotland, *Land Use Policy* 24, 1, 24–34

Chenevix-Trench, H, Philip, L, 2000, *Community and conservation ownership in Highland Scotland: A common focus in a changing context*, www.caledonia.org.uk/socialland/joint_owners.htm

Cohen, AP, 1985, *The symbolic construction of community*, London: Tavistock

House of Commons Scottish Affairs Committee, 2014, *Land reform in Scotland: Interim report, Eighth report of session 2013-14*, paper HC 877, London: The Stationery Office, www.publications.parliament.uk/pa/cm201314/cmselect/cmscotaf/877/877.pdf

Hunter, J, 2000, *The making of the crofting community* (2nd edn), Edinburgh: John Donald/Birlinn

Hunter, J, Peacock, P, Wightman, A, Foxley, M, 2013, 432:50: Towards a comprehensive land reform agenda for Scotland. A briefing paper for the House of Commons Scottish Affairs Committee, www.andywightman.com/docs/432-LandReformPaper.pdf

Johnston, T, 1909, *Our Scots noble families: A general indictment*, Glasgow: Forward Publishing, republished 1999, Glendaruel, Argyll: Argyll Publishing

Lukes, S, 1974, *Power: A radical view*, Basingstoke: Macmillan

Mackenzie, AFD, MacAskill, J, Munro, G, Seki, E, 2004, Contesting land, creating community, in the Highlands and Islands, Scotland, *Scottish Geographical Journal*, 120, 3, 159–180

McCrone, D, 2001, *Understanding Scotland: The Sociology of a Nation* (2nd edn), London: Routledge

McKinney, R, Kahn, H, Jones, D, 2004, *Lottery funding and the UK voluntary sector: Capacity, change and sustainability,* unpublished report by the Social Enterprise Institute, Edinburgh: Heriot-Watt University

Moore, T, McKee, K, 2013, The ownership of assets by place-based community organisations: Political rationales, geographies of social impact and future research agendas, in *Social Policy and Society* (First View*)*, doi: 10.1017/S1474746413000481

Panelli, R, Welch, R, 2005, Why community? Reading difference and singularity with community, in *Environment and Planning A* 37, 1589–611

Rapport, N, Overing, J (eds), 2013, *Social and cultural anthropology: The key concepts*, London: Taylor and Francis

Rural Housing Service, 2001, *Gigha rural housing survey: Assessment and options appraisal*, unpublished report to the Gigha Community Land Steering Group

Rural Housing Service, 2002, *Isle of Gigha housing needs study*, unpublished report to the Isle of Gigha Heritage Trust, Argyll and the Isles Enterprise and Communities Scotland

Samuel, AMM, 2000, Cultural symbols and landowners' power: The practice of managing Scotland's natural resource, *Sociology* 34, 4, 691–706

Satsangi, M, 2005, Landowners and the structure of affordable housing provision in rural Scotland, *Journal of Rural Studies* 21, 349–58

Satsangi, M, 2007, Land tenure change and rural housing in Scotland, *Scottish Geographical Journal* 123, 1, 33–47

Satsangi, M, 2009, Community land ownership, housing and sustainable rural communities, *Planning Practice and Research* 24, 2, 251–62

Satsangi, M, Gallent, N, Bevan, M, 2010, *The rural housing question: Communities and planning in Britain's countrysides*, Bristol: Policy Press

Scottish Government, 2013, *Land Reform Review: Remit*, www.scotland.gov.uk/About/Review/land-reform/Remit

Silk, J, 1999, The dynamics of community, place and identity (Guest Editorial), *Environment and Planning A* 31, 1, 5–17

Skerratt, S, 2011, *Community land ownership and community resilience*, Edinburgh: Scottish Agricultural College

Skerratt, S, 2013, Enhancing the analysis of rural community resilience: Evidence from community land ownership, in *Journal of Rural Studies* 31, 1, 36–46

Smith, DM, 1999, Geography, community and morality, *Environment and Planning A* 31, 1, 19–35

Tönnies, F, 1887, *Gemeinschaft und Gesellschaft*, Leipzig: Fues's Verlag (translated in 1957 as *Community and Society*)

Warren, C, 2000, Scottish land reform: The first act, *ECOS Magazine* 21, 1, www.caledonia.org.uk/land/warren02.htm

Wightman, A, 2004, Scotland's commonweal, *The Drouth*, 14, 8–13, www.thedrouth.org/storage/The%20Drouth%2014.pdf

Wightman, A, Boyd, G, 2001, *Not-for-profit landowning organisations in the Highlands and Islands of Scotland: Sector Review 2001*, www.caledonia.org.uk/socialland/nfp06.htm

Wilson, B, 1994, Recognising land as a vital part of our heritage, *West Highland Free Press*, 18 November, www.caledonia.org.uk/land/bwilson.htm

Young, IM, 1990, Justice and the politics of difference, Princeton, NJ: Princeton University Press, republished as City life and difference, in S Campbell, S Fainstein (eds) (2003) *Readings in planning theory* (2nd edn), pp 336–55, Oxford: Blackwell

Part 3
Planning at the community scale

In the life-cycle of community action, the act of planning – or the broader tendency to become future-orientated – is not automatic. The actions that communities take may be time-limited, restricted to a specific response to a particular set of circumstances: to crises and immediate needs, or the need to provide a specific service over the longer term. The prioritisation of planning requires community groups to recognise the longer-term pressures that are faced and the possibility that, through the articulation of collective vision and will, those pressures can be mitigated or opportunities grasped. It is also the case that time-limited mobilisations are easier to sustain than long-term efforts, and that such efforts need to be framed within structures of informal community activism or formal community governance. Communitarian planning of the type described in Chapter 1 needs to be embedded within community processes, although it can be seeded by the state, with a distinction then drawn between 'communitarian planning as a by-product of community life (with its focus on social goods) and (implanted or hijacked) community planning as a product of the state's search for legitimacy – through extended interaction that delivers a less contentious vision of "what urban change should be like"'. The six case-studies contained in this Part of the book examine examples of both.

We begin in the Netherlands where van der Pennen and Schreuders contrast the 'life world' inhabited by communities with the 'system world' of bureaucracy and the local state. The Dutch New Towns, constructed in the 1950s onwards, provide a context for a coming together of these worlds. Faced with physical deterioration and the need for renewal, residents encounter the slow, incremental and constricted system world of public policy. They become frustrated and attempt to change their environment on their own terms and at their own pace. They take control and begin to lead key projects, but their capacity to do so is heavily influenced by the social characteristics and capacities of their communities, and dependent on effective community leadership. The state, for its part, embraces community action as another tool in its armoury of public policy delivery; though that action is, for the most part, a by-product of community life. In southern California, Dandekar and Main present a case study with some similar characteristics, revealing that community action is indeed an extension of existing community processes and capacities, but in their case they are dealing with processes that have been implanted in order to generate acceptance of planning decisions and outcomes. What we see in California is a form of extended participatory democracy (which is heavily supported) rather than the communitarian planning outlined in the introductory chapter: essentially a form of community planning which is state sponsored in response to the 'disconnect' between the intervention and the heterogeneous needs of community groups. Parker's examination of community-based planning in England, in Chapter 10, traces an extended history from participation through to the drawing up of real community plans and then the absorption of those plans into a revised structure of rescaled official planning. In England, we see what is perhaps the most obvious example of government trying to harness the local energies behind community action as a means of addressing local distinctiveness and winning support (or acceptance) for strategic priorities among community actors. Its efforts have, however, created what is potentially a complex and fragmented planning system with ultimate results that are as yet unclear. The case study of Italy from Ciaffi reveals some very different outcomes. To some extent, communities in England and Italy share a distrust of bureaucracy and the steering centrism of some governments, but while in England this generated a strengthening of community governance, in Italy it has produced a range of local state/community engagements which have not developed into a single strategy but into episodes of militancy, activism and protest. In New York City, we see a clearer line of strategic advantage emerging from community engagement around the community-based housing organisations: not paper plans, but a clear steer as to the future direction of those organisations, constituting an effective form of planning. There, Wolf-Powers is able to point to an 'added strategic value' from community action. Finally, a very detailed account of self-build groups in Freiburg in Germany from Hamiduddin and Daseking shows that the act of building is intricately tied up with community planning, and that both are key to a 'domestication of space' and to the claiming of rights and responsibilities which is central to planning at the community scale.

These different manifestations of planning at the community scale are all unique to place, being linked to context, to particular drivers and to different underlying expectations and cultures. Yet some common themes emerge: these include the link back to social capital, the role of community leaders and innovators, the support provided by the local state (in order to enhance legitimacy and to better connect outcomes to local context), the rarity of 'formal' community plans and the prevalence of community planning by advocacy, the diversity of outcomes within the same country (owing to the complex interplay between place and politics), the broad or sectoral focus of community action, and the link between the development of communities, social capital and aspiration. These themes are explored at length in the chapters that now follow.

8

The Fourth Way of active citizenship: case studies from the Netherlands[1]

Ton van der Pennen and Hanneke Schreuders

Introduction

The 1990s saw the rise of the 'vital city', in which citizens take control and are involved in a kaleidoscope of activities. The vital city is a product, at least in part, of a rescaling of state intervention. Local government has accepted new and heightened responsibilities in the fields of social care, employment creation, education, housing and welfare provision. There has been a transition away from the 'welfare state' to the 'welfare city' which has been given impetus by cuts in government spending and by the expectation that local jurisdictions, and local communities, will design their own responses to the challenges they encounter. In the Netherlands, this state of affairs has recently been labelled the 'participation society' (The Independent, 2013).

What we now call the 'vital city' is not a new phenomenon, but it is becoming increasingly pronounced. In many cities in Europe, and elsewhere in the world, citizens have become more actively engaged in their local areas, accepting a greater degree of responsibility for their own living environment. These 'active citizens' are joining forces with local government institutions to deliver a 'Fourth Way' in public policy, planning and social welfare. In the first part of this chapter, we will seek to conceptualise active citizenship in urban districts, arguing that the idea of a 'Fourth Way' concerns first, a perforation of the boundaries of the welfare state in places with a history of participation, and second, the existence of key community actors who can be described as 'everyday fixers', and who play an instrumental role in delivering the participation society. In the second part of the chapter, we present illustrative cases in a selection of Dutch new towns. These cases reveal how the actions of everyday fixers re-enforces the trend toward the participation society in four civil-collective initiatives focused on the maintenance of public spaces.

The perforated boundaries of the welfare state

In the final decades of the twentieth century, there was a broad political consensus in most western countries that the welfare state was growing beyond the limits of what was practical and desirable and that a process of 'cutting out the dead wood' was required. By the late 1980s, it was being argued that the costs of maintaining the welfare state had become exorbitantly high and ending the policy of dependency of citizens on welfare, social care and social support would bring clear individual and social benefits. Citizens and civil organisations, it was argued, must become more self-reliant and less dependent on state intervention and assistance.

The unintended consequences of the welfare state was a growing bureaucratic rationality (or 'system world') sitting in opposition to the 'life world', or everyday reality, of citizens (Habermas, 1984). Table 8.1 lists some of the characteristics and differences between this bureaucratic system world and the life world of citizens (see also Van der Pennen and Bosch, 2011). These differences are also points of potential tension, between the operation of the formal state and the everyday needs of communities and people. The state operates in a world of normative quality, of benchmarks and of fixed standards. A bureaucracy of quality (assurance) may stand in the way of the practical quality that citizens wish to achieve. The state has a particular rhythm, operating at fixed time scales. Its wheels sometimes turn slowly, whereas the life world of volunteers and activists can be rapidly paced, requiring quick responses and actions (see also Matthews, Chapter 3, this volume). Equally important is the difference in rationale between system world and life world actors: the former are paid employees, while the latter are volunteers driven by emotions, belief and personal or collective goals.

This distinction between system world and life world is important for two reasons. First, it reveals something of the nature of the boundary between state action and community action, characterising the former as slow, rigid, formal and supply-driven, and the latter as rapid, flexible, informal and demand-driven. Second, it suggests that where attempts are made to work across that boundary, there is scope for significant difficulty as contradictory rationales and patterns of working are encountered. The challenge for the Fourth Way is to work effectively across this boundary, to construct effective partnerships, and to marry active citizenship with trust in public institutions.

Table 8.1: System world versus life world

System world	Life world
Specific plans with fixed results and terms	No strict plans
Long-term organisation	Short-term organisation
Short-term horizon	Long-term horizon
Formal	Informal
Official quality norms	Practical quality
Professional distance	Emotion (passion, irritation)
Paid work	Volunteering work
Hierarchical organisation	Horizontal organisation
Supply driven	Demand driven

Source: Brouwer and Engbersen, 2013

Active citizenship and 'everyday fixers'

Across the global north, there is increasing expectation that citizens will be policy-engaged as never before, with their knowledge and energy harnessed in the pursuit of answers to key social problems. Local knowledge of neighbourhoods has become crucial in the effort to gain a clear sense of what communities experience as 'problems' (Engbersen and Engbersen, 2014). Researchers, however, have claimed that citizens deliver more than information or consultancy to the policy process, but are now the owners of initiatives, developing and realising their own policy ideas. Active citizenship has become a new form of urban governance (Houten and Winsemius, 2010), embracing notions of 'collective independence', 'individual responsibility', 'individual empowerment', 'self-organisation', 'basic democracy' and 'citizens' initiatives'. Citizens now act in domains that were formerly the realm of the state and 'focus on improving the quality of the neighbourhood in terms of quality of life and safety' (Denters et al, 2013, 7). Moreover, 'local government and institutions play a stimulating, facilitating or productive role' (Denters et al, 2013, 7). Citizens engage in the public domain, but also work with the former occupants of that domain. They display what Morenoff et al (2001) call 'collective efficacy' but nevertheless remain citizens, retaining their bonds with the state. They aim to address the shortcomings of the state, stepping in to provide services where public funding is not available or accessible. They may seek to bring order to disorder, turning wasteland into a community park for example (Zwaard and Specht, 2013). Their deeds may aim to create a greater sense of community, which can mean the process of community action is more important than the product (Hurenkamp, Tonkens and Duyvendak, 2006; Tonkens and Verhoeven, 2011). Overall, collective efficacy means responding to and improving an existing social reality, but not necessarily accepting the results of system (world) solutions (Specht, 2012).

The theoretical roots of active citizenship can be found in the work of Bang and Sørensen (1999), with their model of the 'everyday worker', which has been reinterpreted for the Dutch context as the 'everyday fixer' (Hendriks and Tops, 2005). The 'everyday fixer' engages in a new form of political–civil engagement, expressing individuality and a strong sense of the collective good. These are citizens with the dedication and drive to get things done. They are networkers, pragmatists, and even the bridge-builders (in the sense employed by Rydin, Chapter 2, this volume) or 'boundary crossers' (Kilpatrick et al, Chapter 5, this volume) who are able to bring different groups or resources together. They are good at brokering relationships and have the ability to 'communicate, to persuade, to imagine oneself in someone else's world and to bring together different worlds' (Hendriks and Tops, 2005, 487). It is these everyday fixers who often become the informal leaders of community action, who relay 'local knowledge' to the system world: that is 'the very mundane, yet expert understanding of and practical reasoning about local conditions derived from lived experience' (Yanow, 2004, S12).

New social capital and trust in the public domain

In Chapter 2 (this volume), Rydin overviews the role that social capital plays in mobilising community action. Active citizenship is an expression of the capacities that communities have to engage with their environment. It has been suggested that social capital is vanishing, and the world is becoming increasingly disconnected and individual (Putnam, 2000; Sennett, 2008). What we have witnessed, however, in recent decades – which is alluded to in both Rydin's chapter and in the introduction to this book – is a 'lightening' (Duyvendak and Hurenkamp, 2004) of social networks and therefore a 'new social capital' (Duyvendak and Hurenkamp, 2004) which is not always a product of traditional social ties. People become involved in community projects for a range of pragmatic reasons, and are brought together within action groups, issue networks, neighbourhood committees, voluntary work, renovation projects, Twitter networks, care services, and so on. Although in many instances the 'socio-spatial community' may have been weakened, relationships are built on 'networked individualism' or as a product of 'multiple inclusion'. New social capital, as described by

Duyvendak, is a product of networked knowledge, opinions, norms, values or narratives. It explains that communities still come together to take collective action despite the erosion of traditional patterns of sociability: relationships can appear less stable (not being based on long-term face-to-face forms of social interaction), but even more fluid forms of sociability can underpin community action.

'Public familiarity', however, retains a role in community building (Fischer, 1982). This familiarity is generated through the meetings that occur as people leave their homes in the morning, collect children from school, take out the rubbish or use local shops and services. It generates trust in the familiar, without people actually having to interact or genuinely know one another. It is a 'familiar trust' in the public domain, with 'trusted strangers' (Lofland, 1985) coming to share some sense or idea of community. Lofland argues that friendship is not a prerequisite to 'neighbourhood engagement', but there need to be nearby places – schools, parks, libraries or shops – where familiarity can take root (Zwaard, 2010). For that reason, reduced spending on public facilities may undermine familiarity, reducing access to what Kilpatrick et al (Chapter 5, this volume) have described as 'interactional infrastructure', though for some forms of community action, prior interaction is not an essential prerequisite.

Engaged/engaging government

As well as providing the context for a growth in new social capital, leading to necessary familiarity, government has a critical role to play in nurturing community action. Blokland (2009) has shown, from research undertaken in Rotterdam, that local government must be 'engaged' in neighbourhood issues: it must demonstrate that it is willing to support active citizenship. If governments abdicate themselves from the responsibility of supporting neighbourhoods, for example through interventions that aim to enhance quality of life, then community action tends to fizzle out. There is a general view that activism fills the void left in the wake of a shrinking state: that people do more when the state does nothing. Yet Vermeij, van Houwelingen, and de Hart (2012) show that where there is less government, there is also less citizen involvement. Interest in an area on the part of the local state shows residents of a neighbourhood that they have not been abandoned. Demonstration of some external faith in an area can be an important catalyst for active citizenship. Conversely, a withdrawal of support is often accompanied by community apathy, which quickly plunges an area into a spiral of decline (Blokland and Savage, 2008; Parmentier, 2009).

Past research reveals that very few citizens' initiatives operate independently, within a policy vacuum (Hurenkamp et al, 2006; Engbersen and Engbersen, 2008). Actions which, at first glance, may appear spontaneous have often been facilitated – and sometimes initiated or orchestrated – by government. Even among those that are genuinely spontaneous, there will at some point be a need for support from local government, from welfare institutions, from other public or third sector services (for example, a housing association), or from established community organisations. Government can seldom 'take a back seat' but rather has a key role and responsibility in the promotion of active citizenship (Zwaard and Specht, 2013, 43), walking what has been described as a 'tightrope' (Tonkens and Verhoeven, 2011) between sensitivity to the independence of community action and the need to provide professional support. There is frequently a tension between official involvement and indifference, between flexibility and control, and between letting go and taking over (Van Ankeren, Tonkens, and Verhoeven, 2010). Independent mediators – or support groups – may be engaged to act as a bridge between community and state actors (see Gallent, Chapter 16, this volume) but in broad terms, the attempt to forge an effective partnership between the state and community action can be described as a 'Fourth Way' in public/community intervention.

The Fourth Way

The ideological basis for the reform of the welfare state, noted in this chapter, can in part be found in the 'Third Way' (Giddens, 1998), which emphasises the combined role of market mechanisms and personal responsibility in producing vital public goods. In this world view, governments must resist intervention where possible, and focus instead on the 'stimulation' of social development. It is a view rooted in social democracy and liberalism: the 'Third Way' calls on citizens to attempt to address local problems before appealing to government for help. The idea of a 'Fourth Way' is of course a derivative of this. It has the same concern for a new relationship between the state and civil society and requires that the latter is not overburdened – through excessive regulation – by the former. Instead, it argues for a partnership between the state, citizens and civil society organisations. Unlike the Third Way, however, it does not prescribe any sequence of responsibility: that is, citizens first, then the state. Rather, the Fourth Way harnesses the power of active citizens in an equal partnership with government institutions: rather than stimulating action, the state works alongside community actors building flat, horizontal rather than vertical, relationships. It stimulates (by creating the conditions in which communities can flourish and by signalling its support for collective action) but then works with those actors towards key social, economic and environmental goals.

New towns

The role of active citizens and their engagement with state actors is now examined in specific *districts* within four Dutch New Towns. The studies focus on community initiatives that have sought to address issues of quality and liveability in the public realm. It is important to note that the focus here is on districts rather than neighbourhoods. The former is a geographical unit in a town or city that has been objectively defined by others and where the building pattern, for instance, defines the physical borders. Neighbourhoods, on the other hand, are much more diffuse in geographical terms with boundaries determined by the lines of communication between citizens. When the term 'local community' or 'neighbourhood' is used in the remainder of this chapter, we are referring to a unit which is socially constructed rather than normatively defined.

Districts are important in the Netherlands as they have become the spatial framework in which the local state interacts with community organisations. Often, permanent outreach teams are tasked with building relationships with these organisations and with networks of local actors operating across different sectors. They seek to promote self-management and to stimulate community development and, thereafter, trust in the public domain. Improving contact between local residents and creating a sense of community is seen as an essential prerequisite for improving the quality of an urban district.

On balance, while many problems can be identified with the *district*, and responses can generally be orchestrated at that level, it is also the case that some issues take root more locally, or community structures align with spatial units that are differently defined. In the case of the Netherlands, however, these districts are relatively small geographical units: they are parts of the New Towns, resembling the 'neighbourhoods' of the UK, for example, rather than its 'districts'.

The new towns of the Netherlands grew rapidly during the 1960s and 1970s as national government responded to high demand for housing with the building of new settlements. The new towns were a product of top-down planning. Half a century on and the new towns are aging, and several are struggling with a range of social and physical problems. Government has intervened to address these problems, and in the remainder of this chapter we examine the initiatives that have been taken forward in five key new towns: Zoetermeer, Almere, Lelystad, Haarlemmermeer and Ede. The outcomes of community action are highlighted, with comments offered on the interaction between the system world of the state and the life world of citizens, and the activities of 'everyday fixers'.

Almere: Citizens take over maintenance of public space

About the district Hoekwierde

Hoekwierde is part of De Wierden, a district in the city of Almere Haven. De Wierden as a whole is an area where incomes are below average and the level of educational attainment is low. Hoekwierde could be described as a 'gold coast' within the larger district. It is close to the waterfront of Lake Gooimeer and comprises solely privately-owned semi-detached and detached houses, with a total of 140 houses set within a large amount of green, public space.

Taking the initiative to maintain public space

Over the last two and a half years, community activities have been initiated to maintain public spaces. This case shows that the 'life world' of citizens has played a leading role in establishing the partnership with local government. The 'Fourth Way' of civic action can also be observed here. Citizens view themselves as equal partners, working alongside the local authority.

This initiative began as a protest group that included a few home-owners who took action to stop the plans of local government to build a high-rise building on the site of local woodland 'in their backyard'. They protested by carefully maintaining the woodland under threat. They raked leaves and cut trees to express their desire to maintain this community space. Their collective action was so strong that the government was forced to abandon its plan when it was blocked through the formal consultation process provided for by Dutch law. The protest enabled members of the community to get to know one another and they came up with the idea of maintaining other public spaces.

'It is so nice to be outside and work together in our neighbourhood. And helping with the maintenance is not complicated, you can even help by just organising a coffee break', tells one of the initiators. Within a few months the group had expanded to 40 people who just enjoyed working together in their forest, being together and teaching and learning from each other: a social infrastructure grew up and the level of neighbourhood involvement rose. '"Friends" is not the right word [to describe] how people see each other, but they get to know each other a little bit more and it is easier to approach a neighbour if you have a problem' added the district manager in an interview.

High ambition: no maintenance role for local government

At a certain point, the team formulated new ambitions. They wanted to take on more and more maintenance work from local government. The people of Hoekwierde demonstrated what we referred to, in the first half of this chapter, as 'collective efficacy': 'We can do this better, more cheaply and it is also more fun than if local government continued to do it.' This is also a typical example of the strong influence of the 'life world'. The citizens see that they have power and take an active interest in organising initiatives by themselves. Sometimes the citizens do a better job of maintenance than the local government, sometimes an inferior job, but it is always on the terms of the citizens and not on the basis of fixed procedures.

Citizens and local government work as equal partners

The citizens started by mowing grass, trimming bushes and cleaning the pond. The ambitions of the citizens of the Hoekwierde are high; they want to maintain public spaces instead of it being done by local government but they had to find a way of financing this work.

The citizens formed an official foundation to apply for various grants so that they could buy the materials to undertake the maintenance work. They also entered into a co-partnership agreement with the local government regarding the regulation of the partnership. This was referred to specifically as a co-partnership and not a subsidiary agreement. Under a co-partnership both parties are equal, while with subsidiaries, one partly is dependent on the other. This is very important in the 'Fourth Way': to be officially equal and to see one another as equal partners.

This contractual agreement regulated how public money for maintaining public spaces in Hoekwierde would be allocated to the citizens' foundation. The co-partnership contract also includes a list of all the types of maintenance activities that the residents are to carry out or not to carry out. This financial agreement is complex and rather interesting. Questions raised from the 'system world' included 'who has a say over how the money is spent'? How can the government influence this citizens' initiative? The agreement states which tasks the citizens are responsible for and how the money is to be used, but nothing more than that. There is no oversight during this process, only a commitment to keep each other informed.

Everyday fixers as an important success factor

Two residents participating in the scheme had professional experience of the spatial planning process and maintaining public space. These two men also had strong leadership skills that helped to recruit and connect people – two special qualities that can be attributed to 'everyday fixers'. These qualities were discernible in the initiators of this project.

How does local government deal with this 'life world'?

The full take-over of the maintenance of public space by residents represented a challenge for local government. The question for the local bureaucracy was how to deal with these citizens? How should they handle the responsibilities involved in the activities; and how should other neighbours and government departments work together? The mayor and alderman were enthusiastic: 'a "thumbs up" for these active and "super" citizens'. At the same time, however, the local 'maintenance department' was a little afraid. 'Wasn't mowing the grass my job?' 'Sometimes it takes more time than expected to trust each other' (system and life world), said one of the initiators. 'Sometimes it is helpful to act as a real negotiator and sometimes it helps to be anarchistic and go your own way', he added in an interview. 'For example, I went to the town hall to explain to the alderman and the department the problem of mistrust of the 'maintenance department' among the initiators of the programme, and I was persuaded to be cooperative.' This way of acting is also typical of an 'everyday fixer', who has local knowledge, leadership skills and knows how to handle both the system world and the life world.

Ede: local government following the speed of active citizenship

About the Schoonenburg district

The Schoonenburg district is a smaller part of the larger district of Veldhuizen. Schoonenburg's urban structure is based around semi-

Image 8.1: Active citizenship in the Hoeckwierde

© Ton Huijzer

detached family houses arranged around small-scale courtyards. The alignment of these houses is not straight and this produces an intimate atmosphere. Around the complex there are large high-rise apartment blocks. The 'small-scale' feel of Schoonenburg contrasts sharply with these high-rise blocks. Schoonenburg comprises mainly privately owned houses in the lower–middle price range.

Volunteer group in Schoonenburg

In Schoonenburg, citizens are active in a volunteer group. It does not have the status of an official foundation and nor does it aim to become one. The initiative began when local government was renovating local public spaces. These residents also thought: 'We can do this work better and more carefully ourselves, and we can do it more cheaply.' They developed their idea, made a plan for a new design for a courtyard and organised and realised the plan themselves, with a little help from the district manager of the local government.

Differences between the life world and the system world

The neighbours developed their whole idea in three weeks. This shows the speed of citizens (life world) compared to the speed of public bodies (system world). When local government makes this kind of plan, it

Image 8.2: Discussion and result I

© Ton Huijzer

takes much longer to organise and realise, because it has to overcome so many bureaucratic obstacles, although this case also shows that the district manager of the local government can react quickly to assist the initiators and understand the life world. 'If you do not react really quickly, there is a big chance that you will lose the energy of the initiators, this energy is exactly what older neighbourhoods in new towns need,' said the district manager. His reaction suggests not only that he understands the life world, but also that he understands the urgent need to work together as partners.

'System world' knows how to work with the 'life world'

The neighbours in Schoonenburg were not only quick to make plans; they also knew how to get funding from the local government. The district manager of the local government was well known in the neighbourhood and can be seen as an 'everyday fixer'. It was easy for citizens to call him to ask how they could secure finance for their idea and he acted as their mediator. The funding was secured from the local authority's 'quality of life budget'. Their only obligation was to fill in an official form and send in their invoices afterwards. The district manager took care of the other bureaucratic arrangements. He was the 'go-between'. This quick and simple access to funding was also one

Image: 8.3 Discussion and result II

© Ton Huijzer

of the success factors of this project. The district manager also showed that he understood how to work with citizens' initiatives.

The district manager in Schoonenburg was very eager to help the citizens quickly; he had a positive attitude, won the trust of residents and secured autonomy from his own 'boss'. The district manager told us that the support of his boss was really important:

> 'I do not need to report everything to him and I can trust my own instincts on how I work, with whom I work, and how I make agreements with citizens. With some citizens I note everything in official documents and with others I only want to see a receipt from a shop and I will arrange the money.'

These are important arguments relating to why he works so efficiently and differently to other district managers.

Almere: from formal participation to active citizenship

About the district of De Wierden

De Wierden in Almere Haven is a larger area of which the smaller district of Hoekwierde is a part. De Wierden is a district with around

70 per cent social housing; socio-economic status and social cohesion are low and the turnover of residents is high. The organisational skills of residents are expected to be low by neighbourhood managers working in local government.

As a result of a large district-based renovation project, the quality of public spaces and social housing has improved. For local residents, however, this top-down intervention was the reason to start their own bottom-up ideas to improve their neighbourhood.

Organisational skills

A few neighbours were already members of the residents' committee which had a longer history, but they were not really active. The committee was regarded as local government's formal partner for reaching people in the district, because the representatives were supposed to have contact with other neighbours. This was not initially the case, but this changed during the renovation process. This was organised by local government and housing associations. Since then, the formal committee has become more active and tried to connect with more people from the neighbourhood in order to influence the plans of the institutions. During these meetings, however, it was not only formal procedures that were discussed; the institutions also consulted the committee about their wishes for the district.

The residents came up with the idea of creating a footpath through the neighbourhood to connect the nicest but often-forgotten spots. 'After the renovation, you could see the beauty of the neighbourhood much better', said the treasurer of the residents' committee. They wanted to organise the footpath themselves rather than through local government. The treasurer of the committee explained that one of the reasons for organising this footpath themselves was that 'as initiator you feel more connected to your project and more engaged with your neighbourhood. It is nicer to go about it this way.' And as he explained in an interview, 'sometimes you discover that you or your neighbours have unknown skills and talents'.

The residents' committee organised several meetings at the home of one of the committee members to hear the ideas of other people. This worked: many ideas were proposed, enthusiasm spread and the 'sleeping committee' awoke. In the space of 18 months, the committee grew from four to 12 members and from zero to 40 extra volunteers.

Taking the plunge

The committee made a formal plan for the footpath and some extra features such as playgrounds, hanging baskets and a small maze. The local government and housing association helped them to develop the plan and introduced them to the national pilot programme. The first funding and activities were organised and the committee started to build the footpath. In fact, the path had already been built, but they installed a paving stone with the 'W' of the Wierden every 10 metres. They did this together on Saturdays so that other people would see what was going on. This began to attract more people and ideas. An artist started the idea of a 'social sofa' which she had built within a few months with the help of children and neighbours under her supervision, and supported by a builder from the neighbourhood.

Image 8.4: Delivering change

© Ton Huijzer

Many participants were inspired and enthused by these activities, and more and more people followed, but they also discovered their own talents. 'This is far nicer than just negotiating and discussing the major plans of local government,' noted the treasurer of the committee. Typically this is an example of the 'Fourth Way' of citizens in participation. People want to do something instead of just talking. The role of the institutions is still important, however. Here the district-based approach to local government and housing associations was the reason for launching this civic initiative. Citizens and institutions also worked together as partners in the larger programme of renovation because this was the way to get the best out of both groups. The footpath project and the role of the formal residents' committee had a positive effect on social contacts, organisational skills and commitment of the neighbours in the district (Brouwer and Engbersen, 2013).

Lelystad: local government's search for the Fourth Way

About the Atolwijk district

This district is one of the oldest and most problematic areas of Lelystad. Most of the houses were built around 1970 and are publicly owned; almost all these houses are terraced family houses. In the 1990s the housing association, the owner of the houses, sold off much of this social housing to the residents (at a discount) because of the organisation's own financial problems. With some of that money, they renovated a small number of social houses, but those properties that had been sold off were not included in this project. Since then, the façades and gardens of these latter houses have deteriorated steadily.

The people who live in the Atolwijk have a low socio-economic status, house prices are low and the neighbourhood is not popular among people from Lelystad. For the government, an important reason for investing in the neighbourhood was to prevent the neighbourhood from becoming less and less attractive.

High level of involvement by government

Local government intended to improve the quality of public space and encourage homeowners to improve their own houses. They did not expect to launch any civic initiatives relating to public space but they did expect residents to repair and maintain their own houses. The level of governmental engagement was high. How could people be encouraged to improve their privately owned houses? And how should government stimulate neighbourhood engagement, while reducing top-down intervention? Those were the central questions for Lelystad in the national pilot project entitled 'Self-organisation in new towns'.

A policy agenda is not automatically a citizens' agenda

The idea of improving the façades and the appearance of the privately owned houses in a neighbourhood where most residents are of a low socio-economic status is an ambitious goal. The local authority in Lelystad had several tools to incentivise residents to invest. They provided grants and low-interest loans to stimulate finances. They also set up a neighbourhood shop where the district manager had office hours and distributed information. This was not a great success: the shop was quiet and only a few grants were allocated in the district. They also organised door-to-door interviews to establish one-to-one contact with the residents about the neighbourhood, but not many people wanted to participate in the interviews. The district manager said in an interview: 'They are simply not interested in the quality of their houses and they also looked a bit afraid when we knocked on the door.'

It is not easy to incentivise residents to invest in the exterior of their houses and there are various reasons for this. Some people cannot invest because of financial constraint; others are too busy with their social and financial problems; and for others still, their house is simply not important enough to them to invest in.

Tapping the energy of the citizens

Local government tried to achieve its aim in another way. The district managers started to look for 'everyday fixers' in the neighbourhood. They invested in their local network and contacted several organisations, institutions and a few residents who were active in the Atolwijk. Together they organised an informal meeting with residents in this district. The goal was no longer to encourage them to improve the quality of their own houses. The goal was to find out which were the most important issues for residents in the neighbourhood: a shift from top-down to bottom-up. Local government abandoned its fixed agenda and started asking questions like: 'Are you satisfied with your neighbourhood?'; 'What aspects might be improved?'; and the most important question: 'What do you want to contribute to your neighbourhood?' This approach worked very well. For the first time in years there was more energy on the part of residents to do 'something for their neighbourhood'. This resulted in two groups being formed by residents. There was one large group that wanted to clean up public spaces and a smaller group that wanted to encourage improvements in the quality of housing.

Organise quick and easy wins

The week after the informal meeting, a group of 15 people started to clean up the public space and a smaller group also started to clean up the gardens and façades. Another resident offered to help his neighbours to contract decorators. These quick and easy wins following the meeting were really important. They started a flow of active people.

The role of the district managers was to encourage the ambassadors and facilitate both the groups by providing materials. In this district, local government could not take a back seat: if they wanted to improve the district, they had to promote active citizenship. This was a lengthy process in a neighbourhood with a low initial level of social cohesion, a low average socio-economic status and where organisational skills were lacking. The case shows that a 'Fourth Way' does not also arise on its own, but needs to be nurtured by a supportive state.

Overview and conclusions

In this chapter, we have linked the idea of active citizenship to positive and equal engagement with the local state, outlining the idea of a 'Fourth Way' in community action with governmental support. This Fourth Way is operating in the context of the 'welfare city', which is itself the product of a growing polemic against the welfare state and top-down government, in the context of fiscal austerity. It involves horizontal relationships and working between community actors and local government. It does not prioritise the former, but recognises that the state has a crucial part to play in stimulating and seeding those actions – at the neighbourhood, community or district level – that lead to essential community development, to familiarity and trust in urban settings, and that can achieve vital local outcomes. Partnership working is the best way to support effective community action and planning.

A 'tightrope' needs to be walked between supporting and controlling community action, however. If support turns into control then it risks undermining the enthusiasm of community actors: keeping a distance is vital for the autonomy of citizenship initiatives, but it is also important that the local state is 'on the spot', giving support and recognition where needed.

The four cases described (drawn from Brouwer and Engbersen, 2013) show that neighbourhood engagement is possible in many different situations, although it is important to take account of varying levels of social cohesion, socio-economic status and the homogeneity, or heterogeneity, of residents. Effective stimulation of neighbourhood engagement depends, first, on understanding the nature of the neighbourhood and therefore the strategy needed to trigger mobilisation. These strategies often have to understand the nature of 'new social capital', the fluidity of social contact, and the importance of 'public familiarity' over friendship in binding together urban communities comprising 'trusted strangers'. While having the right infrastructure in place is important (Kleinhans and Bolt, 2010), the case studies in this chapter have revealed something of the tactics that can be used to stimulate action in what might appear to be hitherto dormant neighbourhoods.

The 'everyday fixers' – the most active of the active citizens – need to be drawn out and encouraged (if encouragement is needed) to become the vanguards of community engagement. Across districts, variations in the level of that engagement, is often explained in terms of the preponderance (or absence) of these 'everyday fixers'. Districts with a history of protest and direct action tend to be home to many of these citizens. Even where they appear absent, however, individuals with the potential and skills to become networkers, bridge-builders and boundary crossers can be drawn out, sometimes by simply asking the right questions and creating a context of open dialogue.

It is not just communities that need these networking pragmatists, however. The local state needs its own supply of pragmatic individuals who see beyond the bureaucratic system world and who are able to work with communities on their own terms: the reflective practitioner who can understand the community view and work effectively at the community/state interface (Van der Pennen and Bosch, 2011). Local bridging to community action is the crucial condition for finding a workable Fourth Way.

Note

[1] The authors are grateful to Radboud Engbersen for his constructive comments on an earlier version of this chapter.

References

Bang, HP, Sørensen, E, 1999, The everyday maker: A new challenge to democratic governance, in *Administrative Theory & Praxis* 21, pp. 325–341

Blokland, T, 2009, *Oog voor elkaar: Veiligheidsbeleving en sociale controle in de grote stad*, Amsterdam: Amsterdam University Press

Blokland, T, Savage, M, 2008, Social capital and networked urbanism, in T Blokland, M Savage (eds) *Networked urbanism, social capital in the city*, pp 1–22, Aldershot: Ashgate

Brouwer, J, Engbersen, G, 2013, *Zelforganisatie gaat niet vanzelf: Evaluatie Experimenten met bewonersinitiatieven in New Towns*, The Hague: Platform 31

Denters, B, Tonkens, E, Verhoeven, I, Bakker, J, 2013, *Burgers maken de buurt*, The Hague: Platform 31

Duyvendak, JW, Hurenkamp, M (eds), 2004, *Kiezen voor de kudde: Lichte gemeenschappen en de nieuwe meerderheid*, Amsterdam: Van Gennep

Engbersen, R, Engbersen, G, 2008, Voorbij de wijk. Over oude vragen en nieuwe antwoorden voor de aanpak van vroeg-naoorlogse wijken, in L Argiolu, R Koos van Dijken, J Koffijberg (eds) *Bloei en Verval naoorlogse wijken*, pp 47–77, The Hague: Nicis

Engbersen, G, Engbersen, R, 2014, *Van buurtbarbecue naar buurtinfrastructuur. Corporaties en het veranderend sociaal domein*, Amsterdam: De Vernieuwde Stad

Fischer, C, 1982, *To dwell among friends: Personal networks in town and city*, Chicago, IL: University of Chicago Press

Giddens, A, 1998, *The third way: The renewal of Social Democracy*, London: John Wiley & Sons

Habermas, J, 1984, *Theorie van het Communicatieve Handelen*, Amsterdam: Boom

Hendriks, F, Tops, P, 2005, *Everyday fixers as local heroes: A case study of vital interaction in urban governance, Local Government Studies* 31, 475–490

Houten, Mv, Winsemius, A (eds), 2010, *Participatie ontward: Vormen van participatie uitgelicht*, Utrecht: Movisie

Hurenkamp, M, Tonkens, E, Duyvendak, JW, 2006, *Wat burgers bezielt. Een onderzoek naar burgeriniatieven*, Amsterdam: University of Amsterdam/NICIS

Hurenkamp, M, Tonkens, E, Duyvendak, JW, 2012, *Crafting citizenship: Negotiating tensions in modern society*, Basingstoke: Palgrave Macmillan

Kleinhans, R, Bolt, G, 2010, *Vertrouwen houden in de buurt: Verval, opleving en collectieve zelfredzaamheid in stadsbuurten*, The Hague: Nicis

Lofland, LH, 1985, *A world of strangers: Order and action in urban public space*, Prospect Hills, IL: Waveland Press

Morenoff, JD, Sampson, RJ, Raudenbush, S, 2001, *Neighborhood inequality, collective efficacy, and the spatial dynamics of urban violence*, Michigan, MI: University of Michigan

Parmentier, MG, 2009, *Reputation, neighbourhood and behaviour*, Utrecht: University of Utrecht

Pennen, T van der, van der Brink, G, van Hulst, M, de Graaf, L, 2012, *Best Persons en hun betekenis voor de Nederlandse achterstandswijken*, The Hague: Boom/Lemma

Putnam, R, 2000, *Bowling alone: The collapse and revival of American community*, New York: Simon & Schuster

Sampson, RJ, 2005, Civil society reconsidered: The durable nature and community structure of collective civic action, *American Journal of Sociology* 111, 3, 673–714

Sennett, R, 2008, *The Craftsman*, New Haven, CT: Yale University Press

Specht, M, 2012, *De pragmatiek van burgerparticipatie: Hoe burgers omgaan met complexe vraagstukken omtrent veiligheid, leefbaarheid en stedelijke ontwikkeling in drie Europese steden*, Amsterdam: Vrije Universiteit

The Independent, 2013, Dutch King Willem-Alexander declares the end of the welfare state, *The Independent*, 17 September 2013

Tonkens, EH, Verhoeven, I, 2011, *Bewonersinitiatieven: Proeftuin voor partnerschap tussen burgers en overheid. Een onderzoek naar bewonersinitiatieven in de Amsterdamse wijkaanpak*, Amsterdam: Universiteit van Amsterdam/Stichting Actief burgerschap

Van Ankeren, M, Tonkens, E, Verhoeven, I, 2010, *Bewonersinitiatieven in de krachtwijken van Amsterdam. Een verkennende studie*, Amsterdam: University of Amsterdam

Van der Pennen, T, Bosch, E, 2011, 'Urban practitioners who make a difference?' in M van Niekerk and L Sterrenberg (eds) *Challenges of urban governance*, pp 21–46, The Hague: NICIS Institute.

Vermeij, L, van Houwelingen, P, de Hart, J, 2012, 'Verantwoordelijk voor de eigen buurt', in V. Veldheer, J. Jonker, L. van Noije, C. Vrooman (ed) *Een beroep op de burger. Minder Verzorgingsstaat, meer eigen verantwoordelijkheid? Sociaal en Cultureel Rapport 2012*, pp 254–76, Den Haag: Sociaal en Cultureel Planbureau.

Yanow, D, 2004, Translating local knowledge at organizational peripheries, *British Journal of Management* 15, S9–S25

Zwaard, J van der, 2010, *Scenes in de Copy Corner: Van vluchtige ontmoetingen naar publieke vertrouwdheid*, Amsterdam: SUN/Transsity

Zwaard, J van der, Specht, M, 2013, *Betrokken bewoners: Betrouwbare overheid*, Rotterdam: Kenniswerkplaats

9

Small-town comprehensive planning in California: medial pathways to community-based participation

Hemalata Dandekar and Kelly Main

Introduction

This chapter looks at the intersection of community groups and city-wide comprehensive planning in the context of small towns in California. City-wide, comprehensive planning in California is finely articulated by state law, which requires the adoption of a 'general plan' that provides the basis for virtually all governance related to planning undertaken by city governments. These comprehensive plans are required to reflect the vision that a city's residents have for the future of the city. All goals and policies included in a general plan must be implemented at the area or neighbourhood plan scale. Any regulations on private property must be consistent with the general plan, and all proposed projects in a city are reviewed for their compliance with it. Thus, the planning that community groups do, whether at a neighbourhood level, or on specific projects or issues, will at some point intersect with goals and policies in the general plan.

By virtue of its requirement to reflect the vision of city residents, and concomitant state regulations that specify cities provide for public input, the process of adopting a general plan or amending it is one in which community groups can participate. Some cities have devised processes that appear to engender meaningful participation; participation in which community members are partners and/or in control of the decision and plan-making process (Arnstein, 1969). Because of the general plan's relative importance to neighbourhood plans and projects, these processes seem a likely place for community groups to attempt to have influence. Despite this, very little has been written about the specific nature of community groups' involvement in the US comprehensive planning process (Sirianni, 2007; Gonzalez, 2006). Indeed, the literature documenting community-based organising around planning issues in the US has focused on intersections with specific projects, both wanted and unwanted, and, to a lesser degree, neighbourhood-level plans. Moreover, literature on project-based participation frequently characterises it as originating from the top (agency-led participation) or bottom (grass-roots, community-based planning), which obscures a more complex understanding of how community groups might be, and are, involved in planning decisions (Cooke and Kothari, 2001; Fraser, 2005; Gonzalez, 2006).

Adding to the limited literature on community group involvement in comprehensive planning, this chapter investigates two avenues for community group participation in processes provided for by cities – the more prevalent and broadly interpreted citizens' advisory committee and the collaborative workshop process. These processes are looked at in two, similarly sized but socio-economically differentiated, small towns in California: San Luis Obispo, a relatively wealthy community with a university, and Delano, a relatively poorer community in which a university-led effort in collaborative planning was exercised in order to illustrate alternative ways for community-based participation to influence general plans. Reviewing these processes on a small-town scale in the State of California, in which the mandate for cities to adopt a general plan and to periodically update its elements is adhered to, offers an opportunity to look closely at processes that enable specific community groups to influence this process and the creation or modification of these influential documents. The lens of advocacy and collaborative planning, two methods frequently utilised by community-based organisations in the US to undertake community-based action, are used in this examination (Gittell and Vidal, 1998; Gonzalez, 2006; Peterman, 2004).

Advocacy planning

During the 1960s, advocacy planning arose in tandem with social movements attempting to address inequities in the US (Davidoff, 1965) and in response to the concepts and outcomes of the rational planning approach – the idea that technical expertise employed by formally trained planners could identify and achieve the 'public interest' through the application of top-down planning for local communities (Diaz, 2005; Harwood, 2003). The primary goal of advocacy planning is the transfer of power and resources from established, well-represented groups to underrepresented groups (Fraser, 2005; Harwood, 2003; Peterman, 2004). Originally, advocacy planning was designed to provide underrepresented groups with a voice through advocate planners, 'guerillas in the planning process' who were familiar with and skilled in formal planning processes (Diaz, 2005; Harwood, 2003).

Early criticisms of advocacy planning pointed out the inherent flaws of expecting planners employed by the existing power structure to advocate for others, as well as the privileging of planning professionals acting on behalf of their constituencies rather than the actual democratisation of the planning process itself (Sandercock, 1998). Discussing the current relevance of advocacy planning, Harwood (2003) writes:

> Today, however, advocacy planning, continues to be held as a viable framework for planning, though with more caution…Advocacy planning has emerged as a centrepiece in progressive local governments' planning efforts at redistribution, especially in the form of local government-sponsored programs that create a bridge between the city and neighborhoods, the rich and poor, and the dominant culture and minority groups. (Harwood, 2003, 26)

Advocates are not limited to those inside progressive city governments but include professionals and non-professionals from many sectors, including non-profits and community-based action groups (Gonzalez, 2006). Literature on advocacy work at the neighbourhood level, via neighbourhood groups, often focuses on community leadership that mobilises residents to protest, march, or rally for residents' rights during the implementation stage of plans and projects (Diaz, 2005; Fraser, 2005; Gittell and Vidal, 1998), which explains why less is known about how community groups, and their leaders and members, actually participate in the planning process, itself (Gonzalez, 2006).

Collaborative planning

Collaborative planning responded to several of the perceived inadequacies of both the rational and advocacy planning approaches. Unlike advocacy planners, collaborative planners do not take centre stage, but instead become facilitators in the process of consensus building among community members and groups (Brooks, 2002). Unlike advocacy planning, collaborative planning is less focused on the representation of a specific group's interests and conflicts and, instead, emphasises a deliberative democratic process in which controversial community issues cannot be resolved until consensus is reached through discussion and persuasion around a particular planning option (Booher and Innes, 2002; Innes and Booher, 2003; Forester, 1999). A diversity of views and community groups is required for the success of a communicative process so that relevant issues will arise and be addressed (Booher and Innes, 2002). Deliberative processes and consensus building can be used within and between community groups and can be organised and facilitated by public planners and community-group leadership (Carpenter and Kennedy, 2001).

The strengths of the collaborative process are that it provides an avenue for conflict management (Gittell and Vidal, 1998), building local coalitions with common interests (Booher and Innes, 2002), and even bridging social capital among stakeholders (Carpenter and Kennedy, 2001). Because this approach does not directly address differential power relationships among groups participating in the process, however, it has been criticised for the limited understanding it provides of social relations necessary for the redistribution of resources to marginalised groups (Fischer, 2004; Sandercock, 1998). The process also assumes that the parties participating in the collaborative processes are negotiating in good faith and willing to compromise, an assumption that appears somewhat naïve in the currently polarised political environment in the US (Brooks, 2002). Still, collaborative planning does provide the possibility of a democratic approach to plan making (Forester, 1999) and has proven to provide lasting compromises in highly conflictive situations between community groups (Gittell and Vidal, 1998); thus, it provides a useful lens through which to view the participation of community groups in comprehensive plan-making processes.

Community participation in the general plan process

California state law mandates that a 'general plan' be prepared for each of the state's current 456 incorporated cities and 58 counties. Representing 'the vision' each city has for its future, all of a city's planning documents, and the regulations that implement them, must take their guidance from the city's general plan (Governor's Office of Planning and Research, 2003). State law defines the content of general plans – land use, circulation, housing and other traditional planning concerns. Many planning benefits can accrue from this centralised common framework for thinking about land use and related issues across a territory. For one thing, jurisdictions are required to think both community-wide and long-term. This formulation of the general plan through localised decision-making, reflects to some extent the country's historical legacy and self-identity, of a county created by frontier settlement of land by homesteading. This largely sweat-equity based investment in westward national expansion, was a means of obtaining absolute, 'fee simple' 'freehold' land ownership.[1] The sentiment that control over most land-use decisions remains at the local level, in local hands, is strong. From the survey and settlement period in US history, private property rights were privileged over public rights. Thus, the acceptance of planning for 'the public good' is a concept that is not broadly embraced or culturally recognised. That there is an agreement to the concept of planning, and a mandate for general plan making, is therefore significant, yet relatively recent.

Along with establishing the content of general plans, state law also sets a minimum level of public outreach that must be completed prior to plan adoption – two public hearings. This low threshold for compliance is, however, moderated by the Governor's Office of Planning and Research (2003), which encourages more extensive participation and recommends that the process addresses issues of diversity and disempowerment. The state, however, is seldom involved in local land-use decisions. These powers are delegated to city councils and county boards of supervisors and the prerogative is assiduously defended. There are, consequently, no requirements for coordination of plans between adjacent entities even with respect to programmes where collaboration rather than competition might be beneficial.[2] The development and design of community involvement in plan making and visioning is, therefore, a quintessentially localised process, bounded within municipal or county boundaries. As long as cities and counties meet the minimum requirements for advertising adoption of, and changes to, general plans and conduct the minimum two public hearings, cities and counties are free to be as inclusive and/or exclusive as they deem appropriate. Culture, historical experience, traditions, networks and connections as well as the structures of power, both economic and of influence, affect the choices that community groups make about action at the city level. Knowledgeable stakeholders are quite cognisant of the fact, and understand that changes they desire must be framed in calls for action within those parameters that are known to be in local governmental control.

Despite ongoing, institutionalised, evolution of the state guidelines designed to encourage participation in local plan making, broad-based participation by the multiple communities that make up a city is consistently lacking (Prowler, 2007). Many city governments struggle with relatively low-participation levels in city-wide plan making, often finding that participants comprise the 'usual suspects', those residents, business-owners and other interested parties with resources, time and connections, who are consistently present, vocal and express their point of view on planning endeavours open for public input.[3] Lack of broad-based participation in city-wide planning efforts has been attributed to factors such as demographic and cultural changes. These arguments suggest that new arrivals, whether documented or not, come from cultures without a tradition of public participation or face cultural and language barriers. Many of these communities experience social and economic marginalisation which, in turn, have a negative impact on civic participation (Derr et al, 2013; Hum, 2010; Umemoto and Igarashi, 2009).

Compounding this problem in California has been a significant demographic shift. California, with its population of 37.3 million people (US Census Bureau, 2010) is, by far, the most populous state in the US. It experienced a 10 per cent population increase over the past decade, a decade in which the Hispanic and Asian population each grew by about 30 per cent, to 14.0 million and 4.8 million respectively. The white non-Hispanic population has declined from its peak of 17 million people in 1990 to 15 million in 2010. Immigration out of the state has been more than offset by international immigration. California is significantly more diverse than the nation: 38 per cent Hispanic, compared with 16 per cent nationally; and, the share of white, non-Hispanics is only 40 per cent, which is significantly lower than its 64 per cent share nationally.[4] California is thus at the cutting edge of demographic change that is making the US population more multicultural, more Hispanic and less white.

A disconnect with sub-populations is not just along the lines of race and ethnicity of new residents. Cities often do not connect with specific demographic groups. Conventional methods of participation fail to engage across age and economic status, to constituencies such as youth and the working poor. They remain disconnected and non-participatory in the community visioning processes (Prowler, 2007). Those whose voices are heard in the comprehensive planning process, often and repeatedly, are those who are connected and understand the influence of the general plan – the affluent, the well-educated, the retirees – and those who are mobilised as members of special interest groups – the bicycle coalition, the wilderness society, the save our downtown group, those networked and part of various electronic or other 'bridging' communities – and, of course, the interest groups of business owners, real estate developers and small proprietors that populate the chamber of commerce.

The broader lack of participation reveals a disjuncture between the mandatory material included in general plans and neighbourhood concerns. The general plan's mandatory seven 'elements' – (1) land use, (2) circulation, (3) housing, (4) conservation (5) open space, 6) noise, and 7) safety – are mostly related to the physical, spatial, and technical sides of the planning enterprise. Broader criticisms of planners' inability to communicate the relevancy of planning concerns (Prowler, 2007) are particularly applicable to the issues covered in a general plan. Discussions regarding land use, circulation, and the environment at a city-wide scale may not match the concerns of residents about access, and control over access, at the neighbourhood and city block scale.

Some cities in California are attempting to design participation processes to address these disparities in culture and income, processes in which community groups representing a variety of interests can work together in the plan-making process. The two cities examined here – one of which, San Luis Obispo, is amenity-rich and has experienced a less significant demographic/cultural shift, and one of which, Delano, is amenity-poor and has experienced significant demographic/cultural shifts – illustrate opportunities for both advocacy and collaborative planning by community groups. The two cases are not directly comparable. They differ greatly in basic and significant parameters – for instance in demographic mix, economy, affluence, education levels, amenity and natural resource base – but they are approximately the same size and exist in the same regulatory framework, that of the State of California. They illustrate that various forms and levels of community exist, and different types of participation are offered and embraced in different contexts. They underscore that context is important in defining 'community'. In San Luis Obispo, participation in a general plan citizens' advisory committee is reviewed. Citizens' advisory committees are meant to provide representation and voice to various city interest groups, offering a natural avenue for advocacy and collaboration. Committee members are appointed by city councils and review and/or develop the goals and policies that go into a general plan. In Delano, a collaborative workshop process is traced. In it community groups/members are invited and sought out to attend public workshops designed to identify and build consensus on the issues and concerns to be addressed in a general plan. In reviewing these two differing processes of community groups' involvement in agency-designed participatory processes, medial pathways for community groups' concerns to intersect with city-wide comprehensive plan making are illustrated.

San Luis Obispo's land use and circulation element (LUCE) citizens' advisory committee

San Luis Obispo is located in California's scenic coast, midway between San Francisco and Los Angeles. With a population of some 45,000 people (similar to Delano's) and California Polytechnic University, San Luis Obispo (with a student body of almost 19,000 at its border and an additional 12,000 students at adjacent Cuesta Community College) is considered an attractive and desirable place to live. Celebrated in the bestseller book *Thrive* as America's 'Happiest City'[5] San Luis Obispo is a city in which modernist planning has transformed what was once a 'sleepy little town with a small college' to a regional touristic destination that at the same time maintains its unique small town identity and architectural/artistic/cultural vitality, making it a livable place with a high quality of life for residents and the transient student community. The city is also a magnet for affluent retirees and a destination location for young couples able to telework. Its Thursday night farmers market is a weekly 'event', a regional draw attended by visitors from a considerable distance. The city has invested in planning and worked to shape and protect environmental, recreation, entertainment and cultural assets and quality of life to make it a go-to attraction for visitors from San Francisco, Los Angeles and the Central Valley. Scenic beaches are only a few minutes' drive away.

The transformation of the city to a destination place, through purposive, community-involved planning, has been aided and abetted by the University's increased prominence. It has attracted academics and professionals who have volunteered to play an active role in the city planning and governance process. Proactive planning has protected the scenic volcanic mountain ranges that ring the city. In 50 years the city has developed an almost contiguous greenbelt that circles the town. It is available for hiking and active and passive recreation and assists in wildlife preservation (bears have been sighted ambling down the well preserved creek to the downtown!). It contributes to the city's small town, rural character and its charm. The city's sustained commitment to a green belt strategy has actively involved multiple stakeholders and is a textbook case of the benefits that accrue from bridging, forming coalitions and implementing a hillside protection ordinance. The impact of protecting a quality of life through planning is reflected in housing values: the median single family home price in the city is $485,000, which is substantially higher than that in surrounding communities. Understanding how modernist mainstream planning by and large has worked in San Luis Obispo is instructive, but not necessarily replicable in communities with fewer fiscal resources and local amenities.

The population of San Luis Obispo has not shifted as much as the state and is 82 per cent white, 7 per cent Asian (US Census Bureau, 2012) and 14 per cent Hispanic.[6] With a median income of $40,000 (skewed by low-income students) and a highly educated population: 45 per cent with college and post-graduate professional degrees, 75 per cent with some college or associates degree,[7] the city has a pool of skilled and aware residents. They volunteer and participate in numerous standing advisory boards (14 currently listed on the city website) and short-term task forces (currently 12 listed) to advise the city council on a breadth of issues. It is considered a 'tough' town to work in by private sector consultant planners. They and the public sector planners who staff departments in the city know that many of the more than 1,000 non-profit organisations[8] registered in the county are tuned into city deliberations on land use and planning that have implications for them and they will be present, active and vocal in their participation in city planning deliberations on these issues.

The city is completing a general plan update of its 1994 Land Use and Circulation Elements (LUCE). It has invested significantly in this process with a total budget of $879,423. The LUCE update process illustrates how community is conceptualised, activated and engaged to participate in the formal city planning process and how mobilised community groups understand and engage with this structure. The community planning involvement in the LUCE update has been run by an established and seasoned planning firm whose approach has arguably been 'textbook correct' in implementing a variety of techniques to obtain community input: hard copy and web-based surveys; community workshops at sites scattered throughout the city; inspirational speakers who have lectured and instructed the public on how to love and sustain their city; numerous workshops to ascertain what residents love and dislike about various parts of the city; opportunities for residents to express their dreams for the city; educational workshops for the LUCE advisory committee on new mandates for general plans such as multimodal streets; design charrettes to vision new futures; and an effort by city staff to deliver broad based dissemination working closely with local news media, community groups and faith-based organisations to get information to residents. All information and documents related to the update are made available to residents on the city's project website (www.slo2035.com/). Social networks and crowd sourcing systems have been established in an attempt to capture the attention of the youthful, 'native' users of interactive technology. Workshops have been held in neighbourhood centres throughout the city. Community members can sign up for electronic news alerts and attend public workshops, they can comment freely and at length at the LUCE Advisory Task Force deliberations, and communicate concerns to city planners and the consultant team. The website states that: 'The City's goal is to engage as many residents, business owners and stakeholders as possible to ensure that the Plan reflects the vision of the entire community.'

Although city staff and the city planning consultants have followed a 'cutting edge' process for community engagement, the discussion and the visioning about futures has been fairly limited in scope, and bounded by the charge from the city council. The LUCE Advisory Task Force consisted of 17 individuals who volunteer their services, were deliberated on, and chosen by the city council after some debate and comments from communities with particular interests in the city such as Save Our Downtown, League of Women Voters, San Luis Obispo Bicycle Coalition, the Homebuilders Association (suggesting that membership on the task force not be restricted to city residents), Residents for Quality Neighborhoods (asserting the importance of appointing only residents on the task force) (city council meetings minutes, San Luis Obispo, 17 January 2012). They represent various city neighbourhoods and stakeholder interests and were appointed by majority vote of city council for a three-year term (March 2012–15) on the basis of their skill sets, the geographic distribution of their primary residence in the city, volunteerism and engagement with non-profit and neighbourhood groups, and their track record of participation.

The 17-member task force includes developers who invest in the city, residents who are protective of the quality of life they currently enjoy in certain residential neighbourhoods, professionals and professors with expertise in affordable housing, historic preservation, habitat preservation and art and culture. The task force painstakingly reviewed the language of the draft LUCE update of the General Plan provided by the consultant, line by line, clause by clause. Thirty-seven meetings, often over three hours long, involved deliberations between members of the task force group debating internal differences, written commentary submitted by the public at large and comments presented in person by residents during the meetings. Community groups such as the Bicycle Coalition, Save Our Downtown, the Chamber of Commerce, local developers and their professional consultants, all appeared before the task force at strategic times when policy related to their interests was being reviewed. In this process, protectionist sentiments and positions were contested, mediated, resolved by vote – local democracy in action, but within the narrow framework of the general plan guidelines as to what is 'includable' in the discussion.

The room to think big, to think inter-sectorally, to think about specific needs of specific groups within the city who were not represented, to think about future economy, to address issues of social access and equity as articulated by task force members or in community participants during this discourse all had to be translated by the task force into implementable policy recommendations pertinent to either the land use or the circulation element. Other issues and concerns, perhaps ones that were of more 'immediate' concern to people in their neighbourhoods were not voiced in this general plan-making process. Attendance at the workshops for gaining input was often times quite limited and familiar faces reappeared at various venues. The update will yield a document that will be incremental, not high on vision, but sound. It will modify two elements of the 1994 plan in their interstices. Out of this process will emerge modifications and technical adaptations that will improve city functions, making room for strategic growth that is sustainable, although the effort offers few visionary leaps to enhance city competitiveness in the next stage in its evolution. There are few radical departures from the strategies of the past that have served the city well but needed to be scrutinised so as to proactively address shifting economic and demographic realties of the state and the region.

Delano and the collaborative workshop process

Delano, with a population of 43,469, is located in the southern part of California's Central Valley, an inland valley stretching approximately 400 miles long and producing approximately 25 per cent of the US's food supply. The surrounding agricultural industry employs a significant number of Delano's residents (30 per cent) (US Census Bureau, 2010). Like many of the small rural communities in the Central Valley's agricultural region, Delano has a relatively high poverty rate (28 per cent), partly explained by the significant number of low-paying jobs in the agricultural sector and a seasonal unemployment rate of 21 per cent, also explained by the seasonal nature of agricultural work in the region (US Census Bureau, 2010). Delano's population is 72 per cent Hispanic. Delano also reflects the growing diversity in California, with 13 per cent of the population identifying themselves as 'Asian Alone,' 7 per cent identifying as 'White Alone', and 5 per cent identifying as 'Black Alone' (US Census Bureau, 2010).

In 2008 the city of Delano, lacking staff and resources to update the city's general plan, commissioned assistance from a comprehensive-planning studio in the City and Regional Planning Department at California Polytechnic State University, San Luis Obispo. Taught in the senior year of the undergraduate programme, the studio offers students real-life experience in the general plan-making process. Students are expected to practice basic principles and techniques of 'community outreach', – here 'community' is used in its broadest sense – everyone who is affected by a plan or project. The studio's outreach efforts include seeking the involvement of the multiple communities – whether they be related to gender, age, ethnicity, economic status, or other concerns, as defined by the communities themselves – that exist in the city.

Prior to the six-month studio, instructors worked with leaders of several Delano community groups to generate interest in a collaborative workshop process to be held between September 2008 and March 2009. Religious leaders, the chamber of commerce, and several non-profits were contacted, including the United Farm Workers (UFW), a national labour organisation that originated in Delano, California. In the 1960s, the UFW, led by Cesar Chavez, was responsible for organising California farm workers for better working conditions and wages[9] (Shaw, 2008).

Five public workshops were scheduled, during which consensus would be built through small-group discussion (Toker, 2012). The workshops were designed to be convenient and unintimidating – a series of picnics held on Saturdays and Sundays at the local community centre (Berry et al, 1993; Prowler, 2007; Sanoff, 2000). The picnics were advertised widely in the paper and on local radio stations and calls were made by the instructors and students to all non-profits, religious groups, business and residents' organisations prior to every picnic.

Of the five workshops, four were actually held before a shift in participation strategy was made. The four workshops were poorly attended. The majority of these participants were decision-makers (city council members, members of other city commissions, a local school district leader and several teachers). Members of two community-based organisations – a local community development corporation and the UFW – attended the last workshop; however, they had missed the earlier workshops, during which most of the framing of the plan was completed. A majority of Delano's community groups were contacted to find out why they had missed the workshops. Their responses were similar: their organisations were overwhelmed with meeting basic needs in the community. Farm workers were busy with the fall harvest. Some organisation leaders questioned the relevance of a general plan to their membership's concerns, particularly in comparison to their other activities. For instance, in fall 2008, UFW members were campaigning to affect the outcome of the 2008 elections for the US President and Congress and the California state legislature.

Delano's staff reported that the comments received during the workshops typified those of the 'usual suspects', the well-connected, who tend to make their concerns known, either through attendance at city meetings or individual meetings with staff and city council members. The demographic characteristics of the workshop participants were tracked, and they were not representative of Delano's diverse population. Fewer than half of the participants were Latino and only two of the participants were farmworkers. Based on limited community participation in the picnics/workshops, students and instructors shifted the location of community outreach efforts to popular community locations and events. This resulted in two events: outreach at the city's annual Holiday Parade and at the primary grocery market in the city. Through these two events, comments were collected from more than 300 community members. Students used the comments to identify groups in the city whose concerns were not represented in the workshops. Students interviewed their informal 'representatives' – people who were not formally organised but shared similar opinions – and featured them in a video they created and presented to the Delano City Council. Comments from members of these 'groups' included:

> They (the city council) only do things for the east side of town [the wealthier side of town]. We don't have anything on the other side of town. No shops, no anything. ('West-siders'' concerns)

> I worked [in the fields] all my life and with a lot of trouble, I got a house. The payments were too high and so they took the house from me. Now I rent. I've been renting for four months. I work very hard, and I can't afford to rent or buy a house. ('Affordable housing/farm workers'' concerns)

> There is a lot of gang activity in Delano...My brother is in a gang, a Delano gang, and I told him you are either going to end up in a coffin or in a jail. (High school students' concerns)

Along with drawing attention to concerns rarely heard in Delano's traditional public processes, the students' general plan included ideas proposed by participants at the Holiday Parade and grocery store. For instance they included zoning for a neighbourhood commercial centre on the west side of town and proposed affordable housing for farm workers. Young people, whose concerns were generally not heard in the workshops, became the focus of one of the proposed optional 'elements' in the general plan, which included recommendations for the creation of a mayor's task force to address gangs and the establishment of a youth commission that would advise the city council on the future of city. In the absence of participation by formal community groups, the students became advocates for 'identified' community groups who had neither the time nor the resources to participate in the collaborative plan-making process.

Reflections and conclusions

The planning process mandated in California, outlined in this chapter, presupposes that communities exist, that they can be identified, and that they understand and are interested in being involved with the plan-making exercise. That 'the shift into planning' of community interests can be facilitated by procedures that allow community participation so these interests are reflected in the vision embodied in the general plan. Our cases studies of community engagement in two cities, similar in size, but quite different in demographic composition, economic well-being, level of education, and other salient characteristics illustrate that this supposition largely holds good for communities such as San Luis Obispo which are resourced to support an extensive and diverse process. The Delano case highlights that exercising an all-round sensitivity to locale and context is essential in community participation-seeking activities. Both cases underscore the limited arena in which collaborative planning can make a difference in the US, largely in interventions in the city's physical domain.

Cities with extensive staff and resources, such as San Luis Obispo, are innovative and garner the funding needed for an extensive and rigorous planning effort to obtain community involvement. Even with resources and the right intentions, however, a citizens' advisory committee such as the LUCE is most responsive to communities that are mobilised and advocate for their interests in an organised, sustained and persistent fashion. As important, in making the plan inclusive and reflecting the diversity of city communities and their interests, are the informed voices of experts on the advisory task force. Their engagement with, and knowledge of, a variety of non-profit communities and interest groups allow these interests to be introduced in the debate and policy formulation exercise. Involvement in a committee such as the LUCE requires substantial time commitments (three years) and is not easy to sustain for individuals and communities that are less established and/or economically marginalised. Such involvement is of little interest to those whose neighbourhood are satisfactory and meet desires and expectations. Project or issue-specific threats to that sense of well-being is what draws these 'passive' communities and interest groups to engage in planning. In a relatively affluent city like San Luis Obispo, the historical evidence suggests that the need for street calming, noise abatement, preventing non-conforming land use, controlling property damaging behaviour, quickly mobilises 'the community' to successfully apply pressure on the city council for actions to remedy the problem. This is the recognised and understood method to implement policies or programmes for 'community-desired' changes, a lesson well learned by long-standing city residents. In such a city, where professional planning skills and resources exist, and there is capacity to draw on robust, informed, diverse advisory committees of informed citizens, the advocacy and collaborative planning effort student planners can provide is less welcome and underutilised. Cal Poly's graduate studio worked in San Luis Obispo on a pre-LUCE effort to raise relevant issues and consult alternative communities in the city. Their findings made little impact on the LUCE driven policy formulation exercise the city undertook.

The Delano case study suggests that open, collaborative processes may not work if community groups and their members are engaged with more immediate and basic needs, lack the resources or time to participate, or are participating in political activities they deem more important. Workshops are not part of normal daily activities, and, thus, not convenient to engage in for people working long hours. The significant time required to participate in collaborative processes deters involvement by disenfranchised people with limited time. Given the paucity of their leisure time, they are unlikely to choose to spend it even at a 'picnic' to talk about land use. In addition, certain participants in cities like Delano may not have formal citizenship, and therefore, may feel that it is not safe to participate. Conclusions from the Delano case study must be made with some caution. The effort was conducted within a short time frame of six months by students. Perhaps, with more time to build community participation, the collaborative process could have seen greater participation by community groups – although staff and financial resources for this were lacking. That it was a student effort may have led some community groups to take it less seriously, although other community members received the community participation processes which students conducted more openly because it was a student effort. The students' brief experiences and findings in communities do not establish that their advocacy efforts are accurate or that they will be adopted by the mainstream and ultimately implemented. Insights obtained through such involvement in the plan-making effort are instructive, however, and further the objective of enhancing community groups' participation in the making of comprehensive plans. With careful attention to the local context the specific collaborative planning processes that are shaped by cities can be effective venues for community-engagement and influence in plan making.

The efforts examined here only partially answer the question as to whether community groups become part of a wider governance and leadership system that delivers benefits for a range of interests, from communities themselves, to policy makers and private enterprise. The fact that comprehensive planning efforts in Delano, San Luis Obispo, and elsewhere, consistently lack significant participation suggests that understanding the detailing of the processes in Delano and San Luis Obispo offer some useful lessons for other communities. In the absence of formal organisations and resources to participate, it is possible that community groups' concerns can be identified with broad and direct outreach to stakeholders. The approach must be flexible and planners must go to where community groups already are. One of the jobs of the planner then becomes the translation of stories and concerns of these groups into outcomes that can rightly be addressed through planning. In more resourced communities spreading the net wide so as to incorporate representation of diverse interest groups in advisory committees may allow alternative community visions and desires to be mediated and consensus achieved through a more formal process.

Notes

[1] Fee simple or freehold ownership was preferred by courts in the common law of the early US. Today it is the most prevalent form of property ownership in the US giving complete ownership of the land and its improvements in perpetuity. Aside from a few exceptions, no-one can legally take real estate from an owner with fee simple title.

[2] The legislative body of each city (the city council) and each county (the board of supervisors) adopts zoning, subdivision and other ordinances to regulate land uses and to carry out the policies of its general plan. See www. opr.ca.gov/s_generalplanguidelines.php for General Plan guidelines and updates. Adjoining cities or cities and counties are distinct and independent

political units which are responsible for the planning decisions within their jurisdiction without a mandate to address adjacencies or overlaps.

[3] This phenomenon may have some universal resonance and is referenced in other chapters in this book and reflected in Gallent's description of those who are co-opted into the Parish plan process (Chapter 16).

[4] In California the Hispanic and Asian population each grew by about 30 per cent, the white, and non-Hispanic population declined by 5 per cent and the black population declined by 1 per cent. Although international immigration added 1.7 million people, it was largely offset by an outmigration of 1.4 million. The population mix in California continues to shift, as the white, non-Hispanic population declines and the Hispanic population increases. The white, non-Hispanic population peaked at 17.0 million in 1990 and has since declined by 12 per cent, falling to 15.0 million in 2010. In contrast, the Hispanic population almost doubled from 7.7 million in 1990 to 14.0 million in 2010. The Hispanic share of California's total population has increased to 38 per cent. The state is on its way to perhaps having the first minority/majority population, the white, non-Hispanic population has decreased to 40 per cent in 2010. See Hayutin et al, 2011, 1–2, http://longevity.stanford.edu

[5] Dan Buettner, *Thrive: Finding happiness the blue zones way*

[6] See www.clrsearch.com/San-Luis-Obispo-Demographics/CA/Population-by-Race-and-Ethnicity. See also, www.city-data.com/city/San-Luis-Obispo-California.html

[7] www.usa.com/san-luis-obispo-ca-population-and-races--historical-education-level-data.htm

[8] Fast Facts about SLO County Nonprofits notes that 1,106 non-profit organisations engaged in activities classified as 501c3 and exempt from federal income tax were registered in the county as of November 2011 and of these 33 per cent had annual revenue greater than $25,000, www.sloccf.org/images/cms/files/nonprofit_overview_for_slo_county_2011.pdf

[9] These efforts included a national boycott of grapes grown in California and well-attended political rallies and marches. These drew national attention including support from national political figures such as Robert F Kennedy, then a US Senator. By the 1970s, the UFW had negotiated the first labour contract in California between growers and farm workers, giving farm workers collective bargaining rights.

References

Arnstein, RS, 1969, A ladder of citizen participation, *Journal of the American Institute of Planners* 55, 4, 216–22

Berry, J, Portney, K, Thomson, K, 1993, *The rebirth of urban democracy*, Washington, DC: Brookings Institute:

Booher, DE, Innes, JE, 2002, Network power in collaborative planning, *Journal of Planning Education and Research* 21, 3, 221–36

Brooks, MP, 2002, *Planning Theory for Practitioners*, Chicago, IL: Planners Press, American Planning Association

Buettner, D, 2010, *Thrive: Finding happiness the blue zones way*, Washington, DC: National Geographic Society

Carpenter, SL, Kennedy, WJD, 2001, *Managing public disputes: A practical guide to handling conflict and reaching agreements*, San Francisco, CA: Jossey-Bass

Cooke, B, Kothari, U, 2001, *Participation: The new tyranny? The case for participation as tyranny*, London: Zed Books

Davidoff, P, 1965, Advocacy and pluralism in planning, *Journal of the American Institute of Planners* 31, 331–8

Derr, V, Chawla, L, Mintzer, M, Cushing, DF, Vliet, WV, 2013, A city for all citizens: Integrating children and youth from marginalized populations into city planning, *Buildings* 3, 3, 482–505

Diaz, D, 2005, *Barrio urbanism: Chicanos, planning, and American cities*, New York: Routledge

Fischer, F, 2004, Professional expertise in a deliberative democracy: Facilitating participatory inquiry, *The Good Society* 13, 21–7

Forester, J, 1994, Bridging interests and community planning and the challenges of deliberative democracy, *Journal of the American Planning Association* 60, 2, 153–8

Forester, J, 1999, *The Deliberative Practitioner*, Cambridge MA: The MIT Press

Fraser, H, 2005, Four different approaches to community participation, *Community Development Journal* 40, 286–300

Gittell, R, Vidal, A, 1998, *Community organizing: Building social capital as a development strategy*, Thousand Oaks, CA: SAGE

Gonzalez, ER, 2006, *Resident involvement in advocacy and consensus planning*, unpublished PhD thesis, Irvine: University of California

Governor's Office of Planning and Research, 2003, *General plan guidelines*, Sacramento, CA: State of California, http://opr.ca.gov/docs/General_Plan_Guidelines_2003.pdf

Governor's Office of Planning and Research, 2010, *Update to the general plan guidelines: Complete streets and the circulation element*, Sacramento, CA: State of California, http://opr.ca.gov/docs/Update_GP_Guidelines_Complete_Streets.pdf

Harwood, SA, 2003, Environmental justice on the streets: Advocacy planning as a tool to contest environmental racism, *Journal of Planning Education and Research* 23, 1, 24–38

Hayutin, A, Kowren, K, Reynolds, G, Rodriquez-SackByrne, C, Teller, A, 2011, *Understanding California's demographic shifts*, Introduction and California overview and excerpts, Standford, CA: Stanford Center on Longevity

Hum, T, 2010, Planning in neighborhoods with multiple publics: Opportunities and challenges for community-based nonprofit organizations, *Journal of Planning Education and Research* 29, 4, 461–77.

Innes, JE, Booher, DE, 2003, Collaborative policymaking: Governance through dialogue, in M Hajer, H Wagner, H (eds) Deliberative policy analysis: Understanding governance in the network society, 33–59, Cambridge, MA: Cambridge University Press

Peterman, W, 2004, Advocacy vs collaboration: Comparing inclusionary community planning models, *Community Development Journal* 59, 3, 266–76

Prowler, D, 2007, *Form foils function*, San Francisco, CA: SPUR, www.spur.org/publications/article/2007-01-01/form-foils-function

Sager, T, 2002, Deliberative planning and decision making: An impossible result, *Journal of Planning Education and Research* 21, 4, 367–78

Sandercock, L, 1998, *Towards Cosmopolis*, Chichester: Wiley

Sanoff, H, 2000, *Community participation methods in design and planning*, Chichester: Wiley

Shaw, R, 2008, *Beyond the fields: Cesar Chavez, the UFW, and the struggle for justice in the 21st century*, Los Angeles, CA: University of California Press

Sirianni, C, 2007, Neighborhood planning as collaborative democratic design, *Journal of the American Planning Association* 73, 4, 373–87

Toker, U, 2012, *Making community design work*, Chicago, IL: APA Planners Press

Umemoto, K, 2001, Walking in another's shoes epistemological challenges in participatory planning, *Journal of Planning Education and Research* 21, 1, 17–31

Umemoto, K, Igarashi, H, 2009, Deliberative Planning in a Multicultural Milieu, *Journal of Planning Education and Research*, 29, 39–53

10

Engaging neighbourhoods: experiences of transactive planning with communities in England

Gavin Parker

Introduction: frames, foci and fragmentation of effort

Those operating within traditional planning paradigms have struggled to capture and reconcile the range of knowledges and diversity of preferences that could inform and shape practice in policy formulation and decision-making arenas. Some may argue that any such aim for all-inclusivity can only ever be aspirational, given the complexity likely to be involved. Notwithstanding the resource limitations and the sheer number of considerations that so often constrain laudable ambitions, however, there are also attitudinal barriers and prevalent power geometries that act to shape method and policy. These factors must bear at least some of the responsibility for the opprobrium so often accompanying plans and development proposals and the ineluctable decisions provoked by such efforts to shape the environment.

A significant issue accompanying the broader imperfections of policymaking and planning systems has been the disconnect between decision-makers and those directly affected by planning policies and new development. That is to say, politicians, as well as professional planners, have struggled to reconcile or mediate individual or group interests with a wider public interest and have failed to communicate or to find satisfactory means of adjusting goals or formulating satisfactory governance arrangements – in short how to shift towards a more consensual pragmatism (Harper and Stein, 2006). This situation has impeded the development of the relations and repertoires envisaged by Healey (1998, 1531) to build 'social networks as a resource of institutional capital through which new initiatives can be taken rapidly and legitimately...fostering the institutional capacity in territorial political communities for ongoing "place-making" activities'. The sentiment is that structures, processes and skills for more inclusive and 'collaborative' planning are needed for a legitimate and effective planning to be fostered to serve a networked yet diverse society.

Thus the development of knowledge and capacity, as well as the structures and processes, conducive to collaborative planning models are claimed to be needed to transform practice, to ease conflict and ultimately to help produce better more sustainable places. Mechanisms to foster such paradigmatic and cultural change (and associated structural accommodations) have remained a feature of planning debate for a generation, and still remain in question given the build-up of attention and the serial and chronic failure to take associated challenges seriously among the planning polity. Thus consideration of community-led planning activity in England is ever more pertinent as it helps point towards potentials for a mainstream shift towards a more transactive planning[1] (Friedmann, 1973) as discussed below, and is a central concern of this book: to understand the characteristics, potentials and constraints of community action and planning. This chapter, given this context, examines how planning at the neighbourhood scale has developed and more recently gained a statutory footing in England. This may be a significant step in the creation of a more collaborative planning, given it is the latest iteration of experiments in community engagement with planning issues.

While the design and operation of the planning system in England clearly structures much community action there are macro-level trajectories of socio-economic change and global political shifts that have inevitably had an impact on attitudes to planning and practices too. These have influenced some efforts at planning reform and participation. Indeed planning and decision-making in the built and natural environment is just one arena where and why governance arrangements have been reformulated or 'modernised'. The broader forces of globalisation, economic liberalisation and communications advances that are key drivers of much change are likewise shaped by the characteristics of policies pursued by governments. This forms an uneven and disjointed dialecticism where change and accompanying discourses of modernisation, competition, efficiency and accountability also act over time to shape the structures and processes of governance that are adopted and contested. Such competing discourses mean that reforming planning and associated governance to achieve collaborative forms of planning are discussed alongside other apparently discordant claims or priorities and produce often incongruent or unstable outcomes.

It is often also argued that individualism and an increasingly dominant neo-liberalism, along with its handmaiden consumerism, plays a part in the disconnect between planning, planners and the public, given its intrinsic identity as a collective endeavour. Attendant attitudes and dissatisfaction with outcomes associated with planning from the citizen-consumer perspective are a feature that can easily bind a diverse population through a shared feeling of resentment towards big government, and a concomitant demand for both transparency and a more participatory approach to governance (Gyford, 1991; Parker, 1999). Expectations of governance systems in terms of process have become more sophisticated and questions of motive, means and method remain ever more relevant in the design of planning and wider governance systems, and are concerns that have found their way into theoretical models for participation too (see Glass, 1979; Forester, 1993; Lane, 2005).

In parallel to the post-war development of urban planning, a concern has grown since the 1960s not only to involve the public more effectively in planning, and latterly to encourage and support community development to build social and institutional capital and ultimately to co-construct policy for places. A twofold emphasis has emerged on 'means and mode' as well as 'information, knowledge and capacity'. Similarly two strands of engagement 'direct' and 'indirect' participation in planning with the latter being organised beyond formal planning systems (Innes and Booher, 2004). These efforts, together with direct (or narrower) participation in planning, reflect a recognition of the so-called democratic deficit apparent in modern planning practice and act to drive attempts to address questions of legitimacy, inclusivity and consensus-building.

In the UK this led to early efforts in encouraging direct participation and were reinforced by the exhortations of a national committee tasked to review public participation in planning (Skeffington, 1969). The seminal Skeffington report advocated a building-in of public participation in planning 'at the formative stages of plan-making' (see Damer and Hague, 1971; Rydin, 1999). Yet this effort to induce direct participation (through the means outlined by Dandekar and Main, Chapter 9, this volume) has tended to result in consultation or otherwise limited engagement effort that rests some way down the routinely cited 'ladder' of empowerment produced by Arnstein (1969) and is viewed with some scepticism as a means to influence outcomes. This situation as well as other perceived shortcomings, led to repeated attempts to reformulate planning systems, structures and process with a view to addressing perceived shortfalls in accountability, speed and inclusivity and with much rhetorical regard given towards involving citizens in planning. Yet, ongoing dissatisfaction and lack of transparency has added to a third strand of engagement that cuts across direct and indirect types – this is a vigorous reactive participation (often presenting itself as oppositional protest) provoked and shaped by issues becoming recognised, but out of the control, or beyond the sight of local populations and is thence latterly contested. This may be read as a rational reaction to being planned for or 'upon' and transcends bureaucratic boundaries. Other community-based or grassroots activity is induced in an effort to genuinely co-construct policy and yet much of both modalities have been seemingly ineffective in shaping planning policies or outcomes and there is a powerful critique about why this is the case rehearsed in the literature (see, for example, Chandler, 2000; Cooke and Kothari, 2001; Brownill and Carpenter, 2007; Sager, 2009a; 2009b; Swyngedouw, 2010; Parker and Street, forthcoming).

Notwithstanding an acknowledgement of the need for the planning process to reflect different views and needs, both a reformed planning and the new community–based development activity in the UK (and its associated rhetorical support), reflects a complex set of historical and economic processes. The de-traditionalisation and diversification of society (see Chapter 1, this volume) has exacerbated tensions between professions, politicians and the public and this leaves us grasping for even basic agreement over the scope and design of planning processes, what is really meant by community and what is a legitimate concern of planning (see Ravetz, 1986). Such issues vie with concerns over representativeness, inclusivity and the degree to which any participatory efforts can truly be considered as 'community action'. Similarly the balance or inter-penetration of power and influence of the local over the national and vice-versa, and the impact of sectional interests in planning are posed as endemic and render collaborative planning and dialogic planning spaces suspect. For Mouffe the dialogical modality required by transactive planning and this form of sub-politics is built on a misguided premise that: 'conflicts can be pacified thanks to the "opening up" of a variety of public spheres where, through dialogue, people with very different interests will make decisions about the variety of issues that affect them' (Mouffe, 2005, 48).

Transactive and collaborative planning with communities

There is an overall normative set of interlinked aims here that are about no less than changing the culture of planning and the capacities within populations to engage with local and strategic planning challenges. This underlies the dynamic approach required in transactive planning, as identified by John Friedmann over 40 years ago. He argued that 'the real solution involves a restructuring of the basic relationship between planner and client' (1973, 172) and the types and sources of knowledge typically deployed by both parties. In Friedmann's view one mindset is typified as abstract and informed by theory and underpinned by evidence, the other by partial and less generalisable experiential knowledge. This immediately sets up important questions recognised also by Healey (1997; 1998) that may be expressed in terms of how to find both structures and processes that accommodate and retain the strengths or benefits of both knowledge fields.

Transactive planning requires the development of interpersonal relations and knowledge into action, including a recognition that 'society needs a heightened learning capacity' (Friedmann, 1973, 193). Advocacy of this paradigmatic approach to the structures and processes of and for planning requires social and institutional capacity to sustain a robust dialogical planning process that transactive planning requires. This shift will also need to reflect pragmatic, incremental realities, given it is also recognised that such efforts are fraught with difficulty and imperfection (Harper and Stein, 2006; Flyvbjerg, 1998; Forester, 1993). Some critics of planning who are sympathetic to similar collaborative planning prescriptions, see that a more engaged and discursive form of politics is needed in application to planning questions. This entails the recognition and support of what Beck (1994) has termed a sub-politics, where a widening of the 'stage of social design' should be established to include 'citizens, technical experts, business people, professionals and other individuals who compete with one another for the emerging power to shape politics' (1994, 22). Power and control, knowledge and responsibility are clearly present as concerns and barriers to the kind of open dialogical or collaborative forms of planning discussed so widely in the contemporary planning literature. In such critiques lie very important warnings about the design and maintenance of dialogic spaces and the required support and capacities needed for what could be a fragile yet necessarily long-term project, as well as a determined effort to maintain the process benefits, cited by Friedmann, and others since, that build capacities and networks – often distilled into the concepts of social and institutional capital (see Rydin, Chapter 2, this volume).

Numerous scholars have further refined and called for more collaborative planning approaches since the early 1970s, also influenced by Habermasian notions of a communicative rationality, as a normative ideal that should underpin planning process – as well as drawing on the insights of Friedmann (see Sager, 2009a; 2009b; Healey, 1997; Forester, 1993; 1999; Clifford and Tewdwr-Jones, 2013). This emphasis has sparked prolonged debate over the possibilities and difficulties of this theoretical-cum-faith position and how apparently collaborative efforts in practice have been subverted or manipulated or appear to lack normative or substantive aims (Tewdwr-Jones and Allmendinger, 1998; Brand and Gaffikin, 2007). Questions of efficiency and effectiveness have also been called into question and how to develop required levels of social and institutional capital remain as part of concerns to find workable models. Thus in examining community-action and community-led planning there are numerous aspects that do require close critical attention.

While debates over the practical and philosophical credibility of collaborative and transactive planning have continued, there have been notable strands of community action in and related to planning taking place. Often this is where particular groups have concentrated on one-off or project based work and sometimes under a banner of 'regeneration' with planners acting as intermediaries and as facilitators and enabling others to become citizen-planners. Other actions may be categorised under the 'social movements' label (which of itself obscures varying degrees of alterity, reactivity and control-taking; see De Souza, 2006; Castells, 1983). Some participatory effort has been linked to formal planning in the UK and has recognised and sought to develop networks of common interest, while other initiatives have attempted to induce more diffuse participation – often this is little more than consultation activity. Yet more examples exist where others work with community members to develop social capital (see for example; Rydin, Chapter 2, this volume, and Rydin, 2003; Holman and Rydin, 2013; Parker and Murray, 2012). This may be instrumental but also develops awareness and understanding of issues and agendas directly relevant to planning and development.

Planning and community action

In the global north at least, attitudes towards efforts to plan from above and the assumption of acquiescence, if not agreement, of populations across whole territories on the part of the state, has been laid to siege for some time. Subsequent debates, as above, have produced a series of challenges to planning as a technical and elitist set of activities to be acted out and imposed on populations 'in their best interest'. A strong theoretical challenge to traditional planning has developed, particularly in the US and then in the UK, as well as a critique to the collaborative models offered up in response. In parallel, an upsurge in self-organisation and efforts to plan from below have emerged and may be categorised across a spectrum of protest or reaction to planning which is organised to challenge, to obstruct and to force change in planning decision-making, both in episodic terms, but also to press for amendments to accommodate community participation in structural terms.

Stung by academic critique and often articulate and organised protest movements from the grassroots and from elite interest groups, many governments have sought to reorganise and rethink planning – both as a means of organising action and policy, but also to use planning and planners as a convenient shield to take the blows directed by constituents and from rhetorical attacks from opposing politicians. The trend to accommodate the collaborative planning model, and a continued frustration on the part of sections of the population, have seen gradual change in planning process and structures *and* interesting organic community action emerging that has been shaping and challenging planning practice. This environment has provided a milieu whereby planning systems have borne serial minor adjustments dressed up as radical reform and often without any clear or coherent underpinning principles. The experience of the UK and England in particular over the past 20 years or so provides a now classic example of this (Prior, 2005) and which has acted to erode, rather than build, the development of trust and understanding that transactive and collaborative planning relies on, while simultaneously experimenting with numerous episodes of public participation, community engagement and community-led planning. Much of the value of these episodes lie in the lessons that such experiments hold for planners *qua* system designers to learn from, rather than examples that are likely to satisfy critics of collaborative planning, strategic planners keen to cascade the priorities of meta-governance, or active citizens keen to have a greater say over change and continuities that affect them.

Thus efforts to think about the role and potential of the community to shape and to contribute to local policy and agenda setting has occupied many academics and policymakers from across the social and policy sciences. This account looks at what is now being termed neighbourhood planning practices (here the term community-led planning is maintained to embrace the three episodes set out below) and cannot therefore be viewed as a comprehensive account of participation in planning in England, nor embrace the full range of activity intimated above. This does, however, indicate the creative tension between engaged citizens and the planning polity and features the English experience of both indirect and direct participation in planning as community action first outwith, and then as part of, formal planning systems since the 1980s.

Three episodes of community-led planning[2] in England since the 1990s

Bearing in mind the above review we now turn to the experiences of efforts to develop indirect and direct participation as part of institutional capacity-building across England. The introductory chapter has already conceptualised some of the differences across forms of community action in planning and places that activity into four drivers and their responses. This demonstrates that we should be aware of how those involved in framing and initiating engagement are actively shaping community action and how this is responded to by participants. The motives of the different parties involved are important and their aims clearly have an impact on design, process and outcome, as well as highlighting related questions of the effective prompts, the focus of concern and the scale of activity. These differ in various examples of community-led planning or community action and shape outcomes.

This review focuses in on one strain of participatory activity or community action traced through the 1980s until the present, and that has led to the current experiment with neighbourhood development planning. This latter episode involves community-led planning becoming institutionalised as part of the UK coalition government's emphasis on 'localism' in England with Neighbourhood Development Plans (NDPs) developed as part of the reformed statutory planning system in England since 2011.

A common thread throughout the series of stages or episodes in the development of community-led planning is that the community itself is forming and shaping the priorities, but within different limits or frames. This trend has been part of a growing recognition of the potential and benefits of activities undertaken by neighbourhoods themselves, in terms of developing capacity and eliciting a better understanding of local issues and preferences as applied to planning or other related local issues and agendas (that is, the 'means and mode' and 'information, knowledge and capacity' strands). The chapter sets out three episodes of planning – all at the community level (that is, as agenda setting and policy formulation exercises rather than in relation to development proposals or contributing to plans prepared by others and largely in the period 1995–2013). As the episodes are outlined, however, we can see continuities but also different frames and purposes imposed and how these cut across the conceptualisation of community action aired in the introductory chapter.

Episode 1: 1995–2001. Evidence gathering as community action in England

This first episode of activity may be characterised as both organic and indirect and demonstrated early characteristics of community-led planning. This saw communities beginning to offer up additional and heterodoxical views and ideas to shape the local policy agenda – primarily in rural England. The work in this phase saw efforts to build on a disjointed and fragmentary self-help approach that had built up during the 1980s, through initiatives such as village and parish[3] appraisals (Moseley, 1997) and which were of themselves influenced by the Local Agenda 21 (LA21) (see Owen, 2002). This work was notably found in those rural areas where planning practice had largely been limited to rather blanket policies of planning restraint and assumed little or no development, unless related to agriculture.

The gap in formal planning in many rural areas was an instrumental and political convenience based both on limited planning resource and lack of political appetite at national and local level to fully embrace rural economic development and social questions such as access to services, rural employment and affordable housing. It is only in the past 20 years that such concerns have been given more prominence and mirror a more integrated analysis of the needs of rural England in the so-called post-productivist era (see Curry and Moseley, 2011). This situation was also a triumph of the environmental lobby and one which suited a significant proportion of the rural population for a time (see Woods, 2005; Sheail, 2002). Thus in such circumstances some community leaders saw a need for more fine grained understanding of community needs and aspirations than that offered by formal planning and a rather unresponsive representative democracy. Yet while research done in this early phase on community action also showed that more affluent and stable communities were more likely to undertake this kind of activity, it also emerged that a shift in attitude among at least a segment of this population was emerging. They were prepared to begin thinking about rural sustainability in a wider sense: in terms of questions of futurity, including confronting social change, balanced economic growth and intergenerational equity.

This phase featured local populations looking to challenge normative assumptions and looking for tools to assist in building a more detailed knowledge of local population demographics, preferences and issues (see Moseley, 1997; Owen, 2002). Much of this activity reflected a frustration at formal planning and represented efforts to fill the gap that formal town and country planning had been unable or unwilling to fill. This involved capturing attitudes, preferences and needs of communities directly through survey work in the main. As a number of such appraisals were generated pressure built on government to examine the potentials of this work. The timing coming into the 1990s also chimed with a re-emergence of a concern with active citizenship and an encouragement to play a more engaged role in local service provision. The Rural White Paper of 1995 tentatively carried a more integrated construction of the countryside and the variety of interests therein, allied to a government aspiration to see more 'governance with communities' (Woods, 2008, 19) and providing a political space for the parish and village appraisal tools (see Murdoch, 1997). Village and parish appraisals were developed as menus of questions for self-constructed community surveys and then as rudimentary software to assist community activists to collate and analyse the data they collected. The kernel of the idea held potential – a potential that involved local populations, led by volunteers, doing much of the groundwork in terms of developing quite detailed local evidence bases to shape community action – and moreover to influence planners and other decision makers. Many of the surveys done were revealing a neglect of rural services and a more diverse set of attitudes towards development than otherwise assumed.

This activity showed up several strategic issues; the lack of proactive planning and the serious underplaying of social considerations and economic development in rural areas. Second, the capacity, appetite and potentials of local populations to actively participate and engage in building evidence bases for policymakers and for their own community leaders to steer local agendas. This was demonstrated in such appraisals and similar survey work and pointed towards a need for support for the activity as well as better more advanced tools and techniques to reflect and address local challenges. Thus, much of this work was rather unstructured and often easily attacked, sidelined or plain ignored by planners and local politicians. The depth and breadth of the work was often limited, resulting in some frustration from within communities wanting to do more and better. So, too, from others raising serious concerns – perhaps obscuring the possible challenge to both professional expertise and to the representative democratic model – over the legitimacy of such outputs and their interpretation, the lack of robust methodology and linked concerns over inclusivity.

Lessons from this episode showed that planning and other service providers had little means to focus on small settlements and rural areas and that minority interests were receiving very little attention in rural areas (Milbourne, 1997). The timing of such community activity did parallel a concern to ensure that local government was more accountable and where possible to examine services and actions that could be undertaken by citizens. The parish and village appraisal work were antecedents of the second episode and indicated that rural populations in particular had not been well served by policymakers and strategic planners since the post-Second World War settlement.

Episode 2: 2001–10. Parish planning in England

The parish and village appraisals experience showed potential to galvanise local populations and develop better knowledge and evidence to shape action (and a common feature that binds the three episodes). Those efforts sufficiently, or perhaps superficially, married with the government agenda directed towards local government modernisation and associated calls for active citizenship and were seen as possible tools to be extended so that 'communities could play a much bigger role in running their own affairs, influencing and shaping their future development' (MAFF/DETR, 2000, 145). The 2000 Rural White Paper rhetorically embraced the idea that citizens should be encouraged to become more actively involved in local governance (see Gardner, 2008) and cited village and parish appraisals as positive evidence of a desire and capacity for communities to play a more proactive role in local governance.

The second phase of community activity reviewed here saw central government take a more active interest in experimenting with what eventually became known as parish planning, a label adopted by the then Countryside Agency who launched a funded programme under that name – the Parish Plan Grant scheme (PPG). The five year programme was initiated in 2001 and represented a consolidation of lessons learned from village appraisals and a means to further develop active community governance. The PPG was launched with little consolidated experience to inform the scheme design at the outset and was put together rather rapidly in the wake of the Rural White Paper. PPG encouraged the formalisation of a community-led planning that was served with national funding and was accompanied with broad aims and loose strictures (Countryside Agency, 2003). The parish planning process was to involve the development of a better understanding of all sections of the community by that community, in terms of self-identified issues and problems, as well as things that were of value. The approach was also conceived to add an action planning element as part of the development of a future vision for the area. Although these sound like the ingredients of a basic planning technique the scheme was non-statutory and communities were able to adopt an holistic approach as an experiment in local agenda setting. A substantial amount of action learning and modification to the structure, processes and guidance for parish planning were developed in that period, as well as the development of practical experience in the communities and on the part of community development workers involved (see Parker, 2008).

Claims about the uptake of parish planning vary and an upper estimate of around 8,700 Parish Plans by 2007 was declared in a report to government by SQW (2007). This figure is likely to be an overestimate given that Action for Communities in Rural England (ACRE) claimed something like 4,000 parish and community-led plans were in place by 2010, but it was clear that there were a very significant number, with some notable hotspots of activity in southern England with the south east of England recording over 1,000 completed Parish Plans by 2010 (Parker and Lynn, 2012). The typical Parish Plan completion period was between 18 and 24 months and many were done with minimal monetary outlay; relying instead on light community development support, in-kind contributions and volunteer time.

The PPG scheme helped tentative partnership working to be developed between local authorities, other service providers and representatives of the communities, despite overestimating the level of activity, the 2007 SQW report looking at parish planning found that in the early period 'parish plans are having difficulty being accepted as long term developmental tools' (2007, 25) reflecting wider attitudes towards community-led action on the part of many local authorities. The aspiration of government was that such initiatives would complement and inform the new planning system under the Planning and Compulsory Purchase Act 2004 which introduced both Statements of Community Involvement and formalised the idea of 'frontloading' participation in the statutory planning system (Doak and Parker, 2005).

While the central government funding for parish planning was cut back after 2005 the intervening period to 2010 saw some significant continued activity – many plans were still in progress with others being initiated using local funds. In some more enlightened local authority areas (see Parker, 2008; 2012) these types of community-led plans were seen as opportunities to develop a stronger evidence base for the organisation of resources, as well as beginning to help shape land use planning. The plans covered a wide range of topics and issues and were making some inroads in influencing decision-makers. The majority of the content and actions were not within the ambit of land-use planning. One important and difficult subject featuring in many plans that did clearly have planning repercussions was the provision of affordable rural housing, with some evidence that the consideration of topics such as this by communities was shifting attitudes (Parker and Lynn, 2012; Gallent and Robinson, 2013; Bishop, 2010). The non-statutory status of these documents, however, meant that they carried very little weight in most cases.

Thus the potentials of parish planning were never fully realised and participants and intermediary organisations were frustrated and rather disappointed that government were, on the one hand supportive in terms of policy rhetoric, as demonstrated in the continued use of active and engaged citizenship rhetoric by the Blair administration, but on the other, in terms of resources, the government was not prepared to put in the quite minimal amount of funding to continue and develop the community-led planning approach (Parker, 2008; 2012; Gallent et al, 2008). The wider funding package, of which PPG took a minority of the overall budget, had only cost £12 million over the five years. One reading of the decision to cease funding is that relatively affluent and largely Conservative areas were perceived as benefiting from this activity while the Labour urban heartlands were not.

Parish planning has remained a niche activity with communities in rural areas. In urban areas other forms of community action were orchestrated around localised projects, or were limited to discussing individual projects, led through neighbourhood forums or decentralisation experiments in neighbourhood or ward level structures (Broughton et al, 2013; Lowndes and Sullivan, 2008), as well as featuring more standard consultation mechanisms that fed into statutory strategies that were to help shape local government decision-making; notably Sustainable Community Strategies since 2000 (Raco et al, 2006). The direction taken in rural England had a more planning-led orientation through parish planning with a theme of evidence gathering and prioritisation, even though it was still outwith the formal planning system and much of the actions were not linked directly to land-use planning. So, given our focus, the community-led planning strand of activity has had a significant influence on governmental thinking about how to organise and direct community action and led to the birth of neighbourhood planning in episode 3. The work by communities themselves with limited financial support in episodes 1 and 2 indicated to policymakers that a new way of orchestrating planning activity was possible on this count at least.

Episode 3: 2011–15? Neighbourhood development planning in England

The last phase discussed here saw the practices and lessons of the first episodes drawn into a model that featured a reliance on the potential of community action being written into the statutory planning system. This move was underpinned by a belief that local people had sufficient interest in planning to invest time and energy in creating community-led plans to be known as Neighbourhood Development Plans (NDPs) enabled under the Localism Act 2011. This policy was presented as a key component of the UK coalition government's 'localism' agenda and tied closely into the second key policy aim of economic growth as enshrined in numerous government proclamations since the May 2010 election and expressed in the Localism Act itself.

The Conservative party, with its strong rural constituency and in search of policy ideas during their period in opposition (1997–2010), were influenced by the successes of the parish planning model as discussed above. The number of Parish Plans produced with quite minimal resourcing gave grounds to assume that similar activity could be mainstreamed successfully and furthermore the approach appealed ideologically; with its association to decentralisation and self-help. Their thinking was expressed in the *Open Source Planning* green paper which set out a vision for a re-orientated planning system where 'local people in each neighbourhood...will be able to specify what kind of development and use of land they want to see in their area' (Conservative Party, 2010, 2). The green paper goes on to claim that: 'This will lead to a fundamental and long overdue rebalancing of power, away from the centre and back into the hands of local people' (Conservative Party, 2010, 2). Thus, when elected the coalition led by the Conservatives duly included neighbourhood planning as part of the wider reforms of the planning system which were set out in the Localism Act (2011) and through the National Planning Policy Framework (NPPF) published in 2012.

NDPs were part of a group of 'community rights' expressed in the Act which were purported to provide a 'powerful set of tools for local people to ensure that they get the right types of development for their community' (DCLG, 2012, para. 184). Although there is little space to discuss the whole set of associated community rights included as part of the Localism Act (see DCLG, 2013), there are some common issues relating to the capacity and support to make effective use of these rights, including neighbourhood planning, that have emerged with some familiar resonance to prior efforts to empower, including questions of resource and support, lack of skills and knowledge, inertias and competing priorities from local government, variable motivation and intra-community conflict and misunderstandings of the requirements needed to meet the neighbourhood development planning regulations.

The challenges in navigating NDPs according to the required bureaucratic frame have been temporarily tackled by funding direct support for many neighbourhood planning groups. The rules in essence are that NDPs must be in 'general conformity' with the NPPF and the strategic policies of the Local Plan – as prepared by the local planning authority. NDPs require certain basic conditions to be fulfilled and may be more or less comprehensive in their scope, but the statutory element of the NDP document produced can only be a matter for land use planning. These tests may present difficulties for non-planners: how do they know with any certainty if their draft plans do meet the criteria? This work becomes not only a technical challenge but a question of confidence and interpretation too. The power to determine legitimacy still rests beyond the neighbourhood and thus far most emerging NDPs have required significant professional support. Pre-examination screening is being strongly advised and there are fears that rejected NDPs will deter new community forums progressing or entering the NDP process.

In relation to the focus on development and growth, the limited scope for action or challenge is also established firmly: '[n]eighbourhood plans and orders should *not promote less development* than set out in the Local Plan or undermine its strategic policies' (DCLG, 2012, para. 184, my emphasis) and the NDP must contribute to achieving sustainable development. This constrains the community in terms of opposing development or change if it is already set out in a superior planning policy document. The freedom to choose the level of development has been restricted and could undermine the motivations of some community leaders.

The Plans when completed have legal weight but are not obligatory; it is up to the community whether they want to produce one. There are a series of required administrative steps involved in the NDP process. Including setting up a community forum (in some areas the parish council, in others with no parish or town council this will be a new group), and this must have at least 21 members. The Forum needs to be formally recognised by the local planning authority and equally the boundary of the neighbourhood has to be agreed too. Meanwhile, early plan preparation may be commenced while such formalities are in hand and lessons from the earlier episodes of community-led planning are clearly useful in terms of community engagement and in preparing a vision for the area. As a result a majority of the early NDPs are from rural areas – often with a track record in undertaking activity outlined in episode 1 and/or 2. Early experiences in urban areas have shown how even the initial stages of NDPs present challenges and delays in these diverse and often contested local areas which are not parished (Parker, 2012).

The NDP can be detailed, or general, comprehensive or narrow in focus. Communities can use neighbourhood development planning to influence the type, design, location and mix of new development. General planning policies for the development and use of land in the neighbourhood can cover where new homes and offices should be built and include matters of design as long as they conform to the local plan. If the local plan says that an area needs to grow, then communities cannot use neighbourhood planning to block the building of new homes – although there is potential to direct where exactly the development might go. The Plan will also need to be in line with local and national planning policies as above (and other relevant law including European environmental law and human rights legislation).

Local Planning Authorities have a duty to support communities in making a NDP within their area during the process. Once a NDP draft has been prepared, an independent examiner will check that it meets the basic conditions required. After satisfactorily passing this screening and making any necessary amendments, a neighbourhood referendum on the NDP is organised by the local authority. If more than 50 per cent of people voting in the referendum support the Plan then the local planning authority must bring it into force. Once a NDP is confirmed decision makers are obliged to consider proposals for development against it.

While NDPs are offered-up by the coalition government as potential routes towards empowerment there are considerable qualifications or obstacles to those already emerging. A number of the immediate issues relating to process and to difficulties presented by community politics and resources have been outlined elsewhere (see Parker, 2012) and many are common to other episodes or other forms of community engagement. The limits of the NDPs, the complexity and difficulties in synchronisation with emerging local plans, disputes over boundaries and the presence of alternative means of tackling some or all of the issues that a NDP may present are additionally shaping the geography and slowing early take-up, progress and attitudes in some places.

In some such areas local planning authorities have been reluctant to commit scarce resources to something that could, to some with a more jaundiced view, be regarded as a laudable but short-lived and inefficient experiment. The period 2011–13 saw community-led planning (NDP) under the Localism Act still developing and momentum had grown by the time of writing, with around 800 communities developing NDPs despite the obstacles, caution and critical voices. A number of others have instead made use of existing tools to achieve aspects of neighbourhood planning or community-led preferences including the ongoing option of developing a non-statutory community-led plan or Parish Plan (see RTPI, 2011; Parker, 2012).

Despite the reservations and teething problems there are clear indications that neighbourhood planning will remain a feature of planning in England. There appears to be a growing political consensus that some form of neighbourhood scale planning is important and should be encouraged. Thus community-led planning is likely to remain in some form beyond 2015, yet how it is designed and orientated is likely to change, with moves to direct more attention to disadvantaged communities being discussed and a perceived need to find ways to simplify the process and requirements likely to feature in a 'fourth episode' of community-led planning in England. The key point is that moving community action developed in episodes 1 and 2 from non-statutory status into the statutory system is forcing LPAs and the wider culture of planning to confront the challenges of the collaborative planning paradigm more squarely. It is also developing an understanding of the difficulties and challenges faced by professional planners within the wider community and both will need time and consistent support and resourcing to grow the mutual learning that is a key feature of transactive planning. In short, there is emerging evidence that both community activists and professional planners are developing mutual learning. NDPs are opening up spaces for locally derived knowledge and evidence to be drawn in and upwards into formal policymaking and governance above the neighbourhood scale. These are early days indeed for NDPs but there is some cause for optimism amid the caution.

Conclusion: community planning at the neighbourhood scale in England

Experience with community-led planning activity, over the past two decades in England using the lens of three linked 'episodes' have generated a rich if fragmented set of experiences. A significant moment came with the passing of the Localism Act in 2011 – this saw neighbourhood scale, community-led planning activity enshrined in law and made part of the statutory planning system. Given just how much has been written about collaborative planning in various forms and guises in the past 40 years it is, at first glance, surprising that practice in England has taken so long to catch up with the theoretical debates over collaborative planning.

Yet community-led planning as discussed above is only one grouping of a variety practices and experimentation tried in England. Governments have been cautious about the possible resource and possible delays or barriers to development that collaborative planning at the neighbourhood scale could imply in the statutory process. For advocates of forms of transactive planning community-led planning can help to 'promote the deliberative aspect of and create and protect the conditions for deep and genuine civic discourse' (Sager, 2009b, 3) and help develop associated necessary mutual learning. Yet the persuasive critique from post-political theorists warn of the dangers of participants being either co-opted or marginalised, or neighbourhood-scale activities being kept isolated and compartmentalised and thus making very little difference. This concern reflects the idea that community-led planning may represent little more than the reorientation or consolidation of neo-liberalism (Haughton et al, 2013). Swyngedouw, for example, argues that such spaces can 'forestall the articulation of divergent, conflicting and alternative trajectories of future socio-environmental possibilities' (2010, 195) and the experience and research in community-led planning in this regard is admittedly mixed (see Parker and Murray, 2012; Parker and Street, forthcoming).

There are a series of inertias and vested interests that have acted to slow or subvert the aims of community-led planning in England but others doggedly see the potentials, despite the difficulties, that these mechanisms can offer. So putting grander debates to one side and suspending disbelief to a degree, it may be that community-led planning in England in this period together represents a significant step and there is clearly a momentum that is bringing elements of transactive planning into being. At least the latter two stages bear some of the credentials that reflect Friedmann's aspirations for the development of a transactive planning (and/or the schema set out in Chapter 1). Much is still in play, however, and the first period of neighbourhood planning will be under scrutiny from several different perspectives. The experiences of communities that have been active in one or more of the episodes outlined above are such that the process has been useful in terms of developing knowledge and awareness and networks within and beyond the neighbourhood. Relations between community activists and planners and others have often improved in areas where community-led planning has settled in (Parker and Murray, 2012). Yet the latter episode is revealing more of the difficulties and issues that statutory status brings given the legal requirements and the imposition of a frame that requires 'growth' and the associated likelihood of challenge by some developers keen to search for weaknesses and opportunities. Conversely the weight of statutory duty necessitates that local government and others take neighbourhood development planning seriously. There is every indication that neighbourhoods need support and continuities in order to develop knowledge and understanding and new skills for both communities and planners. Aspirations to build capacity that could see communities planning for themselves are somewhat off the mark however; community-led planning experiences thus far demonstrate that intermediaries and professional input is critical.

Given the above there are a series of issues and questions to be addressed from varying conceptual and practical perspectives:

- Critical academics – They are looking for purity against the ideals of collaborative planning theory and empowerment in the context of the post-political critique. They are concerned that similar approaches can actually be used to marginalise dissent and prevent change. Is this happening?
- Local Planning Authorities/public sector planners – They are pragmatic and resource driven and there is a tension between what is possible and what is desired, with competing priorities, and a use of alternative tools may be instrumentally useful but they will not develop the transactive ideal.
- Local politicians – community-led planning is a threat to representative democracy, cross-boundary considerations are problematic.
- National government and strategic planners – Their ability to deliver on strategic goals and matters that transcend the local is an issue, together with the difficulty of maintaining trust when localist priorities are trumped by larger concerns.
- Communities and community groups – Do they make a difference? Can they manage it? Is it worth it? These are linked to the transaction cost question. What alternatives are there to community-led planning or NDP? What is learned and gained in process as well as outcome terms? Will government continue to support the community-led planning approach?

Overall there are considerations of how community-led planning can assist in: 1: developing social capital, as well as 2: shaping tangible change, and 3: the reformulation of planning and decision-making structures (Holman and Rydin, 2013; Rydin, Chapter 2, this volume).

Associated to this threefold question there are issues that relate to the process and the design of neighbourhood planning itself. At least six factors are relevant and can be distilled down into the mnemonic of PROAKT: Process; Relations; Outcome; Attitudes; Knowledge and Trust, and are otherwise explained as *how* the system/process is designed and operationalised, with *whom*, and the need to bring required actors onside by whatever *means*, for what *purpose* and how the aims and limits are constructed and, latterly, the associated need to *educate*, inform and develop trust so that community-led planning will be robust, high-quality and durable.

Another issue that is marginalised in these debates but cannot be avoided is how to integrate and deliberate on the views, preferences and needs of local communities with the policies and strategic needs derived from 'greater than local' sources as intimated earlier in this chapter. Furthermore, bridging the accompanying mindsets or rationalities that can frustrate the vertical integration of ideas, needs and interests has been neglected. There is a need to find ways to learn from the community development model and to focus effort at vertical two-way integration of knowledge and needs at global, national, regional and local/neighbourhood scale. Both need to be reconciled and decisions about what is most usefully kept outwith the statutory process and what is required as part of a statutory element of planning in England is still moot.

The transactive examples discussed are indicative of how different rationalities and emphases can affect participatory spaces. The opportunity and aspiration of transactive planning is derived not only from developing capacity and awareness on the part of communities, but also in shaping a new sensibility in planners and encouraging new roles for elected politicians. The cumulation of the episodes outlined here and the 'crossing of the Rubicon' that the Localism Act represents, provides an opportunity to firmly embed the transactive ideal in formal planning – it remains to be seen what the costs (and benefits) of such transactions really are. For sure, there needs to be a great deal of work done in developing wider awareness and civic engagement with planning challenges. That task is one that needs to be taken up by government, public authorities, schools, universities and professional institutes: to name just a few.

Notes

[1] Here transactive planning, as process, is read as part of a wider collaborative planning paradigm.

[2] The term community-led planning is used to denote all activity that is discussed here at the lower than district level, that is, parish planning, community-led planning and neighbourhood development planning under the Localism Act (2011), see also Parker and Murray (2012) and Parker (2012).

[3] A parish is the smallest unit of government in England, initially an ecclesiastical term, most parishes are overseen by elected parish or town councils. Numbering well over 10,000, most of these units of administration are found in rural areas.

References

Arnstein, S, 1969, A ladder of citizen participation, *Journal of the American Institute of Planners* 34, 216–25

Beck, U, 1994, The reinvention of politics: Towards a theory of reflexive modernization, pp 1–55, in U Beck, A Giddens, S Lash (eds) *Reflexive Modernization*, Cambridge: Polity Press

Bishop, J, 2010, From parish plans to localism in England: Straight track or long and winding road?, *Planning Practice and Research* 25, 5, 611–24

Brand, R, Gaffikin, F, 2007, Collaborative planning in an uncollaborative world, *Planning Theory* 6, 2, 282–313

Brenner, N, Theodore, N, 2002, Cities and the geographies of 'actually existing neoliberalism', *Antipode* 34, 349–79

Broughton, K, Berkeley, N, Jarvis, D, 2013, Where next for neighbourhood regeneration in England?, *Local Economy* 28, 7–8, 817–27

Brownill, S, Carpenter, J, 2007, Participation and planning: Dichotomies, rationalities and strategies for power, *Town Planning Review* 78, 4, 401–28

Castells, M, 1983, *The city and the grassroots*, Berkeley, CA: University of California Press

Chandler, D, 2000, Active citizens and the therapeutic state, *Policy and Politics* 29, 1, 3–14

Clifford, B, Tewdwr-Jones, M, 2013, *The collaborating planner: Practitioners in the neo-liberal age*, Bristol: Policy Press

Conservative Party, 2010, Open source planning, *Planning green paper/ Discussion paper* 14, London: Conservative Party

Cooke, B, Kothari, U (eds), 2001, *Participation: The new tyranny?*, London: Zed Books

Countryside Agency, 2003, *Parish plans: Guidance for parish councils*, Cheltenham: Countryside Agency

Curry, N, Moseley, M (eds), 2011, *Reflections on rural change in Britain and Europe*, Cheltenham: Countryside and Community Press

Damer, S, Hague, C, 1971, Public participation in planning: A review, *Town Planning Review* 42, 3, 217–32

DCLG (Department of Communities and Local Government), 2012, *National planning policy framework*, London: HMSO

DCLG (Department of Communities and Local Government), 2013, *You've got the power: A quick and simple guide to community rights*, London: DCLG

De Souza, M, 2006, Social movements as 'critical urban planning' agents, *City* 10, 3, 327–42

Doak, J, Parker, G, 2005, Networked space? The challenge of meaningful community involvement in the new spatial planning, *Planning Practice and Research* 20, 1, 23–40

Fallov, M, 2010, Community capacity building as the route to inclusion in neighbourhood regeneration?, *International Journal of Urban and Regional Research* 34, 4, 789–804

Flyvbjerg, B, 1998, *Rationality and power*, Chicago, IL: University of Chicago Press

Forester, J, 1993, *Critical theory, public policy and planning practice*, Albany, NY: SUNY Press

Forester, J, 1999, *The deliberative practitioner*, Cambridge, MA: MIT Press

Friedmann, J, 1973, *Retracking America: A theory of transactive planning*, New York: Anchor/Doubleday

Gallent, N, Morphet, J, Tewdwr-Jones, M, 2008, Parish plans and the spatial planning approach in England, *Town Planning Review*, 79, 1, 1–29

Gallent, N, Robinson, S, 2013, *Neighbourhood planning: Communities, networks and governance*, Bristol: Policy Press

Gardner, G, 2008, Rural community development and governance, in M Woods (ed) *Rural policy under New Labour*, pp 169–88, Bristol: Policy Press

Glass, R, 1979, Citizen participation in planning: The relationship between objectives and techniques, *Journal of the American Planning Association* 45, 2, 180–9

Gyford, J, 1991, *Consumers, citizens and councils*, Basingstoke: Macmillan

Harper, T, Stein, S, 2006, *Dialogical planning in a fragmented society*, New Brunswick, NJ: Rutgers University Press

Haughton, G, Allmendinger, P, Oosterlynck, S, 2013, Spaces of neoliberal experimentation: Soft spaces, postpolitics, and neoliberal governmentality, *Environment and Planning A* 45, 217–34

Healey, P, 1997, *Collaborative planning*, Basingstoke: Macmillan

Healey, P, 1998, Building institutional capacity through collaborative approaches to urban planning, *Environment and Planning A* 30, 9, 1531–46

Holman, N, Rydin, Y, 2013, What can social capital tell us about planning under localism?, *Local Government Studies* 39, 1, 71–88

Innes, J, Booher, D, 2004, Reframing public participation: strategies for the 21st century, *Planning Theory and Practice* 5, 4, 419–36

Lane, M, 2005, Public participation in planning: An intellectual history, *Australian Geographer* 36, 3, 283–99

Lowndes, V, Sullivan, H, 2008, How low can you go? Rationales and challenges for neighbourhood governance, *Public Administration* 86, 1, 53–74

MAFF/DETR, 2000, *Our Countryside: The Future. A Fair Deal for Rural England*, Rural White Paper. Cm 4909, The Stationery Office

Milbourne, P (ed), 1997, *Revealing rural 'others': Representation, power and identity in the British countryside*, London: Pinter

Moseley, M, 1997, Parish appraisals as a tool of rural community development: An assessment of the British experience, *Planning Practice and Research* 12, 3, 197–213

Mouffe, C, 2005, *On the political*, London: Routledge

Murdoch, J, 1997, The shifting territory of government: Some insights from the Rural White Paper, *Area* 28, 2, 109–18

Owen, S, 2002, Locality and community: Towards a vehicle for community-based decision making in rural localities in England, *Town Planning Review* 73, 1, 41–61

Parker, G, 1999, Consumer-citizenship and environmental protest in the 1990s, *Space and Polity* 3, 1, 67–83

Parker, G, 2008, Parish and community-led planning, local evidence bases and local empowerment: An examination of 'good practice', *Town Planning Review* 79, 1, 61–85

Parker, G, 2012, Neighbourhood planning: Precursors, lessons and prospects, paper given to the *Oxford Joint Planning Law conference*, 14–16 September, reproduced in *Journal of Planning and Environment Law*, 2012 Winter Supplement, www.quadrilect.co.uk/Gavin%20 Parker.pdf

Parker, G, Lynn, T, 2012, *Localism and growth? Neighbourhood planning and housing, Town and Country Planning* 83, 1, 15–19

Parker, G, Murray, C, 2012, Beyond tokenism? Community-led planning and rational choices, *Town Planning Review* 83, 1, 1–28

Parker, G, Street, E, forthcoming, Planning at the neighbourhood scale: Localism, dialogic politics and the modulation of community action, *Environment and Planning C: Government and Policy*

Prior, A, 2005, UK Planning reform: A regulationist interpretation, *Planning Theory and Practice* 6, 4, 465–84

Raco, M, Parker, G, Doak, J, 2006, Reshaping spaces of local governance? Community strategies and the modernisation of local government in England, *Environment and Planning C: Government and Policy* 24, 4, 475–96

Ravetz, A, 1986, *The government of space: Town planning in modern society*, London: Faber & Faber

RTPI (Royal Town Planning Institute), 2011, *Localism Bill: Existing tools for neighbourhood planning*, RTPI information note, 24 May, London: RTPI

Rydin, Y, 1999, Public participation in planning, in B Cullingworth (ed) *Fifty years of British town planning*, pp 184–97, New Jersey: Athlone

Rydin, Y, 2003, *Conflict, consensus and rationality in environmental planning*, Oxford: Oxford University Press

Sager, T, 2009a, Planners' role: Torn between dialogical ideals and neo-liberal realities, *European Planning Studies* 17, 1, 65–84

Sager, T, 2009b, Responsibilities of theorists: The case of communicative planning theory, *Progress in Planning*, 72, 1, 1–51

Sheail, J, 2002, *An environmental history of twentieth-century Britain*, Basingstoke: Palgrave

Skeffington, A, 1969, *'People and planning': Report of the committee on public participation in planning* (the Skeffington report), London: HMSO

SQW, 2007, *Integration of parish plans into wider systems of governance: Report to the Department for Environment, Food and Rural Affairs*, July 2007, London: DEFRA

Stoker, G, 2004, New Localism, progressive politics and democracy, *Political Quarterly* 75 (supplement), 117–29

Swyngedouw, E, 2010, Impossible sustainability and the post-political condition, in M Cerreta, G Concilio, V Monno (eds) *Making strategies in spatial planning: Knowledge and values*, pp 185–205, Dordrecht: Springer

Tewdwr-Jones, M, Allmendinger, P, 1998, Deconstructing communicative rationality: A critique of Habermasian collaborative planning, *Environment and Planning C* 30, 11, 1975–89

Woods, M, 2005, *Rural geography*, London: SAGE

Woods, M (ed), 2008, *New Labour's countryside: Rural policy in Britain since 1997*, Bristol: Policy Press

11

Active communities of interest and the political process in Italy

Daniela Ciaffi

Introduction

A thousand years ago, the Arabs had already concluded that the Italian peninsula was too long to govern effectively (Ruffolo, 2009). More recently, urban regeneration policies promoted in Italy have encountered significant challenges, especially the challenge of coordinating public, private and third sector actors (Bobbio, 2004). Moreover, there has been a general failure to connect to community interests as part of the regeneration process. Although there have been notable exceptions (for example, in Bologna, see Ginocchini and Tartari, 2007), the general picture in Italy is one of weak engagement of communities with the politics of urban policy. This chapter is primarily concerned with the openness of those politics to community voices. It considers the drivers of community action in terms of why communities seek engagement with development processes, and why some policy makers are more receptive to that engagement. A series of Italian cases are used to dissect the interaction of active citizens with local politics, often in situations of mistrust and in a country where professional networks tend to dominate and exclude non-professional actors.

There are a number of fast and easy explanations as to why Italy has begun to embrace community input into planning. First, European funding sources may only be accessible where particular engagement practices are adhered to (Ciaffi, 2005). Second, there is a closer affiliation between grassroot movements and specific political groupings, which gives an uneven geography of engagement based on political leaning. Third, the specific goal of alleviating conflict has a role to play in promoting engagement (Saporito and Ciaffi, 2013). The reasons why community groups have become more active in the planning arena tend to mirror the factors determining institutional support. They also want the funding, and political ties secure political activism. There are also more general drivers, however: many groups are responding to what they see as a malaise of over-development in some cities, and therefore come together to oppose new projects. In response, some urban authorities have tried to harness the 'negative energy' of communities and refocus it not on the quantity of development, but its quality – asking them to think about what they would like to see rather than what they wouldn't. In this context, some active citizens and communities have emerged. Mannarini (2009) has argued that some groups, seeded by authorities looking to secure external funding, have become too 'obedient'. Community action in Italy is characterised by the extremes of militant opposition (to major infrastructure projects and new building) and passive obedience (communities mobilised to win cash funding). In between, there is a hesitancy in Italian society to get involved in the qualitative aspects of urban change.

The lifecycle of community action and planning

In the remainder of this chapter, I present three case studies of community action and planning in Italy. The first – in the earthquake-hit city of L'Aquila – is a short-run, aborted case. The second – in the Sicilian city of Palermo – is at an embryonic stage. The third – in the town of Canelli, near Asti in Piedmont – might be described as a mature and ongoing community action. Together, these three cases reveal the 'life-cycle' of community planning as suggested in Chapter 1, but they do not track a 'progressive' life-cycle, but rather the drivers and obstacles within this cycle, some of which can result in a failure, or stalling, of community mobilisation. The three cases deal with very different contexts and challenges. The Pettino neighbourhood of L'Aquila (in Abruzzo) was badly damaged by an earthquake in April 2009, triggering a short-term emergency and a longer-term need for reconstruction. The Favorita Urban Park in Palermo has become a focus of what might be described as a 'hesitant' and complex community mobilisation, which is poorly understood by the municipality and which receives intermittent support. Finally, community action surrounding the regeneration of Canelli's town centre – which began four years ago and is now winding up – is perhaps the most 'Anglo-Saxon' (Podziba, 2006) of the cases. Community actors, frustrated by what was viewed as an opaque and inaccessible planning process, came together in an attempt to lever change and shape planning outcomes.

From my experience, the life-cycle of community planning seems to comprise five stages. These five stages come together to form a general model for describing the relationships between communities of interest, the focus provided by a proposed local transformation (or some other challenge), and the local state. The *first stage* is dialectic and involves an open testing of ideas and reaching agreement around goals that are underpinned by particular values and interpretations. A proponent group sets out a position (relative to the proposed transformation, or other challenge) and on the basis of that position, alliances form and the network takes shape. There is also, at this stage, an estimate of the human, economic and institutional resources available and how these will determine the nature of possible actions. The *second stage* involves early programming in the sense that a general programme of action is agreed, aligned with the skills that are present within the group. At that stage, some network members may fall away, feeling that they have nothing to offer. Also, new members may be drawn in by the remaining group in order to fill particular resource or skill gaps. This early programming also involves understanding the broader demand or appetite for action within the wider community. The *third stage* is the bulk of 'community action'; it is the continuous work of activism and planning, of taking specific actions and planning new projects. It is in part about achieving outcomes through lobbying, through dialogue and through engagement with the challenge at hand. It is also about continuing communication, the organisation of events, consultation and monitoring, and maintaining a sense of empowerment (Arcidiacono et al, 1996). This stage may last for years or decades and is characterised by the ongoing interactions that sustain trust and deliver specific outcomes (Paba, 2010). The *fourth stage* is that of conclusion, and may never be reached, depending on the focus and nature of the community action. Where it is reached, it may be due to the sudden trauma of failure (an unwanted project goes ahead) or the slow decline as enthusiasm in the action ebbs away. On the other hand, the group may achieve what it set out to achieve and either dissolve or move on to new projects or challenges. The *fifth and final stage* is iterative, in which lessons learnt are transferred to other neighbourhoods (being channelled either through existing network connections or because of the active learning of a 'community practitioner'; see Gallent, Chapter 16, this volume) or assimilated by the group and used in new projects. This life cycle of community planning now provides the lens through which to examine processes and outcomes in L'Aquila, Palermo and Canelli.

The case studies

Over the last ten years, the author has been involved directly in a number of local actions, acting as a consultant to a small group of active citizens in the Pettino neighbourhood in L'Aquila, an 'action researcher' in Canelli, and – most recently – an active member of the informal group 'Towards La Favorita' in Palermo. The case studies draw on this experience and on consequent analysis of the processes and outcomes of community action in these three locations. My 'positionality' as an 'insider' in the community planning processes documented in this chapter needs to be acknowledged: during all these studies, but particularly in Palermo, I have been on the inside, looking out. Certainly, my closeness to these various local struggles will have had some impact on the conclusions reached. There is more research to be done, in Italy, at the political and practice interface with community action. More analysis is needed from a policy and practice perspective.

Pettino neighbourhood in L'Aquila

L'Aquila has a population of just under 70,000 residents. It is located in Abruzzo in central Italy and became a focus of international media attention in 2009 following an earthquake that killed almost 300 people. The old historic centre was badly damaged and had to be completely evacuated of population because of the risk of further building collapses. The displaced residents were decanted to 20 temporary settlements around the centre. Pettino is one of the largest neighbourhoods in the city, located about three kilometres north-west of the city centre. It sits directly on a seismic fault. About three-quarters of its 15,000 residents were displaced by the earthquake.

In response to the disaster, a community group of about a dozen active citizens formed, led by a young woman who is the local representative of an international development organisation with more than 40 years of experience of development planning in different parts of the world. The view of the group, and of its leader in particular, was that the official response to the earthquake had been inadequate. There had been a failure to communicate with the affected communities (in the aftermath) and then a continuing failure in the weeks and months that followed to involve residents, to build the necessary partnerships for reconstruction and to work with people to ensure that the planned reconstruction was attuned to local aspirations and need. In short, the community felt a sense of abandonment: as if its needs and its opinions were being ignored.

This provided the trigger for the group, who not only decided to develop their own neighbourhood plan (because of perceived shortcomings in local engagement) but also sought external assistance from experts in community-led planning (including the author) in

Italy, who might be able to direct the group to examples of successful participatory planning elsewhere in the country. Their aim was twofold: to connect to the wider Pettino community and to produce a neighbourhood plan that would embrace different ideas and would have public space, and opportunities for community interaction, at its heart. The group had a very particular make-up: it comprised professionals with direct interests in planning and construction. Besides the international development member, others in the group were involved in the protection of cultural heritage, in self-build projects, in building design and in various forms of community liaison. This was a group endowed with a range of key skills, which had also been angered by what it considered to be the 'heavy handed' approach of local government after the earthquake, its failure to be open to local input and its slowness in standing down the military control of the quake-hit zones.

The relationship this group shared with the authorities was not a positive one. Local politicians, and the city's mayor in particular, were thought to be remote from the community, adopting a 'command and control' attitude, which may have been appropriate for the hours and days following the quake, but which should have given way to a softer, more open approach in the years that followed. Indeed, a documentary film by Alberto Puliafito in 2010 titled *'Comando e Controllo'* articulated the view, felt by a great many L'Aquila residents, that the approach taken to reconstruction, especially the failure to work with communities, had resulted in the city becoming a 'ghost town'. Also, while the politicians were slow to embrace the aspirations of Pettino's citizens, they were quick to open up what were now vacant sites to speculative interest. Communities had wanted to see L'Aquila become a more 'sociable city' – a place of inclusion, community rights and expression, art and participation – delivered largely through better quality

Image 11.1: A plea for greater transparency during a meeting of the Pettino group in L'Aquila

© Silva Ferretti

public space; what they got was a continuing focus on preserving and extending private interest.

The Pettino community group never progressed past the second stage of the life-cycle. Within a year, it disbanded, being unable to take forward any of its agreed actions. Clearly, in this case the success of the group depended on the willingness of the local authority to embrace its activities and ambitions. The nature of the challenge required partnership working, but local government remained entirely closed to community input. It was not, however, completely immune to criticism: in February 2013, the authority announced a programme of 'participatory budgeting' for the city. The initial reaction of those community members less scarred by the experience of the post-earthquake years was to think that the mayor and his political allies had woken up to the need for greater transparency and dialogue. But these hopes were quickly dashed. Consultation on how to spend €3 million of public money on various local projects lasted just six weeks and comprised 11 staged events and the opening of a virtual portal for community comment. Half of the meetings had the sole purpose of canvassing views on fixed options, and the other half were dedicated to telling residents how money would be spent. There was no empowerment of citizens through the open management of a portfolio of public works (Allegretti and Sintomer, 2009) and in relation to the life-cylce of community planning, what we see in Pettino is a determination on the part of the local state to resist any erosion of its own power. It is committed to the worst kind of 'tokenism' (Arnstein, 1969).

La Favorita in Palermo

Palermo is a city of just over 650,000 inhabitants. In recent years, plans have taken shape to rejuvenate the city's major urban park: La Favorita. In October 2012, an event was held to discuss ideas and plans for the park. This was attended by around 60 residents of nearby neighbourhoods and representatives of a number of local associations. The event – labelled 'Towards the Favorita' – was organised by a private consultancy specialising in participatory planning (the Syracuse Hub) using European funding from a larger project called 'Gardmed: the network of Mediterranean gardens'.

La Favorita covers an area of 400 hectares and is located at the confluence of three Palermo neighourhoods. It is the city's green lung and how the park can be used is regulated by national rules on the management of nature reserves. Besides its environmental value,

La Favorita has considerable socio-economic (and tourism) potential, for nearby residents and for the city as a whole. During the 2012 event, many proposals emerged from seven round-table discussions. These were largely concerned with the future planning of the park and focused on accessibility, the pedestrianisation of roads penetrating into the park, the design of places for socialising, and the insertion of a network of 'urban gardens' (for food growing). There was also a concern for better understanding the challenges faced by La Favorita, and so it was suggested that residents should get involved, over a longer period, in 'mapping out' key challenges and ultimately in indentifing alternative management approaches.

During the event, a member of the local council announced that a Land Use Plan for La Favorita would be drawn up. It is notable that this particular councillor had been heavily engaged in the community-led regeneration of a neighbourhood garden (at Uditore) in the city. Some of those involved in the Uditore project were present at the La Favorita event and it was clear that the involvement of this particular councillor instilled them with a great deal of confidence and trust in the proposed La Favorita process. During the next seven months, there was intense media interest in the project, and particularly in the suggestion that certain roads running through the park should be closed to vehicular traffic. Pedestrianisation was not a central concern for the community actors, whose focus at this stage was on coordinating different community interests under the collective banner: 'Towards La Favorita', but for the local authority, pedestrianisation was an easy message to communicate and seemed to convey its emphasis on improving 'environmental quality' in the park.

A second event took place in 2013, this time attended by around 200 people. The coalition of community actors remained firmly in the first stage of the life-cycle, still testing ideas, developing its position and assessing its resources. It reasserted its strong desire to work with the local authority towards community-focused solutions for La Favorita, however. In response, the trusted councillor (who was once again present) and the municipal architect responsible for the Land Use Plan for the park, restated the importance of maintaining a dialogue with the community. They also set out three key components of the La Favorita Plan, however: pedestrianisation, the return of food growing to the park, and investment in new sports infrastructure. While the community was still at the stage of testing ideas and working out its guiding values, the local authority had sped ahead and was now setting out firm priorities. The partners were clearly working at different speeds and to very different schedules (see Matthews, Chapter 3, this volume).

A few weeks after the second event, a number of the most active citizens within the coalition of community groups (many of whom were architects or landscape professionals) requested a technical meeting with representatives of the local authority to discuss possible and potential new uses at various sites within La Favorita. The meeting took place, but there was widespread disappointment among participants at the answers provided by the local authority: some felt that the politicians knew too little about the ongoing planning process, so provided vague answers to specific questions; but others, although disappointed, expressed the view that they should continue engaging with the local authority and not become 'antagonistic'. It was clear at the second meeting, and at this follow-up session, that a technical process – led by 'experts' – was now in full swing. Some community members felt disempowered. The active citizens expressed their determination to continue working on the La Favorita project, but wider support fell away. Further events were organised – workshops, walks through the park, and mapping exercises – but all these activities were now stricken by a nagging doubt: that none of this community activity would influence final outcomes at La Favorita. A great deal of trust in the process had been lost.

The current state of play at La Favorita is that the community coalition, which remains fairly strong, continues to engage in events designed to draw support to its now clearer vision for the park. It wishes to eliminate the physical barriers between the edge of the park and the

Image 11.2: Exercising in the Favorita park during the 2013 event

© Simona Sansone

adjoining neigbourhoods. Its vision is of communities that spill into and use, on a daily basis, the communal space that the park provides. The active citizens have managed to mobilise support behind this vision, but relations with the local authority remain strained and the prospect of direct influence over the planning process seems uncertain.

In reality, the 'Towards La Favorita' coalition has progressed to the third stage of community action and may remain there for some time. It is seeking, in a sense, to appropriate the park from the local authority: to assert and demonstrate support for its own vision. The local authority, for its part, continues to follow at a distance the community action without providing direct support. The coalition organised and ran an 'Inside La Favorita' two-day event in November 2013. This community fair provided an outlet for the 30 associations, youth and sports clubs, and numeorus small business that remain active in the coalition. Thousands of local people attended, but few councillors were seen at the event. A complex dynamic seems to have undermined the partnership between the public and community actors in this case: the technical planning process has proceeded at a pace that the community is unable to keep up with; the local politicians appear content to let that process drive ahead (it is, after all, an expression of their executive power), but are uncomfortable with negative publicity and growing antipathy on the part of some residents; they continue, therefore, to lend tacit support to the community action and, for its part, the community is divided on whether they should continue to work with the authority or seek to realise their own vision of La Favorita through opposition to official planning and perhaps even through antagonistic action.

The town of Canelli in Piedmont

Canelli is a small town of 11,000 inhabitants near Asti, in Piedmont. In the summer of 2007, the mayor of the town called a meeting with planning experts from the Politecnico di Torino. A resident architect, who happened to be a graduate of the Politecnico and who now leads an association of local stakeholders, joined the meeting. The meeting was triggered by a sudden explosion of local protest at the town's residential expansion and, more particularly, at the felling of nearly 100 plane trees to make way for new housing. Very quickly, a number of interest groups formed, all expressing concern over the pace and quality of new development. One of these was led by a local producer of sparkling wine, who organised a series of lectures (with invited international experts) on the wine-growing landscapes of the area. These lectures focused on the tension, in and around Canelli, between the poor quality architecture and environment of the town and the cultivated beauty of the surrounding landscape.

The mayor and his administration was suffering a crisis of public credibility. Local anger had reached boiling point and it had become necessary to vent that anger. Following the initial meeting, the team from the Politecnico was tasked to work with the interest groups (and also try to connect to hitherto silent residents) and assimilate, where possible, their concerns into the strategic planning process leading to a revised Canelli Master Plan (Fubini and Ciaffi, 2011). Two years later, an international workshop run at the Politecnico focused on the problems of Canelli. A professor and seven students from MIT in the US became involved in how to de-jargon and make a number of technical documents underpinning the planning process understandable to non-planning specialists. The aim was to change the visual language of planning as a means of opening it up to community actors, and develop a long-term vision for the town with the community as an equal partner. Following this exercise, the team from the Politecnico used a new set of visualisations to explore, with different groups, the reuse of old industrial sites, options for a greenway adjacent to the River Belbo, revitalisation of the central area, the insertion of new urban squares, and better traffic management for the town. Discussions also focused on the deliverability and viability of various strategies and projects. The mayor's term of office came to an end in 2009. His reflections on 'better governance' and his own journey from 'dentist' (concerned only with intervention) to 'community planner' were deemed significant enough to end up on the pages of *Il Sole 24 Ore* (a national newspaper dealing mainly with economics and politics), testimony perhaps to the perceived innovativeness of this form of more open local government in Italy.

The mayor was succeeded by a young pragmatist, who followed his predecessor's example of paying close attention to local feeling. He placed new emphasis, however, on the regeneration of Canelli's town centre. The new mayor retained the academic experts but also brought in new advisors on urban quality. He mixed an emphasis on community input with professional knowledge of how public spaces can be revitalised, meeting the different needs of a range of user groups. The assembled team visited other towns in the region and sought to transfer lessons back to Canelli. At the beginning of 2012, the mayor's proposed project for a new centre was presented to a packed town hall. Dubbed the 'urban living room', a design project was conceived which was the outcome of focus groups with resident associations, retailers, local employers, professional groups and children. It immediately won the support of the wine-growers, one of whom described it as 'a beautiful proposal', adding that 'after so many years of words, we at last have a coherent intervention...for the redevelopment of Piazza Cavour'.

Image 11.3: Canelli's new urban square: the outcome of the participatory process

© Alessio Studio

The committment to a participative approach in Canelli sets this example well apart from Pettino and La Favorita. The community was the first to mobilise, in a series of associations, but this mobilisation was quickly embraced by the town's political leadership. This marriage of protest and intervention was concerned as much with planning *for* the community as planning *with* the community. What we see in Canelli is the progression through to the fourth stage of the life-cycle, with recent completion of the mayor's 'urban living room' at a final cost of €500,000. We also see a powerful role for independent mediators between community aspiration and conventional planning, who are able to make that planning more accessible to a lay audience and who faciliate the open dialogue that is crucial to the building of trust within a broadened community planning process. The project was not without its problems. During the works phase, there was considerable criticism of pedestrianisation and the impact of construction on local businesses. The mayor, however, stuck to his message that the revitalisation of the Canelli's heart was central to the renewal of Canelli itself. He is currently up for re-election and is arguing that, through an open planning process, Canelli has achieved in five years what most towns fail to achieve in ten.

Conclusions

In the three case studies presented in this chapter, community action grew from very particular development challenges: responding to disaster in Pettino; shaping a key piece of the urban fabric at La Favorita; and saving a town from the demoralising effect of poor development in Canelli. The recurrent theme, that ties these cases together, is the need to change the prevailing style of planning and make it more transparent, more interactive, and more open to innovation.

In Pettino, activists were insensed by the closed nature of the planning process and knew from their own professional experiences that those responding to post-disaster situations have a resonsibility to communicate with the local population and to involve them in the rebuilding of their own lives and neighourhoods. This happens in international cooperation all over the world; that it was not happening in the heart of Europe was a source of considerable frustration and palpable anger. When attempts to engage with the local state failed, and all the aspirations of residents came to nothing, anger seemed to be the only remaining emotion. The local politicians picked up on this and engaged in a tokenistic act of reconciliation: consultation on a 'participatory budget' with limited project options and an even more limited time-frame. The Pettino case serves as an example of local government entirely closed to community input, although, obviously, it must be serving some interests for it to retain its mandate: but that was not a focus of this research.

The situation in Canelli was very different; it has been held up as an example of healthy interaction between community actors and the local state (Podestà and Vitale, 2011). We are able to observe, in this example, a full cycle of community planning from trigger and inception, through to the adoption of a clear position on the local challenge, all the way to conclusion and reflection. Facilitation also played a big part in the process though, significantly, it was a crisis of trust and a key political decision that led to that facilitation in the community planning process. Although both of the political leaders in that process – the old mayor who made the jump from 'dentist' to 'community planner' and the young pragmatist – were ultimately sensitive to community input, the second brought the project to a close through what was in the end an executive decision: to execute a particular urban intervention. Canelli's brand of community planning was ultimately one that mixed strong leadership with open dialogue.

In comparison to the dire failure of Pettino and the apparently good outcome in Canelli, the situation at La Favorita was much messier. The public and community actors were unable to work to the same time-line. There, the planning bureacracy *seemed* to outpace the political process, but the likely reality is that those politicians who appeared receptive to dialogue with the community, and attended the events, were not necessarily the ones taking the key decisions. Someone, behind the scenes, was pushing the planning process along and either not giving it time to assimilate community input, or viewing that input as unimportant. There had, however, been past positive experiences in Palermo and perhaps for that reason, or because the various community actors believed that there were still victories that could be won without immediate political support, the community action did not fizzle out as it did in Pettino.

In all three cases, community action was built on a platform of internal dialogue. The group came together at La Favorita because European funding was available for the first event; but the appetite to shape the future of the park was already there. The appetite to do something was present in all the cases, but it is clear that in Italy *political support* plays an important role in turning that appetite into sustained action. In Pettino, its absence caused consternation and anger; at La Favorita, it seemed to be present in the background but it eventually vanished; in Canelli, it saw the project through to completion. At the beginning of this chapter, I observed that between the extremes of miltant protest and passive obedience, there are a range of hesitant urban actions in Italy that either quickly fold or rumble away without achieving a great deal. This seems to happen because groups expect, and look for, political support. There is probably a natural divide between those people who seek help and those who look to help themselves. At La Favorita, the latter group seemed almost emboldened by the loss of political support, engaging in self-organisation and working to coordinate the creative energies of a diverse community (Susskind and Sclavi, 2011).

There is a tendency in Italy for community planning to be seen, exclusively, as planning *with* communities. Without political sponsorship (and without strong external network connections), there is an automatic assumption that such planning is toothless. This suggests a lack of faith in the intrinsic benefits of communitarianism: the question asked of community action is what can it *lever* rather than what it can achieve on its own. This is, however, very much an instrumental perspective on community action and one that is informed by a number of large and successful urban projects, in cities such as Bologna and Turin, that have brought together active communities with city planners and their political masters (Sclavi, 2002; Boschini, 2009). There are of course also many examples of regression (Romano, 2012) and instances where much more could have been achieved had local government placed greater trust in community partners or had resources been available for communities to do more on their own.

References

Allegretti, G, Sintomer, Y, 2009, *I bilanci partecipativi in Europa: Nuove esperienze democratiche nel vecchio continente*, Rome: Ediesse

Arcidiacono, C, Gelli, B, Putton, A, 1996, *Empowerment sociale*, Milan: FrancoAngeli

Arnstein, RS, 1969, A ladder of citizen participation, *Journal of the American Institute of Planners*, 55, 4, 216–22.

Bobbio, L, 2004, *A più voci: Amministrazioni pubbliche, imprese, associazioni e cittadini nei processi decisionali inclusivi*, Naples: ESI

Boschini, M, 2009, *Comuni virtuosi: Nuovi stili di vita nelle pubbliche amministrazioni*, Bologna: EMI

Ciaffi, D (ed), 2005, *Neighbourhood housing debate*, Milan: FrancoAngeli

Ciaffi, D, Mela, A, 2011, *Urbanistica Partecipata*, Rome: Carocci

Fubini, A, Ciaffi, D, 2011, L'uso strategico del documento programmatico di un piano regolatore, *Urbanistica* 145

Ginocchini, G, Tartari C, 2007, *Leggere e scrivere la città. Mercato: una storia di rigenerazione urbana a Bologna*, Bologna: Urban Center Bologna

Mannarini, T, 2009, *La cittadinanza attiva: Psicologia sociale della partecipazione pubblica*, Bologna: il Mulino

Ministero delle Infrastrutture e dei trasporti, 2002, *Il programma Urban e l'innovazione delle politiche*, Milan: FrancoAngeli–DIAP

Owen, H, 2008, *Open space technology: guida all'uso*, Milan: Genius Loci

Paba, G, 2010, *Corpi urbani: Differenze, interazioni, politiche*, Milan: FrancoAngeli

Podestà, N, Vitale, T, 2011, *Dalla proposta alla protesta, e ritorno. Conflitti locali e innovazione politica*, Milan: Bruno Mondadori

Podziba, S, 2006, *Chelsea story: come una cittadina corrotta ha rigenerato la sua democrazia*, Milan: Mondadori

Romano, J, 2012, *Cosa fare, come fare. Decidere insieme per praticare davvero la democrazia*, Milan: Chiarelettere

Ruffolo, G, 2009, *Un paese troppo lungo*, Turin: Einaudi

Saporito, E, Ciaffi, D, 2013, Two democracies work better together: French and Italian decision-making processes for the Turin-Lyon railway project, in A Römmele, H, Schober, H (eds) *The governance of large-scale projects: Linking citizens and the state*, Baden-Baden: Nomos

Sclavi, M, 2002, *Avventure urbane. Progettare la città con gli abitanti*, Milan; Elèuthera

Susskind, E, Sclavi, M, 2011, *Confronto creativo. Dal diritto di parola al diritto di essere ascoltati*, Milan: et al/Edizioni Review

12

New York City's community-based housing movement: achievements and prospects

Laura Wolf-Powers

Introduction

This chapter offers as a 'community planning' case study the experience of community-based not-for-profit housing organisations in New York City and their relationship (from the 1970s through to the present) with that city's elected officials and executive agencies.[1] I argue that in New York City, community-based organisations have unambiguously added strategic value in the social housing arena, becoming 'part of a wider governance and leadership system that delivers benefits for a range of interests' (Gallent and Ciaffi, Chapter 1, this volume). Moreover, their political participation and advocacy have helped to bring about many of the policies that currently structure this system. Their role has been in constant flux, however, changing with shifts in city, state and federal political regimes; with the contingent relationship between their development work and their political advocacy; and with the transformation of the city's housing markets.

The chapter begins with a discussion of the unique political experience of the US, specifically the efflorescence of social movements at the neighbourhood scale during the 1960s and 1970s and the emergence of a branch of planning practice that embraced these movements' anti-systemic perspective. It then describes the birth and evolution of community-based housing organisations in New York City, originally the product of maverick efforts to stabilise neighbourhoods that had been virtually abandoned by both the public and private sectors. In the late 1970s, faced with a mounting inventory of multi-family apartment buildings that they had repossessed for tax delinquency, city government officials gradually and steadily integrated community-based organisations into an organised system for rehabilitating and managing these buildings. By extension (and because of legislative and policy actions that enabled them to produce new affordable housing as well), community-based organisations in New York City became responsible in the next several decades for governing the provision of safe and affordable accommodation to tens of thousands of low- and moderate-income households. While highlighting the interdependence of the city and the housing organisations as an example of 'co-production of public policy' (Gallent and Ciaffi, Chapter 1, this volume), this case also gently challenges Chapter 1's implicit assertion of a clean distinction between planning professionally produced by experts and local community action.

The final part of the chapter discusses current challenges facing the community-based not-for-profit housing sector in New York City. As more and more of the city's neighbourhoods have 'come back', becoming desirable to market-rate renters and buyers, non-profit organisations have increasingly found themselves in competition with conventional developers and property managers. This has again changed the terms and the tenor of their relationship to local government. In this context, debates have arisen about what unique value neighbourhood-rooted, mission-driven organisations deliver to the city's communities as against market-sector counterparts which can, in many cases, produce affordable housing units more quickly and manage them with greater efficiency.

Neighbourhood social movements and planning: the US experience

In many cities in the US, one consequence of state- and market-driven cycles of disinvestment and redevelopment during the second half of the twentieth century was the emergence of oppositional social movements rooted at the neighbourhood level (Fainstein and Fainstein, 1983; Beitel, 2013). Community-based social movements in US cities sprang, in the 1970s, from networks of organisations whose founders, active in the civil rights, anti-war and student movements of the previous decade, had discovered that housing and neighbourhood issues presented opportunities for political engagement around fundamental issues of social structure (Beitel, 2013; Taylor and Silver, 2003). 'Why talk about a vacant lot or a neglected building, or even a neighbourhood?' one New York City housing advocate asked rhetorically when being interviewed for this chapter. His answer: 'Because talking about specific places was a way of talking about inequality…in the American idiom' (Dulchin, 2013).

What is perhaps unique about the US experience is that a large number of those engaged in movement politics identified as planners (see Wolf-Powers, 2008). In response to struggles over urban renewal-era policies, a sizeable minority of individuals trained in architecture, planning and urban design during the 1960s and 1970s became intent on counteracting what they saw as the elite-driven shaping of the urban physical and social environment, and embraced community-led approaches. Members of this constituency asserted the potential of planning to challenge established institutions of governance and decision-making power while acting within established institutional contexts (Davidoff, 1965; Friedmann, 1971; Clavel, 1986; Krumholz and Clavel, 1994). The primacy of local planning as a framework for social movement claims of this type can be ascribed to the fact that under American federalism, planners and other actors in local government exert an unusual level of control over land use and development decisions. It can also be attributed to the advantages that professional skill and legitimacy conferred on neighbourhood-based activists; it helped their cause to have credentialled planners in their midst and to be capable of speaking in the language of zoning variances, building codes and intergovernmental financing schemes.

Understanding the historically specific emergence of a counterhegemonic strand of planning in the US is relevant to this case because it provides a starting point for examining the relationship of New York City's community-based housing movement to traditional political institutions and processes within the city. The organisations at the heart of neighbourhood housing movement were concerned with defending local populations from displacement, with improving housing conditions in poor and working-class neighbourhoods, and with strengthening political participation and getting the voices of the non-affluent into conversations about the city's future. As such, in the mid- to late-1970s they oriented themselves toward influencing municipal planning and housing policy from the outside, often using confrontational means. Over time, their successful efforts to shape policy situated them at the centre of a vast system governing social housing provision in the city.

The strategic alliance between government and the self-help housing movement in New York City

In the late 1960s and early 1970s in New York City, deindustrialisation and the shift of jobs and population to suburban municipalities led to massive private disinvestment from the city's residential real estate, particularly multi-family buildings occupied by low- and moderate-income renters. The mayoral administrations of John V Lindsay (1965–73), and then Abraham Beame (1974–7) faced accelerating job loss and working-class flight. Practices in which mortgage lenders, real estate agents and (in some cases) federal government housing officials colluded, such as block-busting and property flipping, further destabilised poor and working-class communities – places whose residents, because of their means, their race, or both, had extremely limited housing choices (see Wilder, 2000; Pritchett, 2002). In many neighbourhoods, neither banks nor developers were making sustainable investments. Basic physical infrastructure in low-income areas of the city received increasingly poor maintenance at the hands of a fiscally strapped city government.

In the context of urban disinvestment and rising operating costs (between 1971 and 1981, heating oil prices increased by 431 per cent and overall operating costs by 131 per cent), many landlords not only stopped paying property taxes to the city but also ceased to provide basic services in their buildings (Braconi, 1999; Saegert and Winkel, 1998). In response, neighbourhood activists, many of whom identified as planners, began to take control of local assets themselves (Susser, 1982; Leavitt and Saegert, 1990). In some cases, these assets consisted of empty buildings, but more frequently they were partially occupied multi-family structures in advanced states of disrepair. Sociologist Nicole Marwell describes the birth of self-help housing on the Southside of Williamsburg in Brooklyn in about 1970:

> The [Southside] activists set themselves a modest goal: to work with the Puerto Rican and other Latino residents of the Southside to restore individual apartments to livable conditions. They began identifying landlord-abandoned buildings, where basic services – heat, hot water, garbage removal, maintenance – were no longer being provided. They then encouraged the tenants to pool the funds they would have spent on rent to purchase these services themselves. In buildings with vacant apartments in need of rehabilitation to make them habitable, organisers found new tenants, moved them into the apartments, and allowed them several months before they were required to start paying into the building services fund. This practice allowed new tenants to spend 'rent' money on initial renovations, and then integrated them into the larger structure of the

building, making the entire building more viable. (Marwell, 2007, 45–6)

The non-profit organisation formed by these activists in 1972, Southside United Housing Development Finance Corporation (or Los Sures) has since rehabilitated or constructed nearly 3,000 units of affordable housing in 300 buildings; it currently manages a portfolio of 580 units of affordable housing in 25 buildings, as well as providing assistance to low income tenant co-operatives (Southside United HDFC, 2013). The Urban Homesteading Assistance Board (UHAB), founded in 1973 to institutionalise the formation of tenant-owned housing co-operatives in distressed buildings, has helped tenants preserve 1,700 buildings and 30,000 units (UHAB, 2013). The Association for Neighbourhood and Housing Development, a 94-member coalition and trade association, estimates that its members have rehabilitated and developed 100,000 housing units since 1974. As of 2008, they were acting as property managers for 35,000 households (ANHD, 2008).

Responding to very concrete problems in the built environment, then, New York City's housing organisations have, over the past four decades, linked a generalised critique of mainstream planning with action and mobilisation at the neighbourhood level. They first engaged their members in taking local control of assets that the private sector did not see profit in preserving, and that the public sector lacked the capacity to maintain. They advocated successfully for public policy that was favourable (in a variety of ways) to the preservation of these assets. As will be further discussed below, they nurtured neighbourhoods' social infrastructure, by supporting block associations and crime prevention efforts, running youth programmes, and assisting local businesses.

Yet the success of this form of community action has rested in part on policy decisions taken by New York City's local government. First, on an informal basis, local officials tolerated urban homesteading efforts in the 1970s. The city's legal department agreed to use an obscure provision in state housing law, the Housing Development Fund Corporation (HDFC), as a vehicle for turning over abandoned and distressed homes (buildings that the city had seized for non-payment of taxes) to community groups for the purpose of establishing tenant-owned cooperatives. While activists were constantly frustrated by the difficulty of obtaining city grants and loans for the renovation of buildings (Finney, 1987; Baldwin, 1978), the HDFC provided a crucial legal mechanism (Reicher, 2013).[2]

Second, the city integrated communities and their residents into its larger strategy for disposing of the property it had come to hold. Local

Law 45, passed in 1976, shortened from three years to one the period of tax delinquency required before the city could foreclose multi-family properties. Rather than hastening tax collection as expected, the law prompted many owners to forfeit their buildings, leaving the city with a massive inventory of what was known as 'in rem' housing stock, much

Figure 12.1: *Street* magazine, issue IV (cover)

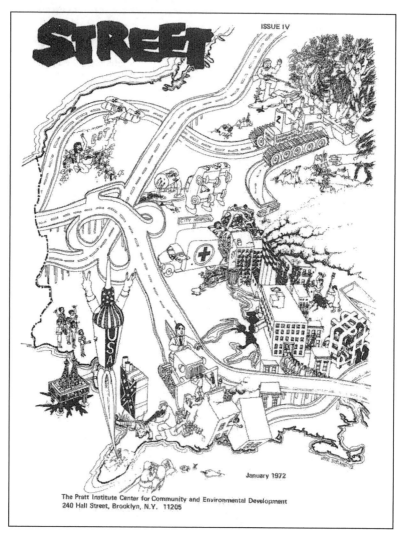

Publications like Street magazine, issued by the Pratt Institute Centre for Community and Environmental Development between 1971 and 1975, exemplified the political positions and cultural values of the counter-hegemonic strand of the city planning profession in the US. The cover of issue IV of *Street*, drawn by Uffe Surland, critiques urban housing disinvestment and calls on neighbourhood residents to counter it with self-help efforts.

of it severely dilapidated (Braconi, 1999; Saegert and Winkel, 1998).[3] In 1978, the city formed the Department of Housing Preservation and Development (HPD) and 'established an array of disposition programs utilising virtually any potential source of alternate ownership' (Braconi, 1999, 93).[4] The three main approaches were transfer to for-profit owners, transfer to tenant ownership (via an initiative called the Tenant Interim Lease (TIL) programme), and transfer to non-profit owner-managers which either owned and managed the buildings or helped tenant co-operators take ownership.[5] Both for-profit and non-profit owners received funding from the federal Community Development Block Grant programme and the city's capital budget to undertake repairs to building systems and individual units. While buildings conveyed to tenant cooperatives and non-profits have accounted for only about 25 per cent of all transfers under the city's *in rem* re-privatisation programme, the system as a whole can be seen as a strategic alliance between communities and the local government – an alliance formed to do what market institutions, in the 1980s and 1990s, were not doing, particularly with respect to highly distressed buildings in low-income neighbourhoods. The city relied on neighbourhood non-profits to work with the most deteriorated housing stock in the most troubled communities in other words, stock that private landlords were not interested in owning.

The organisation of non-profit groups into a networked social housing sector – in New York City and elsewhere – also owes much to the influence of federal policy. Many of the organisations that became active housing rehabilitators and developers were originally initiated through federally funded programmes designed to promote inner-city economic development and political participation during President Lyndon Johnson's Great Society era: the Community Action Program, the Model Cities programme, and the Special Impact Program (SIP). SIP, realised in 1965 by Senators Robert Kennedy and Jacob Javits, gave birth to the first groups that claimed the title of community development corporations, or CDCs (Weir, 1999; Ryan, 2004). While CDCs were envisioned chiefly as engines of economic empowerment and job creation, several factors colluded to reshape their mission. First (as discussed below), a legal, financing and technical assistance infrastructure developed around housing rehabilitation and development with the support of government, banks and major foundations (Rosen and Dienstfrey, 1999; Erickson, 2009). Second, in the absence of a parallel infrastructure to support business and job generation in low-income communities (see Weir, 1993), many groups floundered in their attempts to create jobs and nurture entrepreneurs (Mueller and Schwartz, 1998).

In the mid-1970s, neighbourhood-rooted advocacy organisations across the country were instrumental in Congress' passage of the Community Reinvestment Act (CRA), which opened up a new source of private financing for social housing (see Squires, 2003). This federal law set up a system by which bank regulators evaluate bank lending practices on the basis of these institutions' responsiveness to need and opportunity in low-income neighbourhoods. Loans made under the CRA were originally a financing source for rehabilitation of deteriorated housing, and have since been used by community organisations to develop new infill housing, both for rent and for sale. In New York City, an influx of immigration and an economic upturn tied to the growth of advanced producer services stimulated the market for new housing in the 1990s; it also helped shrink the city's *in rem* inventory. In response, the community housing network leveraged low-interest financing made possible by CRA, along with the federal Low Income Housing Tax Credit (instituted by Congress in 1986), along with city- and state-sponsored programmes, to develop new affordable units. Community groups inspired to action by the neglect of their neighbourhoods in the 1970s were now developing below-market housing options that enabled low- and moderate-income households to remain living in neighbourhoods that were experiencing new waves of investment.

Via their involvement in the production and management of social housing, community-based housing organisations in New York came to exist squarely within the ambit of local government planning. This partly reflects the city's opportunism and expediency (Braconi, 1999), but it is also a product of the communities' readiness and capacity to move from planning to action. In envisioning a better future for their neighbourhoods and constituents amid devastating disinvestment, community-based groups initiated political advocacy and convinced city officials to rely on them and their members to rebuild (rather than write off)[6] the city's distressed neighbourhoods. They also built a set of technical and social capabilities that enabled them to play a crucial role in that work. These capabilities, along with the constrained-yet-substantive political power they wield, make it possible for them to continue claiming a role in determining the trajectories of their neighbourhoods. In doing so, they work between the state and the market, as an integral part of what Erickson (2009) calls a 'decentralized housing network' implicating public, private and non-profit actors (see also Wylde, 1999).[7] Their experience thus challenges Chapter 1's implicit assertion of a clean distinction between planning professionally produced by experts and local community action. Activist planners in the community housing sector have developed substantial technical and policy expertise. To complement this, local government has opened up its model of governance to the participation of community groups.

Community-based housing and social capital

While the number of housing units rehabilitated, developed and managed by community groups and tenant cooperatives is a key index of the importance of the community housing sector, simple unit counts obscure the less quantifiable value these groups have created and maintained in the city's neighbourhoods across fluctuating property market cycles. Organisational work that reinforces formal and informal social relationships among residents of a neighbourhood, and which activates the resource potential of these relationships, can be conceived in terms of social capital (see Coleman, 1988; Rydin, Chapter 2, this volume). Saegert and Winkel (1998) present empirical evidence that social capital adds value to government investment in housing by leading to enhanced housing quality, security and reduced criminal activity (p 18).[8] Additionally, organisational initiatives not directly related to housing yet indirectly supported by housing revenue – after-school programmes, urban gardening and agriculture projects, participatory vision planning – are argued to enable residents to gain information and skills, and to build trust and reciprocity (with one another and with neighbourhood and citywide institutions) that are useful in the achievement of individual social and economic goals.[9]

As previously noted, the very neighbourhoods mentioned above (along with other formerly distressed neighbourhoods like Harlem, Clinton and the Lower East Side in Manhattan) have seen new waves of private investment and settlement by affluent households since the early 1990s, presenting community-rooted housing organisations with dilemmas very different from the ones that brought them into being. As the city has largely completed the re-privatisation (of its *in rem* housing stock, the work of many groups has shifted from rehabilitation to new housing production (although UHAB continues to support tenant-owned cooperatives in existing buildings). Community groups have also taken on new advocacy challenges. While political mobilisation in the 1970s and 1980s centred on drawing attention to neglect and abandonment and holding the city's housing disposition and subsidy programmes accountable, it currently aims to curb tenant harassment and illegal evictions in gentrifying neighbourhoods where units vacated by below-market tenants would now command premium rents (Reicher, 2013).These groups have also pressed the city to ensure that government-subsidised housing production better serves their neighbourhoods' needs (ANHD, 2012; 2013a).

These developments are taking place amid ongoing controversy as to whether community-based housing groups, sometimes known as the 'non-profit housing industry', have become too fully assimilated into a government- and market-prescribed *status quo*. Some planning scholars assert that the multiple partnerships and networks linking community housing organisations to the state, to mainstream financial institutions and to philanthropic organisations, enforce their adherence to a system that does as much or more to injure low-income neighbourhoods today as it did in the 1970s (see DeFilippis et al, 2010; Eisenberg, 2000; Stoecker; 1997; 2003). For these observers, community housing groups are too busy correcting market and state failures to question or challenge the social system that produces them. Further, community-based organisations that own and manage rental buildings have focused on improving housing quality by adopting more efficient management practices; these may cut against tenant participation and engagement objectives (Marwell; 2007; Saegert and Winkel, 1998).

As a counterweight to this in New York City, individual housing groups and the Association for Neighbourhood and Housing Development (ANHD) have successfully directed resources toward coalition building and leadership development, involving themselves in city- and state-wide organising campaigns aimed at preventing residential displacement, reforming outdated housing subsidy programmes, and inscribing affordable housing obligations in city zoning laws (Stallings, 2012). A different kind of counterweight is offered by tenant co-operatives, whose members tend to be less overtly involved in political mobilisation, but whose commitment to maintaining safe and high-quality buildings and to keeping housing affordable for future generations of owners embodies the potential of a 'shared equity' model for home ownership that achieves the goal of permanent affordability. It is perhaps because of the partnership role that the community housing network plays in the system for rehabilitating and managing affordable housing in the city that local government officials have been generally responsive when these groups have confronted the city over policy.

Consequences of recent housing market transformation

The city's three-pronged re-privatisation strategy for its *in rem* housing stock (conferral to private owners, tenant cooperatives and community groups, along with significant investment from the city's capital budget) has been hailed both as a stabilising influence on New York City's housing markets and as a factor in the revitalisation of many of the city's distressed neighbourhoods (Schill et al, 2002; Schwartz, 1999). Starting in the 1990s, the city's population (after having declined by nearly 800,000 in the 1970s), began to grow, and developers again began to create new market-rate as well as subsidised units. At the same time, competition for existing stock increased, and composite prices rose, increasing by over 150 per cent from 1980–9 and, after a small dip in the early 1990s, appreciating 124 per cent between 1996 and 2006 (Furman Center for Real Estate, 2008). Price appreciation – and neighbourhood change – has been particularly pronounced in East and West Harlem and in Brooklyn neighbourhoods close to Manhattan. While the for-sale housing market cooled somewhat during and after the recession of the late 2000s, the typical New York City renter did not see rental prices decline; median rent increased 8.5 percent between 2007 and 2012 while real household incomes dropped sharply (Furman Center for Real Estate, 2012).

With vacancy below 5 per cent, purchase prices high even in an off market, and nearly one third of renter households paying more than 50 per cent of their income in rent, community-based housing organisations working in low- and moderate-income neighbourhoods, now find themselves responding to a crisis generated by prosperity. They are responding to this in part through heightened advocacy. Between 2000 and 2010, efforts by these organisations have shaped city policy governing the up-zoning of land;[10] opposed investors who purchase multi-family buildings in changing neighbourhoods with the purpose of evicting poor tenants; and drawn public and official attention to the risk of expiring use, which occurs when privately-owned subsidised units are income- and price-restricted only until their subsidised financing expires (usually 30 years). If housing created with public subsidy, tax abatements or state and city land is not permanently available to low- and moderate-income households, argues ANHD, 'the city may not be developing housing for "the next generation," since for every affordable unit added or preserved, at least one other may be lost due to expiring affordability restrictions' (2010, 1).[11] Housing groups have consistently been friendly critics of Mayor Michael Bloomberg's housing policies on these and other grounds.

While advocating for policy change, mission-driven housing groups in New York City have also continued in their role of housing rehabilitators, producers and managers. But in the past 25 years, they have been joined by private developers and management companies. 'Affordable housing, here in New York,' ANHD's Benjamin Dulchin argues, 'is not risky. If properly underwritten, it will be occupied fully and it's a solid investment...The for-profit sector noticed that.' Conveyance to private owners had always been one of the three prongs of the city's *in rem* strategy; in the late 1980s, private developers began using subsidised financing from the city and other sources to create affordable housing. Of the approximately 235,000 units renovated or developed with city subsidy between 1987 and 2007, about 171,000, or 72.8 per cent, were developed by for-profit firms working in partnership with the city.[12] City officials, particularly in the Bloomberg Administration, have focused on maximising the production of affordable units – which can be done more efficiently by firms – and had little use for the intangible local value contributed by mission-driven non-profits. Further, community groups have found the property management function challenging (Bratt et al, 1998); many buildings that were not organised into tenant-owned co-operatives were divested by their owners and are now owned and managed privately. This data suggests that while the community-based housing movement was a crucial actor in a time of disinvestment, its development and management functions now play a smaller part in the city's overall system for housing low- and moderate-income residents.

Conclusion

In 1998, Saegert and Winkel wrote that 'The history of New York City's re-privatisation programs shows the trade-offs between programs that support social capital and those that promise to produce more units in a shorter period' (p 58). Considered in retrospect, their statement frames a discussion about the recursive nature of community mobilisation, planning, and policy implementation over time. In New York, the on-the-ground mobilisation and innovative capacity of neighbourhood-based groups influenced the city's response to the housing disinvestment crisis, shaping officials' attempt to rehabilitate distressed buildings in areas of the city which they had considered razing. The groups then assumed an important role in building back those areas, implementing the policies they had participated in creating. In an economically transformed New York City – one in which there is fierce competition for land, and in which the city's inventory of *in rem* housing is much smaller – community-based housing groups may evolve again. The groups may develop or reinforce their capacity as agents of commercial corridor revitalisation, small business assistance and workforce training (ANHD, 2013b). Some are also redoubling their focus on advocacy – for policies related to jobs and economic development as well as housing.[13] Arguably, the worsening of economic stratification and poverty (including working poverty) in wealthy New York City is, as a policy issue, nearly as intractable as housing abandonment four decades ago. Whether there is a community-based policy solution to these problems as there has been in housing, however, remains in doubt.

It is important to think about what may be lost in the social and political realms with a diminution of the strategic partnership that has prevailed between the public and not-for-profit sectors in low-income housing development and management. First, in the housing itself, there may be less of the tenant solidarity and social capital fostered by community-based non-profits. Second, if neighbourhood housing groups earn fewer development fees from housing rehabilitation and construction, it may be difficult for them (unless they are able to raise philanthropic dollars) to support community organising, or to sponsor resident involvement in visioning and planning for neighbourhoods. Third, it is possible that they will see a diminution in their traditional policy and governance roles, to the extent that those roles have emanated from the city's reliance on their participation in the city's low-income housing development system.

The success of New York City's community-based housing movement up to this point is certainly a function of its spatial and temporal context. A number of factors – the prevalence of multi-family buildings in the housing stock, the predominance of renter households in the city's housing market, the coincidence in time of deindustrialisation and population loss with massive increases in building maintenance costs – contributed to the debacle of private sector abandonment during the 1970s. Several of these same factors – plus the skill and enthusiasm of activist planners bent on using place to galvanise social action – enabled the evolution of a locally-based, mission-driven housing sector that is unequalled in size or capacity in other US cities. How that network of organisations will evolve, and in what form it will survive, depends greatly not only on markets and policies, but also on the agility and adaptability of the network itself.

Notes

[1] The author wishes to thank Eileen Divringi for superb research assistance and Susan Saegert for useful comments on an early draft.

[2] 'Under Article XI of the Private Housing Finance Law, a corporation may be created for the exclusive purpose of developing a housing project for persons of low income and for the benefit of persons and families who are entitled to occupancy in the housing project by reason of ownership of shares in the corporation' (Mallin, nd).

[3] According to Braconi, the city owned 60,000 vacant and 40,000 occupied apartments in 1979.

[4] One of the early leaders of the urban homesteading movement, Philip St George, was appointed head of the Division of Alternative Management Programs (DAMP) within the Department of Housing Preservation and Development.

[5] A number of tenant cooperatives, supported by UHAB and other organisations, did not go through the TIL programme but simply organised on their own and won funds from the city (and, briefly, the federal government) for rehabilitation.

[6] At the time, the notion that the city might cut off services to large portions of the Bronx and Brooklyn, subsidising residents to relocate to more densely populated areas within the city, was the subject of serious public discussion, much as it is in Detroit today (Carlson, 2004).

[7] As Erickson (2009) illustrates, non-profit community development corporations play an important part in the functioning of the social housing sector in many US cities, most notably Boston, San Francisco and Chicago (see also Rosen and Dienstfrey, 1999). New York's self-help housing movement shares a federal policy lineage with these other places, but it is also unique both in terms of scale and in terms of the extent to which community housing organisations have shaped local government housing policy and practice.

[8] Saegert and Winkel's granular study of currently or formerly *in rem* multi-family buildings in Brooklyn addressed the relationship between housing quality and security, social capital, and ownership structure (that is, whether a building was owned and managed by the city, a community-based group, a private landlord, or a tenant co-operative). Buildings owned by tenant co-operatives were found to have the highest building quality and safety; quality

and safety levels for landlord-owned and community group-owned buildings were roughly equivalent, while city-owned buildings measured lowest on these variables. Social capital was higher in tenant-owned and community group-owned buildings, and, as expected, mediated the effect of ownership on building conditions (p 48).

[9] Evidence for the contribution of community groups to the maintenance of the social fabric in times of severe disinvestment is available in contemporaneous accounts and oral histories of life in the city's disinvested neighbourhoods in the 1970s and 1980s (see, for example, Carlson, 2004; Leavitt and Saegert, 1988; 1990; Marwell, 2007; Neubauer, 1993). Others sources are *Street*, a magazine produced from 1971 to 1975 by the Pratt Institute Center for Community and Environmental Development in Brooklyn that publicised and celebrated community-initiated efforts to improve quality of life in Brooklyn neighbourhoods (Wolf-Powers, 2008) and *City Limits*, which began in 1976 as the city's non-profit housing sector began to institutionalise. The current community- and social capital-building efforts of neighbourhood-based groups continue to be chronicled in *City Limits* as well as in the publications of the Association for Neighbourhood and Housing Development and UHAB.

[10] Successful community mobilisation in the early 2000s led to the city's current policy of voluntary inclusionary zoning: in the event of a re-zoning that allows builders to build more stories, the city grants a 'density bonus' to developers who agree to include affordable units. Advocates want inclusionary zoning to be mandatory.

[11] According to this report, nearly 170,000 subsidised units will be 'lost' by 2037 if their owners decide to opt out of the income and price restrictions placed on them by the terms of their original financing.

[12] Some of these developments involved neighbourhood-based organisations working in partnership with private developers.

[13] The exception here is UHAB, which remains squarely in the housing sector, organising tenant associations in subsidised housing, assisting existing tenant co-operatives, and taking advantage of opportunities to develop new tenant cooperatives in foreclosed or city-owned buildings.

References

ANHD (Association for Neighbourhood and Housing Development), 2008, *Roadmap to permanent affordability: Analysis, observations and the future of subsidized housing in New York City*, New York: ANHD

ANHD (Association for Neighbourhood and Housing Development), 2010, *A permanent problem requires a permanent solution: New York City's next affordable housing expiring-use crisis and the need for permanent affordability*, New York: ANHD

ANHD (Association for Neighbourhood and Housing Development), 2012, *From collaboration to transformation: The initiative for neighbourhood and citywide organizing and the power of grassroots community development*, New York: ANHD

ANHD (Association for Neighbourhood and Housing Development), 2013a, *Real affordability: An evaluation of the bloomberg housing program and recommendations to strengthen affordable housing policy*, New York: ANHD

ANHD (Association for Neighbourhood and Housing Development), 2013b, *Roadmap for equitable economic development: expanding the toolkit of the community development movement*, New York: ANHD

Baldwin, S. (1978) *New self-help loan aids poor in housing*, City Limits

Beitel, K, 2013, *Local protest, global movements: capital, community and state in San Francisco*, Philadelphia, PA: Temple University Press

Braconi, F, 1999, In re in rem: Innovation and expediency in New York's housing policy, in MH Schill (ed) *Housing and community development in New York City: Facing the future*, pp 82–108, Albany, NY: SUNY Press

Bratt, R, Vidal, AC, Schwartz, A, Keyes, LC, Stockard, J, 1998, The Status of non-profit-owned affordable housing: Short-term successes and long-term challenges, *Journal of the American Planning Association* 64, 1, 39–51

Carlson, N, 2004, *UHAB comes of age: Thirty years of self-help housing in New York City*, New York: UHAB, http://community-wealth.org/content/uhab-comes-age-thirty-years-self-help-housing-new-york-city

Clavel, P, 1986, *The progressive city: Planning and participation, 1969–1984*, New Brunswick, NJ: Rutgers

Coleman, J, 1988, Social capital in the creation of human capital, *American Journal of Sociology* 94 Supplement, S95–S120

Davidoff, P, 1965, Advocacy and pluralism in planning, *Journal of the American Institute of Planners* 31, 4, 334

DeFilippis, J, Fisher, R, Schragge, E, 2010, *Contesting community: The limits and potential of local organizing*, Piscataway, NJ: Rutgers University Press

Dulchin, B. (2013) Interview by Author, New York City, 1 November.

Eisenberg, P, 2000, Time to remove the rose-colored glasses, *Shelterforce Online* 110, www.nhi.org/online/issues/110/eisenberg.html

Erickson, DJ, 2009, *The housing policy revolution: Networks and neighbourhoods*, Washington, DC: Urban Institute Press

Fainstein, A, Fainstein, N (eds), 1983, *Restructuring the city: The political economy of urban development*, New York: Longman.

Finney, A. (1987) *Homesteading: New reforms, old problems*, City Limits

Friedmann, J, 1971, The future of comprehensive urban planning: A critique, *Public Administration Review* 31, 3 (Special Symposium Issue), 315–26

Furman Center for Real Estate and Urban Policy (2008) *State of the city's housing & neighborhoods*, New York: New York University, (http://furmancenter.org/research/sonychan/2008-report)

Furman Center for Real Estate and Urban Policy (2012) *State of the city's housing & neighborhoods*, New York: New York University, (http://furmancenter.org/research/sonychan/2012-report)

Katz, A, 2005, Reflecting a moment: Media's role in community engagement. Remarks presented at City legacies, A symposium on early *Pratt Planning Papers* and *Street* magazine, New York, NY: Pratt Institute Manhattan Campus

Krumholz, N, Clavel, P, 1994, *Reinventing cities: Equity planners tell their stories*, Philadelphia, PA: Temple University Press

Leavitt, J, Saegert, S, 1988, The community-household: Responding to housing abandonment in New York City, *Journal of the American Planning Association* 54, 4, 489–500

Leavitt, J, Saegert, S, 1990, *From abandonment to hope: Community households in Harlem*, New York: Columbia University Press

Mallin, B. (nd) *Limited Equity Cooperatives: A legal handbook*, Prepared for the New York State Division of Housing and Community Renewal, (www.uhab.org/sites/default/files/doc_library/Limited_Equity_Cooperatives_A_Legal_Handbook_0.pdf)

Marwell, N, 2007, *Bargaining for Brooklyn: Community organizations in the entrepreneurial city*, Chicago, IL: University of Chicago Press

Mueller, L, Schwartz, A, 1998, *Why local economic development and employment training fail for low-income communities*, in R Giloth (ed) *Jobs and economic development: Strategies and practice*, Thousand Oaks, CA: SAGE

Neubauer, E, 1993, *Advocacy planning at Pratt: A case study in social change*, Unpublished master's thesis, New York: Graduate Center for Planning and the Environment, Pratt Institute

Pritchett, W. (2002) *Brownsville, Brooklyn: Blacks, Jews, and the changing face of the ghetto*, Chicago, IL: The University of Chicago Press

Reicher, A. (2013) Interview by Author, New York City, 1 November

Rosen, K, Dienstfrey, T, 1999, Housing services in low income neighbourhoods. In RF Ferguson, WT Dickens (eds) *Urban problems and community development*, Washington, DC: Brookings Institution

Ryan, WP, 2004, Bedford Stuyvesant and the prototype community development corporation, in M Sviridoff (ed) *Inventing community renewal: The trials and errors that shaped the modern community development corporation*, New York: Community Development Research Center, New School for Social Research

Saegert, S, Winkel, G, 1998, Social capital and the revitalization of New York City's distressed inner-city housing, *Housing Policy Debate* 9, 1, 17–60

Schill, MH, Ellen, IG, Schwartz, A, Voicu, I, 2002, Revitalizing inner-city neighbourhoods: New York City's ten-year plan, *Housing Policy Debate* 13, 3, 529–66

Schwartz, A, 1999, New York City and subsidized housing: Impacts and lessons of the city's $5 billion capital budget housing plan, *Housing Policy Debate* 10, 5, 839–76

Southside United HDFC (Southside United Housing Development Finance Corporation), 2013, About Southside United HDFC, www.southsideunitedhdfc.org/index.php/about-us

Squires, G, (ed), 2003, *Organizing access to capital: Advocacy and the democratization of financial institutions*, Philadelphia, PA: Temple University Press

Stoecker, R, 1997, The CDC model of urban redevelopment: A critique and an alternative, *Journal of Urban Affairs* 19, 1, 1–22

Stoecker, R, 2003, Understanding the development organizing dialectic, *Journal of Urban Affairs* 25, 4, 493–512

Susser, I, 1982, *Norman Street: Poverty and politics in an urban neighbourhood*, New York: Oxford University Press

Taylor, J, Silver, J, 2003, The essential role of activism in community reinvestment, in G Squires (ed) *Organizing access to capital: Advocacy and the democratization of financial institutions*, Philadelphia, PA: Temple University Press

STREET, nd, *STREET* magazine: a publication of the Pratt Center for Community and Environmental Development, archived at www.pratt.edu/academics/architecture/sustainable_planning/pspd_in_print/

UHAB (Urban Homesteaders Assistance Board), 2013, *About UHAB*, http://uhab.org/about

Weir, M, 1993, *Politics and jobs: The boundaries of employment policy in the United States*, Princeton, NJ: Princeton University Press

Weir, M, 1999, Power, money, and politics in community development, in RF Ferguson, WT Dickens (eds) *Urban problems and community development*, Washington, DC: Brookings Institution

Wilder, C. S. (2000) A *covenant with color: Race and social power in Brooklyn*, New York: Columbia University Press.

Wolf-Powers, L, 2008, Expanding planning's public sphere: *STREET* magazine, activist planning and community development in Brooklyn, NY 1971–75, *Journal of Planning Education and Research* 28, 2, 180–95

Wylde, K, 1999, The contribution of public–private partnerships to New York's assisted housing industry, in MH Schill (ed) *Housing and community development in New York City: Facing the future*, pp 62–81, Albany, NY: SUNY Press

13

Community-based planning
in Freiburg, Germany:
the case of Vauban

Iqbal Hamiduddin and Wulf Daseking

Introduction

When prospective households embark on building homes together, they set out to create communities. In Freiburg, a small city of southern Germany famous for the strides it has taken in becoming Germany's unofficial 'Environmental Capital' (Buehler and Pucher, 2011), such community-build ventures have already occurred on three large sites across the city and several more large schemes are underway at the present time. Indeed, group self-build has emerged as a significant pathway for the delivery of new housing in Freiburg, through which over 1,100 new homes have been delivered in the city since 1993. Part of the appeal for this collaborative approach to building is financial, and particularly the 20 per cent cost reduction in comparison to developer-produced housing that may be achieved when commercially driven profit margins are removed from the build process, and economies of scale are created through collaboration (Hamiduddin and Gallent, 2014). Evidence from group members themselves, however, indicates that the social nature of the group-build approach can also be a critical factor in the decision of whether to pursue a collaborative build project (Hamiduddin and Gallent, 2014). The social nature of the approach means, rather inevitably, that it is not for everyone.

This chapter explores one of the city's large group self-build sites at Vauban – a renowned urban quarter on a former military site in the south of the city heavily lauded for its socially and environmentally progressive design features, participative planning and resident-led housing schemes. The case study investigation is formed from both a body of academic field research, comprising semi-structured interviews, household surveys and documentary research (see Hamiduddin, 2014a; Hamiduddin, 2014b; Hamiduddin and Gallent, 2014) together with narrative insights from Freiburg's former head of planning. Vauban has been held up as an exemplar of sustainable urbanism (Hall, 2013), by bringing together best practices in green design – notably in building architecture, infrastructure and traffic-free residential areas where cars are physically separated from homes, and also in social design – where shared street spaces, extensive green areas and community amenities support high levels of informal contact between residents.

Elements of Vauban's emergence are drawn by way of four structuring questions. First, what factors led to the initial emergence of community-led planning and housing development at Vauban? Second, how have municipal planners encouraged and facilitated this approach? Third, to what extent has a collaborative approach to planning and housing development influenced the profile of the Vauban community and internal relations within it? Finally, the fourth question considers the extent to which learning points can be drawn from the Vauban case. This last aspect examines the issue of residential self-selectivity and the potential problems posed by the creation of large narrow age-range cohort communities. Experience from Freiburg's older suburbs suggests that – in the absence of dynamic housing market churn – large residential age cohorts can create downstream problems of service provision from ageing in place and depopulation. A significant emerging learning point has been to use resident-led development approaches at more modest scales, and within ageing neighbourhoods to draw younger families to depopulating areas.

Building, dwelling, thinking

The idea of a group of households collectively building their homes seems rather quaint; as if to obey a primeval instinct for communitarian living, at odds with the high mobility and consumerism of the age and a fringe activity immovably embedded in a specific place, with only very limited outside relevance. The people of Freiburg, however, have historic form in ignoring fashionable thinking within urban planning circles. Notably, the inner city was rebuilt entirely to its old structure after the devastation of the Second World War, in contrast to the experimentation and remodelling towards the new age of the automobile in other German cities. The forces of modernisation caught up with the city in the late 1960s, however, when planners began to approve the creation of low density suburbs and modernist inspired tower blocks to meet the need for new housing to accommodate a post-war 'baby boom' generation. Even, however, at a time when Melvyn Webber (1964) began to describe shifting geographies of social relations – 'communities without propinquity' – at the intersecting nodes of new communications technologies rather than in fixed geographical places, Martin Heidegger (1975) was ruminating on very physical, place-related notions of *dwelling*; places that mankind sought to provide permanence and rootedness in the world, among social relations and in spiritual certainty. For Webber the low density suburban forms served by automobile-oriented lifestyles and telephone communications demonstrated that 'the social' need no longer be subordinate to spatial form. By contrast, the tight spatial 'bundling' of the physical, social and spiritual in Heidegger's interpretation of the term 'dwelling', illustrated by way of the idealised model of a Black Forest farmstead, is derived from tracing the term's evolution rather than any contemporary social analysis. Because '*language* remains the master of man' (Heidegger, 1975, 146), Heidegger is provided with firm, enduring insights into humankind's fundamental need to know his or her place among established reference points, which he describes as *the* 'four' of earth and sky (physical), divinities (spiritual) and mortals (social). Thus, the post-war housing shortage had not just caused a crisis of shelter but a 'plight of dwelling', whereby 'mortals ever search anew for the nature of dwelling...that they must ever learn to dwell' (Heidegger, 1975, 181). Furthermore, because 'we attain to dwelling...only by means of building' (Heidegger, 1975, 145), the *quality* of building seems inextricably linked to the *quality* of dwelling, itself invoking non-material attributes including cherishing, protecting, caring and nurturing, which give places distinctive character and form. Simply put, if dwelling is to be attained, mankind must build and live within environments which represent their place among 'the four'.

In an apparent echo of 'Heideggerian' thought, significant numbers of Freiburg's residents have been given the opportunity to shape their home environments. Although collaborative or group self-build was first adopted at a new urban extension at Rieselfeld, from the start of construction in 1993, it was more extensively applied at the newly constructed Vauban suburb. Moreover, at Vauban collaborative house building may be viewed as one – if significant – element of community engagement in the neighbourhood design and realisation process. The purpose of the next section is to determine *why* community-led planning took root in Freiburg and the extent to which municipal planners facilitated this approach.

Building and dwelling in Vauban

Accounts of Vauban's physical development tend to begin with the occupation of the site by environmental protestors following withdrawal of the French garrison from the site in the early 1990s, and to portray the scheme as organic – the end result of grass roots activism – and also rather opportunistic: the product of a windfall site left by the departing military. These accounts tend to give less prominence to Freiburg's longer term political culture and particularly the green movement which began to influence planning profoundly from the 1970s, and the organisational system which offered residents the opportunity to participate in planning processes. The two elements – political culture and organisational system – suggest answers to two important questions; first about why collaborative build emerged as a mainstream method of housing delivery in Freiburg specifically and, second, over the role played by the planning system in facilitating this approach to development. In fact, the two elements are intrinsically linked: organisational structure serving as the conduit, channelling local political fervour into the corridors of decision making and ultimately to a democratically accountable executive mayor empowered to respond. Freiburg is by no means unique in Germany for having a strong local political tier, but considerable variability in local government structure exists nationally after the extensive regional restructuring which took place in the immediate post-war period.

Organisational structures can only facilitate processes, however; they seldom create paradigm changes in themselves and even where strong local governance structures are in place, strong local fervour will not automatically transform policy. Well-placed champions can be essential at critical moments in time. In relation to Vauban specifically, the groups pressing for environmentally and socially progressive development of the site faced the two immediate and common obstacles of land and finance. They did not own the land and nor at that time did the municipality; the site comprised a military facility belonging to the German Federal State. Nor did the groups have the finance to buy the site from the state or to compete with large speculative developers who had already identified the potential gains from a large brownfield site located a short distance from the centre of a city in the middle of a long-term housing shortage. For Freiburg's municipal leadership, therefore, the straightforward option would have been to have allowed the Federal government to sell the site off to large developers and facilitated the redevelopment of the site into new housing. That, however, was not the course chosen. The municipality blocked proposals for developer-led housing, bought the bulk of the site itself at 'cost price' from the state[1] and harnessed the input of local groups for the generation of a set of guiding principles as the foundations for a socially and environmentally 'progressive' masterplan. Perhaps the most radical departure, however was the fragmentation of the site and the sale of individual development plots to cooperatives, individuals and groups of self-builders. What led to this course of action? Two factors are particularly important. First was the weight and momentum of popular environmental fervour pushing for an 'alternative' project from below, a factor which forms the focus of the next section. The second was a well-placed champion in the then Mayor of Freiburg, Dr Rolf Böhme, who seized the opportunity to address practical problems of housing and sustainability, making a definitive statement for the city and political capital for his office.

Freiburg's political protest fervour

Freiburg's political protest fervour, which developed during the student-led social justice protests of the late 1960s and culminated in campus uprisings across Germany in 1968, might be regarded as a 'carrier wave' for two reactive movements that are particularly important in Vauban's history. The first – providing the underlying ideological basis for Vauban (or at least the groups and individuals responsible for establishing the scheme) was a local protest movement formed in the early 1970s to oppose plans for a nuclear power station at Wyhl, approximately 20 km to the southwest of Freiburg. Following mass demonstrations in February 1975 the plans were withdrawn, but fuel crises earlier in 1973 and later in 1978 had created an energy 'crunch' of increasing demand but diminishing supply. The protestors forced a strategic change away from increasing supply to reducing demand through greater efficiency, and towards a diversification of energy production through domestic micro generation to large renewable energy plants. Capitalising on the region's high daylight levels, a solar industry had already begun to emerge in the city in the late 1960s, led by local architect Rolf Disch, who later created Vauban's 'Solar Ship' building and solar quarter. More generally, the fervour of reactive environmental protest begin to find expression in the physical planning of Freiburg, notably through the city's second Transport Plan in 1979 (Buehler and Pucher, 2011), which prioritised public transport and 'green' modes of travel over the private car, in contrast to the prevailing thinking of the day among planners. The importance of this plan as groundwork for the large, suburban car-reduced development by creating robust networks for car-alternative travel is difficult to overstate.

The second reactive movement – essentially formed from the ranks of the first, established itself to petition for access to the Vauban site, following the French departure in 1992. The site became occupied by a multitude of different groups – informal squatters, activists and travellers. Some were simple opportunists and others were anarchists, but an important concept was conceived during this period – the principle of collaboration between households to create housing. The idea was not entirely new; housing cooperatives had already emerged from the squatter communities of Berlin, but Freiburg was a small city in a rural region and scarcely avant-garde therefore. On the Vauban site the *Selbstorganisierte Unabhängige Siedslunginitiative* or self-organised independent settlement initiative (SUSI) embraced this new collaborative thinking as a means to re-purpose the existing barrack buildings as low-cost housing. It established itself formally as a cooperative, survived eviction by purchasing a small portion of the site (34 ha of the 38 ha site were sold to the municipality) and set an important precedent for the subsequent master-planning and approach to redevelopment.

A collection of communities

What followed from an initial reactive phase – which shaped the overall strategy for Vauban's redevelopment – was a community-building project, founded on a collection of smaller sub-communities. Governing the development of the overall site, an apparatus for stakeholder input from residents and representative groups was established around the Forum Vauban – a central point of liaison with the municipal government's Vauban Committee. With the Vauban barracks site newly under its ownership, the Freiburg municipality ran a competition for the development of a land use plan to serve as the framework for future development. The winning design was selected and formally adopted in 1997. At the heart of the idea for this 'sustainable living quarter' were three important principles. The first was to limit traffic by separating vehicles from homes, the second was the 'city of short distances' concept to reduce travel need through mixed land uses and land use patterns to favour pedestrians and bikes, and the third was to capture a broad spectrum of housing tenures, from SUSI style cooperatives, through collaborative self-build or *Baugruppe* schemes, to private family homes.

Figure 13.1 shows the organisational framework of bodies established to oversee the development of the Vauban site. At first the arrangements appear complex, but because ultimate decision-making power for planning was concentrated in the city council's Vauban Committee the network orientated itself towards this body via two coordinating groups. The first was the broadly top-down 'Project Group Vauban' representing the views of the municipality and the region. The second was the broadly 'bottom-up' Forum Vauban – the representative group for the organisations, bodies and self-build groups on the site, directly in the case of the larger groups (such as the car-free living association and the Genova older people's cooperative) or indirectly via a citizens' (residents') association for smaller groups. Although it played an important role in setting the overall tone for the Vauban scheme, SUSI was not directly represented because it had already acquired its own sizable parcel of the site. As a consultative member of the city's Vauban Committee, the Forum Vauban served as the conduit for community participation in the planning process and scored some notable early successes, for example in designating the inner area of Vauban as a 'car free' site.

Although these arrangements are important in understanding Vauban's evolution and the physical shape of the present-day development, it is arguably the flexibility and freedom granted to the group self-builders and cooperatives that has left a striking legacy on Vauban's physical and

Figure 13.1: Organisational framework governing Vauban's development

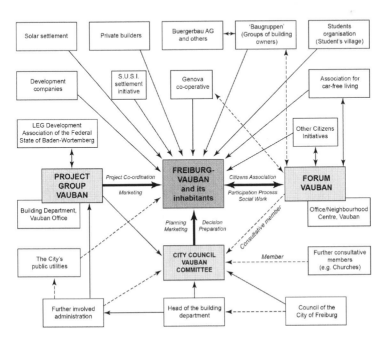

Source: Forum Vauban

social qualities. Five hundred of the site's 2000 homes were realised by these sub-communities of up to 25 households, occupying single or adjoining buildings. Although each building design had to comply with an overall framework set out in the site masterplan, covering basic aspects such as footprint, roof heights and factors affecting development patterns, the detailed design elements including building style, materials and internal layouts were left to the discretion of each group. Although the approach gave residents considerable freedom to shape individual homes to their own needs, the practical need to achieve compromises made for intense social experiences (Hamiduddin and Gallent, 2014). The architectural diversity and expression encouraged by this process resulted in a highly distinctive neighbourhood environment (Image 13.1): a 'common wealth' produced by the collective community input of households intent on attaining dwelling in a physical setting that they have themselves shaped, and in strong social relations catalysed by the collaborative build process.

Image 13.1: Vauban street scene

© Iqbal Hamiduddin

The 'Baugruppe' approach

Although Vauban has become well known for its self-build groups or Baugruppen, it is in fact one of a number of major sites within the city in which this process has been used as a means to deliver new housing; and Freiburg is one of a number of cities across Germany where the approach has been used. Other notable schemes exist in Berlin, Cologne and in Tübingen, where the large 'Südstadt' contains a high proportion of Baugruppen housing. Research conducted in a number of different sites across Germany by Hamiduddin and Gallent (2014) shows that the groups may form in a variety of different ways and for a variety of reasons. Some emerge from existing social networks and may be largely motivated by social objectives, such as the desire live in close proximity to friends or relations, or to be able to choose one's neighbours; other groups may be initiated by a professional in the development industry – typically an architect – who is motivated by the project itself and the prospect of cost-savings compared to more traditional house-purchase. Although these two approaches – dubbed 'organic' and 'professional', respectively – suggest slightly different primary drivers behind group-build, the social factor tends to remain dominant, causing groups to come together and sometimes to break apart as differences in beliefs and values become apparent.

Although it is important to understand why some prospective households are drawn to this approach, it is equally important to consider the groups that are potentially excluded. Evidence from Freiburg (Hamiduddin, 2013 and 2014a) suggests that low income or financially vulnerable groups as well as older home-seekers may be significantly less likely to be able to access these schemes. Conversely, those most likely to be in a position to pursue group self-build are those who enjoy preferential access to the property market anyway – namely, younger more prosperous households. The barriers identified vary between groups and have cultural inflections. As group self-build is predicated on private finance, this is perhaps the chief barrier and is itself contingent on individuals being able to raise it. Furthermore, because house purchasing typically occurs just once or twice in a lifetime in Germany – to provide a home in which to raise a family – mortgage finance has tended to be heavily associated with this stage of life. Although this is a cultural norm rather than a hard barrier it can, as the next section shows, have pronounced effects on the overall composition and profile of the community as a result.

The Vauban community

What characterises Vauban's residential community? This section compares official demographic data compiled by the municipality and data from household surveys conducted by Hamiduddin (2013). In order to see how Vauban compares with other neighbourhoods, three sites are compared. Vauban where approximately a quarter of homes have been delivered through group self-build, Rieselfeld where the proportion is around 10 per cent, and Haslach, a 'traditional' suburb where there is no group-build housing.

Residential profile

Figure 13.2 presents the age profiles of residents from the three Freiburg neighbourhoods, together with overall mean values for the city, and shows that the greatest differences in age structure between each development occur at the younger and older extremes. Both Vauban and Rieselfeld have nearly double the city's average proportions of under-18 year olds. The two schemes also have significantly fewer older people with Vauban recording only 2.1 per cent of its population in the over-65 bracket, compared with the city average of 16.9 per cent. Vauban and Rieselfeld record slightly higher than average proportions of their populations in the middle 35–60 year age bracket. In other words, the communities of Vauban and Rieselfeld are typified by households of middle-aged adults with children, while Vauban in particular has markedly fewer older residents.

Reflecting the significantly higher proportions of children in each of the two newer schemes, Table 13.1 shows that Vauban and

Figure 13.2: Age profiles of the three neighbourhoods and the city

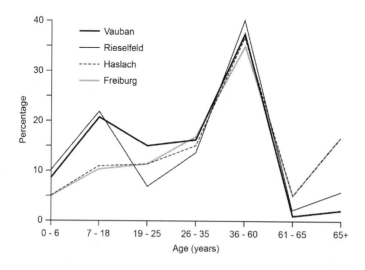

Source: Freiburg City Authority (2010c)

Table 13.1: Household sizes

	Vauban	Rieselfeld	Haslach	Freiburg
Household occupancy (N)	2.95	2.56	1.89	1.92

Rieselfeld's household occupancy rates of 2.95 and 2.56 respectively, are significantly greater than the Freiburg average of 1.89.

Table 13.2 summarises the overall characteristics of each of the three neighbourhoods from a range of official data collated by Hamiduddin (2013). Compared with the Freiburg average, Haslach's residents are slightly less likely to be car owners, less likely to be working and also less likely to be receiving social support. Haslach's age profile and household occupation rates closely correlate to the city average and residents' voting habits have recently swung from red to green. Rieselfeld residents display average levels of car ownership and social support receipt, but also a younger age profile, a higher than average household occupation rate and a committed green electorate. Last, Vauban residents are markedly less likely to be car owners, but are younger with higher household occupancy, have average levels of worklessness and social support receipt, which might be related to the location of a student hall of residence, and are committed green voters throughout.

Table 13.2: Summary of district population characteristics

	Car Ownership	Worklessness	Social Help	Age profile	Occupation Rate	Politics (2006 and 2011 elections)
Haslach	10% lower	Above average	Lower than average	Average	Average	SDP 2006 Green 2011
Rieselfeld	Average	Lower than average	Average	Younger	Above average	Green & SDP 2006 Green 2011
Vauban	30% lower	Average	Average	Younger	Above average	Green Throughout

Social relations

Can the nature of social relations between residents within the three neighbourhoods be attributed to the different ways in which these areas have been produced? Harvey (2000) suggests – with specific reference to new residential schemes which attempt to encourage strong sociability – that community relations may be bought at the price of exclusion and homogeneity. Here, the development of community is considered at three different levels – along streets, across each development, and in terms of how residents in each location judge their neighbourhood's level of integration into the wider city. Residents were asked how many people they knew by name on their street. The results are shown in Table 13.3. Although the range of results was considerable, varying from zero in the case of residents who had recently arrived to 150 for one long-time resident in Haslach, the average from each development tells an interesting story of neighbourly relations in which Vauban residents know an average of three times as many of their neighbours as residents of Haslach, with Rieselfeld residents approximately halfway between the two.

Table 13.3: Street relations in the three neighbourhoods compared

	Vauban	Rieselfeld	Haslach
Sample number (N)	89	86	73
Min	0	0	0
Max	120	100	150
Average	39	25	13

Residents were asked how often they greet a neighbour in the questionnaire survey and the results appear to support the patterns of street and development friendship noted above: 73 per cent of Vauban residents greeted a neighbour daily, compared with 48 per cent in Rieselfeld and 36 per cent among Haslach residents (see Figure 13.3). Three principal factors may have influenced these patterns. In the first instance a basic sociability between neighbours must exist, and in Vauban this is likely to be affected by the group-build approach which was most prevalent in Vauban. Second, residential design may exert an influence on social interaction – such as through incidental contact (resulting, perhaps, in the familiarity noted by van der Pennen and Schreuders, Chapter 8, this volume) which relates to a third factor; the travel patterns of residents and particularly the likelihood of residents achieving propinquity through being in the same place and at the same time.

Corresponding patterns emerge in relation to friendship development at the neighbourhood scale. On average, Vauban residents know nearly five times as many people in their neighbourhood as residents of Haslach (Table 13.4). These measures are, for the most part, just estimates. The pattern may relate to substantial differences in household size, revealed in official Freiburg City Authority data. The average in

Figure 13.3: Neighbourly contact in the three neighbourhoods compared

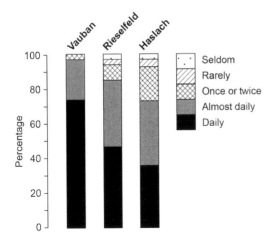

Source: Iqbal Hamiduddin

Vauban is 2.95, as many households contain young children.[2] This figure compares to 2.56 in Rieselfeld and 1.89 for Haslach. The overall Freiburg average is 1.92. If 'persons known' are converted into 'households known' using the household occupancy (size) data for each of the developments, the differences narrow somewhat to an average 32 households for Vauban residents, 25 households at Rieselfeld, and 11.5 for Haslach residents.

Table 13.4: Persons known on development

	Vauban	Rieselfeld	Haslach
Sample number (N)	89	88	73
Min	5	5	0
Max	1000	300	200
Average	95	64	22

Perceptions of relative community cohesion were gauged through questions about how residents thought people of different ages and backgrounds mixed, the sense of belonging to their neighbourhood, and their impression of community cohesion. As Figure 13.4 shows, the results on age and background mix from Vauban and Rieselfeld are very closely matched, with about 80 per cent of residents in each stating that different age groups mixed together well or moderately well, and

Figure 13.4: Community perceptions in the three neighbourhoods compared

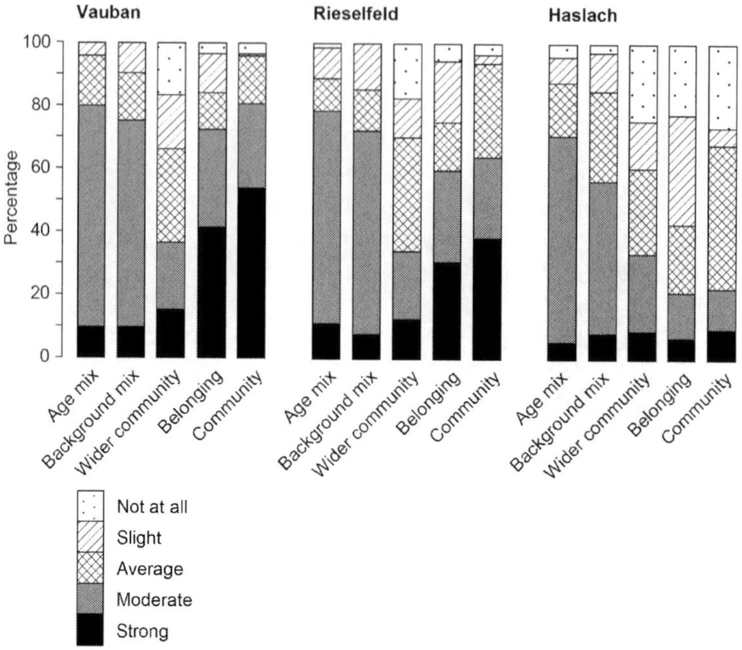

Source: Iqbal Hamiduddin

over 70 per cent in each thought that people of different backgrounds mixed well or moderately well. In Haslach these results were slightly less positive at 70 per cent and 57 per cent, respectively although a greater proportion of residents thought that the neighbourhood was 'average' in respect to how different age and background groups mixed with the result that similar and small proportions of residents in all three developments responded negatively.

Results for the 'sense of belonging' that residents felt to their community diverged much more dramatically: 70 per cent at Vauban, 60 per cent at Rieselfeld but just 22 per cent at Haslach. Last, over 80 per cent of Vauban residents thought that their neighbourhood had a strong or moderate sense of community, approximately 65 per cent at Rieselfeld and just 23 per cent at Haslach, where about one third thought there was a slight or only a weak sense of community.

Indicators of community cohesion from resident questionnaire surveys are by their nature subjective, and individuals' perceptions are shaped by a range of different factors, not least experience and aspirations. Yet the patterns that emerge from a range of different questions and measures are consistent, and this is likely to relate to the patterns of social interaction shown earlier, and also to the community-based mode of housing delivery at Vauban and Rieslefeld.

In order to investigate whether introversion and insularity are evident (and indeed could be a corollary of strong community development) residents were asked about the extent to which they felt part of a wider local community outside their immediate area. Figure 13.5 suggests that Haslach residents were less likely to feel a sense of wider belonging than the residents of Rieselfeld and Vauban, although potential survey bias needs to be acknowledged. There was a greater proportion of younger respondents in Haslach and in all the areas, younger people tended to express a weaker feeling of 'wider belonging'. So Haslach is disproportionately affected by this sense of 'disconnection' among the young, which may be explained in terms of 'rootedness' or particular social preferences which are age-specific. Despite this potential bias, a 2007 study by the City of Freiburg (2007) found that 72 per cent of Rieselfeld residents and 65 per cent Vauban residents had moved in from other parts of Freiburg, meaning that many perhaps retained social networks across the city, offering an alternative explanation for the differences seen in Figure 13.5.

Figure 13.5: Perceptions of belonging to a 'wider community' compared

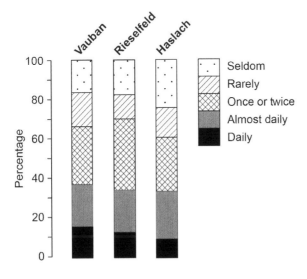

Source: Iqbal Hamiduddin

Building, dwelling, excluding?

One of the intrinsic difficulties of 'cohesive' communities is that they may be inwardly oriented and defined in terms of exclusion (see Rydin, Chapter 2, this volume). As Harvey (2000, 70) put it: 'well-founded communities often exclude, define themselves against others, erect all sorts of keep-out signs (if not tangible walls), internalize surveillance, social controls and repression'. The 'glue' of bonding social capital between members can act as a deterrent to those on the outside. Thus, although the notion of dwelling in a safe and cherished physical place and within a secure web of social relations holds a certain nostalgic caché, Heidegger's exploration of the original meaning of the term, its associated forms and the cited example of the Black Forest farmstead presents some challenges in modern, mixed and socially progressive societies. Yet although the socio-spatial community in which 'mortals find dwelling' has had its demise in western societies predicted, charted and elegised, it has in reality failed to disappear altogether. Indeed, Vauban seems to respond to this need for dwelling, which has itself been nurtured at the site in three distinctive ways: first through the collaborative method of delivering housing through building groups and cooperatives (allowing distinctiveness and expression), second through a socially-oriented neighbourhood designed to encourage propinquity, and third, the ambitious car-free living philosophy governing the core of the development allowing green spaces to be extracted from would-be car infrastructure. These distinctive elements of Vauban, which have been important in shaping the overall physical and social characteristics of the site, are perhaps the most unequivocally positive end results of community participation and empowerment during planning and development. Perhaps more difficult to evaluate is the relatively narrow demographic range of residents in comparison with other neighbourhoods and the city's overall profile. Three specific questions are raised. First, could more have been done by the major stakeholders to make the scheme more inclusive? Second, what are the likely longer-term social consequences of demographic concentration? And last, what lessons can be taken away for future schemes?

As the last question forms the basis of the next section, the first two questions are initially addressed. It is perhaps important to note first that Freiburg has had a burgeoning younger demographic since the 1950s. In a sense, the city has been struggling with its own successes in drawing large student cohorts to its prestigious university and in maintaining a quality of environment and a knowledge-intensive economic base that has restrained the outflow of graduates, perpetuating a long-term shortage of housing. Vauban's relatively narrow demographic range must be viewed against this backdrop of skewed market demand. Could the major stakeholders have done more to encourage a social mix? Privately financed projects, including self-build, are always likely to exclude some groups from the mix, but a number of deliberate steps were taken to include lower income and older residents through the Genova and SUSI initiatives. Perhaps the more important question, however, is whether projects that are, in the main, likely to be attractive to a limited set of social groups with a very particular demographic, a good idea. Similar concentration has become an issue in other suburbs of the city, including Mooswald, Landwasser and Vauban's near-neighbour St Georgen where, as at Vauban, a large number of younger families settled, remained, and aged *in situ*. In response, the city's planners have turned to the idea of 'fresh cell therapy' (Daseking, 2010; Hamiduddin, 2014a), attempting to bring scaled-down group build projects to aging parts of the city through enhanced forms of urban infill.

Learning from Vauban

Scaling down

Although Freiburg's growing population continues to generate pressure for new housing, its planners have turned away from new large-scale urban quarters such as Vauban and Rieselfeld and have instead focused attention on promoting small-scale developments in districts in where population decline has set in. The 'injection' of 'fresh cells' – of younger families – into aging neighbourhoods aims at stabilising demand for local services and amenities. Fresh cell schemes are typically in the order of 100–200 homes, although a number of different schemes may be situated within a single district. In addition to increasing the overall population density and stretching the age profile, the approach has distinct practical advantages in utilising smaller pockets of brownfield land situated within the urban perimeter. This is not an uncontroversial approach as several neighbourhoods have lost allotment gardens and cherished green spaces, but it has allowed city planners to extend a long-term policy of 'smart growth' within the city, by focusing new housing around the city's light rail network.

Though a fraction of the scale of its suburban forebears, the new fresh cell schemes have adopted some of the key design approaches of Vauban and Riesefeld, emphasising social elements of residential design including shared street surfaces, using the group self-build approach (exclusively in some instances) to create the housing, and separating vehicles from homes to create traffic-free communal spaces. The 'dwelling' intent therefore has a lingering presence in the approach, albeit at a more modest scale. The difference in scale, compared to Vauban, has meant that a streamlined approach to planning has been possible. Master-plans provide the overall framework in which the

Image 13.2: Wiehre Bahnhof

© Robin Hickman

Baugruppen operate and continue to harness the power of social and professional networks to deliver new homes.

Early examples of the fresh cell approach are to be found in Freiburg's westerly Wiehre suburb, with the largest located on the site of the district's former railway station, on publicly owned land belonging to the national rail infrastructure provider (Image 13.2). Over 180 apartments were built by a number of different groups, and these radiate from a single shared surface 'home zone' street in a 'Wilhelmsian' style, which conforms to the traditional pattern of built form across the wider neighbourhood. Car access to homes is limited to setting-down and collection only and car parking, provided at the overall city statutory level of 1.3 spaces per home, is located in a subterranean garage accessed from the side of the development in a manner which prevents through-traffic. The scheme, however, has been deliberately situated with convenient, high quality public transport access with high frequency tram connections into the city centre obtained from the tram stop located 300 m away.

Conclusions

The examples of group-build led development cited in this chapter suggest that high quality urbanism, place-making and strong social relations can be nurtured when residents are given the freedom and flexibility to shape their physical environment. At Vauban, groups occupying the site after the military withdrawal provided the initial impetus to set the course of reutilisation away from the commercially-led redevelopment that was initially mooted. The realisation of Vauban owes perhaps as much to the dogged local campaigning – itself the descendent of earlier environmental protest – as an enabling structure of local government led by a sympathetic mayor. Both elements have been critical in Vauban's genesis. The momentum generated by campaigning groups led to the creation of the Forum Vauban: a body set up to shape the neighbourhood masterplan, and to act as a conduit between the individual building groups and the municipality. Social relations developed during the scheme's realisation continue to manifest themselves in the present-day, making Vauban an evidently strong social community, dwelling within a distinctive place setting.

The important question remains, however: *is Vauban simply a 'one off' or can wider lessons also be drawn?* The question is particularly pertinent to countries with contrasting approaches to planning for housing. In Britain, with its centralised planning system and propensity towards volume house building, a trend of political devolution begun under a

Labour government in the first decade of the century and currently being pursued under the present coalition administration's 'localism' agenda, two recent and related policy streams appear to draw from the Heidegger dwelling-building instinct, characteristic at Vauban. The first is the creation of institutional space to allow local communities greater control in decision-making on planning matters in a tier of neighbourhood planning (see Parker, Chapter 10, this volume). Theoretically, neighbourhoods could be empowered to deliver Vauban-style simplified planning arrangements, allowing residents freedom of physical expression, as long as such arrangements are broadly consistent with higher plans, as is also the case in Freiburg. The second is a modicum of support for the self-build sector, including for collaborative schemes, in apparent recognition of the financial, tangible and social rewards that the alternative models to volume house production may bring. Vauban has caught the attention of practitioners and policy makers internationally (Hall, 2013), and although the scheme's evolution pertains in large part to local societal context and political circumstances, it illustrates the potential of community power under an enabling governance framework. Moreover, the social outcomes described in this chapter evidence the enduring social outcomes of this apparently radical but arguably instinctive approach to residential development.

Notes

[1] The site did not have planning permission and the municipal government indicated that they would not give permission to a developer. In effect the state had no choice but to sell to the city.

[2] Children tend to act as a social bridge: parents get to know one another through schools.

References

Buehler, R, Pucher, J, 2011, Sustainable transport in Freiburg: Lessons from Germany's environmental capital, *International Journal of Sustainable Transportation* 5, 1, 43–70

Buehler, R, Jungjohann, A, Keeley, M, Mehling, M, 2011, How Germany became Europe's Green leader: A look at four decades of sustainable policymaking, *The Solutions Journal* 2, 5, Online

City of Freiburg, 2007, *Die Neubaugebiete Rieselfeld und Vauban* [The New Developments of Rieselfeld and Vauban], Freiburg: City of Freiburg

City of Freiburg, 2012, *Demographischer Wandel in den Freiburger Stadtbezirken* [Demographic Profiles in Freiburg's Districts], Freiburg: City of Freiburg

Daseking, W, 2010, *The sustainable suburbs of Vauban and Rieselfeld*, unpublished paper, Freiburg, City of Freiburg Department for Building Construction

Hall, P, 2013, *Good cities, better lives*, London: Routledge

Hamiduddin, I, 2013, *The social implications of residential car reduction: Exploring community and mobility at the neighbourhood scale*, unpublished PhD thesis, University College London

Hamiduddin, I, 2014a, Social sustainability and neighbourhood form: Learning from the evolution of residential design in Freiburg, Germany, *Town Planning Review* forthcoming

Hamiduddin, I, 2014b, The car in the neighbourhood: Residential design and social outcomes in southern Germany, in R Hickman, M Givoni, D Bonilla, D, Banister, 2014, *An international handbook on transport and development*, Cheltenham: Edward Elgar

Hamiduddin, I, Gallent, N, 2014, '*Custom build*' *neighbourhoods: Examining the 'double win' of housing production and community development through group-build*, unpublished, available from the author

Harvey, D, 2000, *MegaCities: Lecture 4*, Amersfoort: Tynstra Gudde Management Consultants

Heidegger, M, 1975, *Poetry, language and thought*, New York: Perennial

Ryan, S, Throgmorton, JA, 2003, Sustainable transportation and land development on the periphery: The case of Freiburg, Germany and Chula Vista, California, *Transportation Research Part D* 8, 37–52

Webber, M, 1964, *Explorations into urban structure*, Philadelphia, PA: University of Pennsylvania Press

Part 4
Scales, influence and integration

The experience in many countries is that community action and planning should not automatically be viewed as an attempt to shape the policy environment or to influence political decision-making. Those engaged in such action are often motivated by a desire to achieve outcomes on their own, without the strings that are often attached to external support. However, because of the political and professional desire to secure legitimacy (often in a context of frustration with representative forms of democracy) by connecting in some way to the 'grass roots', and also because of a recognition that the wider political and policy environment presents place-based communities with particular risks and opportunities, there is a tendency for those communities to seek influence and governments to pursue the integration of community inputs into broader governance processes. Connection across different scales, and the attempt to bridge the private interests of community actors with sometimes abstract notions of the public good (see Chapter 1), throws up a number of challenges. The case studies that follow try to address the issues of scale, influence and integration in planning and the design of public policy.

There are three chapters in this part of the book. Reflecting on experiences in Canada, Filion begins by examining the necessarily 'integrative nature of planning' and what this means for planning across different scales. He examines issues of scaling by taking a transect from the province of Ontario, through the city of Waterloo and down to a neighbourhood organisation. He observes that 'scaling fosters the emergence of communities of interest specific to each scale' and that the interaction of these communities determines the extent to which messages are clearly communicated up and down and whether interventions at the top are shaped by aspirations at the bottom. This chapter provides a general critique of scaling in planning, applied here to the wider decision-making environment in which community or neighbourhood organisations find themselves. The remaining chapters then consider how community action engages with the scale issue: in Chapter 15, Amdam brings different actors and scales together in a depiction of Volda (Norway) as a complex adaptive system, arguing that the effects of scale can be nullified where there is a genuine devolution of power to community actors; that, essentially, there are decisions that are best made at a community scale though 'self-governed community development'. Such mechanisms are specific to context, but many conceptions of planning allow the separation of strategic from local development decisions, and the argument that power should be devolved as far as possible is not an unusual one. These debates, however, inevitably return to the view that community action will always exist within the shadow of hierarchical authority: that there are 'strategic dilemmas integral to governing' (Davies, 2008, 11) that always need addressing. The trick is to ensure that strategic direction is not only supported by a weak electoral mandate (see Messaoudène and colleagues, Chapter 6, this volume), but that democracy is open and based on constant dialogue. Chapter 16 takes us back to a position set out in the first chapter: that there is a need to 'connect to the citizenry' to inform all levels of decision making. That connection depends on community development and a vibrant community sector. It also depends on effective bridging to community actors in order to ensure an open channel to policy development. Returning to England for a second time in this book, Gallent offers an analysis of the role of support groups in community-based planning, arguing that these have an important role to play in extending the democratic credentials of community building beyond the 'usual suspects' and in connecting the many good ideas that communities have to the local state and to service providers. Support groups can be effective, in many contexts, at broadening the reach and activities of community groups, at providing technical support, and in developing and extending 'networked community governance' in ways that do not merely legitimise top-down interventions but gives resource and capacity, and therefore power, to different communities.

This final section looks at the integration of community action and planning into wider governance structures, and its influence over a broader policy-making and strategic planning environment. Not all communities seek that influence, but for some it is part of the life-cycle of community planning. Here, we show that there are critical scaling issues to overcome, as well as issues of capacity and the question of how far localised community action can and should set the strategic direction for planning.

Reference

Davies, JS, 2008, Double-devolution or double-dealing? The Local Government White Paper and the Lyons Review, in *Local Government Studies*, 34, 1, 3–22

14

The scaling of planning: administrative levels and neighbourhood mobilisation as obstacles to planning consensus

Pierre Filion

Introduction

Integration should be at the heart of planning because of its need to find common ground between diverse interests and engage multiple categories of actors in coordinated interventions. The integrative nature of planning has been emphasised over the last decades by the attention theorists have given to the description and promotion of participatory models suited to the achievement of consensual outcomes. The importance of integration within planning has also been brought to light by attempts at large-scale transformative planning strategies in response to pressures for a shift away from prevailing urban development trajectories. Such transformative strategies require a tight coordination of numerous actors over long periods.

The integrative aspirations of planning have to contend with the interest, income, value and power cleavages that traverse society. These societal divisions represent barriers to successful consensual participatory processes as well as to the deployment of wide-scale planning interventions over long time horizons. This chapter concentrates on another type of fragmentation, which, while the object of less treatment in the literature, represents nonetheless a major source of obstacles to planning processes and outcomes: the impact of scaling. Unlike societal divisions, which are deeply embedded in the structure of society, scaling effects on planning are closely tied to the administrative arrangements in which this profession operates. The scope of scaling is broader than that of administrative levels, however, because it incorporates their geographies and attendant socioeconomic distributions. Scaling also encompasses interests, cultures and worldviews to which administrative levels and their respective geographies give rise. In this sense, the present chapter provides a spatial complement to Matthews' concern with time (Chapter 3, this volume).

Consistent with this book's focus on community action and planning, the present chapter emphasises the relation between the neighbourhood mobilisation level and the other scales relevant to planning. It portrays neighbourhood activism as both unique among the different scales at which planning operates and an influence on its other scales and, therefore, on planning decision-making. Neighbourhood mobilisation brings to the planning system issues arising from local living conditions. These issues are shaped by the common socioeconomic attributes and values characteristic of many neighbourhoods. Planning outcomes bear the mark of the confrontation between neighbourhood reactions, which are not filtered by the elaborate institutional structures encountered at other scales, and planning proposals, which are the product of formal political and expert-based processes.

The chapter first discusses views on integrative planning, from a process and implementation perspective. The next section introduces the literature on scaling from which it draws to formulate a definition relevant to the difficulties that integrative planning encounters. The third section consists of a case study of large-scale long-range transformative planning: the Growth Plan, which encompasses an extensive region focused on Toronto. The case demonstrates how each scale generates its own perception of this planning strategy, and examines the effects of these competing perspectives on its deployment. The chapter closes with a discussion of the inevitability of scaling effects on planning and of their consequences on large-scale planning interventions and, thereby, on their ability to address crises, of an environmental nature or otherwise, confronting contemporary society.

Integrative planning

The very nature of planning involves the integration of different social groups and actors into its processes. How else could it forge coalitions over proposals affecting parts of or, indeed, entire urban areas? Or how could it maintain support from groups and organisations, each pursuing its own interests, over the duration of long-range planning strategies? Hence the importance theorists give to the integrative dimension of planning in their reflections on how this profession does or should operate.

Planning theory is largely about how to improve the inclusiveness of decision-making processes so as to achieve planning outcomes that are more consensual and thus socially equitable. From the 1980s, inspired by the thinking of the Frankfurt School and, more specifically, Jürgen Habermas (1984) on conditions for consensual dialogue, planning theorists have concentrated on how to foster conditions for wide-scale participation in planning processes and the adoption of forms of communication respectful of all involved (for example, Forester, 1989; 1999; Healey, 1992; 1997; 1998). They believe in the transfigurative virtues of open dialogues, which, in their view, sensitise participants to each other's reality and interests, and thereby contribute to the achievement of consensual outcomes (Healey, 1999, 1132; Innes, 1996, 461). The paradigmatic status of the dialogical/consensual approach underscores the importance planning theory attributes to the integrative nature of planning: integrative in terms of the presence of different actors around the decision-making table, mutual respect among these actors, the consideration of their respective positions in decisions, and planning outcomes that heed the experience of different social groups.

The dialogical/consensual perspective is vulnerable to critiques targeting its tendency to gloss over the effects of societal divisions on communication processes. Researchers in disagreement with this perspective have pointed to its utopian nature, which fails, in their view to heed how societal cleavages and conflicting interests impede unbiased dialogues and, to an even larger extent, consensus building (Allmendinger and Tewdwr-Jones, 2002; Huxley, 2000; Tewdwr-Jones and Allmendinger, 1998). Some of the most scathing critiques concern lack of attention to the impacts of political and power-laden relations on planning processes. They stress the need to acknowledge the embedding of planning in society's power structure (McGuirk, 2001; Mouffe, 2000).

While all forms and stages of planning involve different categories of actors, it is in the formulation and deployment of large-scale and long-range strategies that integrative needs are most glaring. To meet their objectives, such strategies indeed require a tight coordination of the actions of multiple actors over long time horizons. The present time is conducive to the adoption of such strategies due to the popularity of mega-projects and, perhaps above all, pressures, felt with special acuity in North America, for planning to reverse prevailing urban development trajectories. After 65 years of low-density and near fully automobile dependent dispersed urbanisation, there is rising awareness of the negative consequences of this form of development. Dispersed patterns are blamed for high urban growth expenses (especially in the case of horizontal infrastructures), lack of stimulating urban spaces, the health consequences of sedentary lifestyles and a string of environmental sequels including the contribution of car travel to the atmospheric accumulation of greenhouse gases (for example, Burchell, 2005; Carruthers and Ulfarsson, 2003; Kunstler, 1993; Richardson and Bae, 2004). Opponents of dispersed development put their faith in planning as an instrument of urban transformation. This represents a tall order for planning given powerful path dependencies sustaining the ongoing production of dispersed urban patterns (Atkinson and Oleson, 1996; Downs, 2005; Filion, 2010; Marshall et al, 2009). In its effort to abate dispersion and foster a return to more concentrated urban forms, planning must overcome the tight interconnection between low density, specialised land use and near universal automobile reliance, as well as entrenched habits and interests vested in urban dispersion (Marshall, 2000).

Only wide-scale and long-term planning strategies have any potential for bringing about the desired change of the urban development trajectory. These types of strategies must rally large contingents of actors, which expose them to the same societal division effects as those that burden dialogical/consensual planning. Societal divisions may hinder the alignment and coordination of the different interests essential to the pursuit of these strategies. Transformative strategies must further contend with the need to harness divergent interests over long periods in order to assure the consistency of planning interventions.

Scaling obstructions to integrative planning

The chapter adds an additional layer of planning obstacles to those originating from societal divisions: the impact of scaling. While scales and administrative levels overlap, they should not be confused. The concept of scales embraces administrative levels, but also geographies under their jurisdiction, the respective socioeconomic makeup of these geographies and cultures and worldviews these layers and geographies generate (Neumann, 2009, 401). In this sense, scales are to the broad concept of governance what administrative levels are to the narrower concept of government.

Despite their serious impacts on processes and interventions, effects of scales on planning have been given scant attention within the planning literature. Things are different with the geography and political economy treatment of scales. Rising interest in the geographical dimensions of societal phenomena has prompted within these disciplines an exploration of scaling and its varied consequences (Marston and Smith, 2001; Smith, 1995). Much of the writing on scaling originates from Neil Brenner, who has investigated spatial restructuring provoked by the passage from Keynesianism to neoliberalism (Brenner,

2001; 2009). He has documented the creation of new political spaces to accommodate the rise of the 'Rescaled Competitive State Regime' (Brenner, 2004, 295). In his view, new administrative arrangements favour sub-national and supranational scales, at the expense of the traditional nation-state. Power is delegated to city regions, which are major assets in international economic competition. These regions thus become beneficiaries of important infrastructure investments and governance arrangements meant to secure their global standing (Brenner, 2004, 214; Swyngedouw, 1997). At the same time, certain responsibilities of the nation-state, especially those pertaining to economic management, are uploaded to supranational organisations (Brenner, 2000).

When transposed to planning, scaling brings to light difficulties in achieving the integration needed for dialogical/consensual processes and wide-scale interventions to meet their objectives. It represents a factor of fragmentation, which compounds the effects of divisions embedded in the structure of society. Some scaling-related segmentations are a direct outcome of features that distinguish administrative levels from each other: different mandates and related expertise, their respective intervention capacity, and available resources. Administrative levels are also singularised by their respective organisational architecture, especially their electoral system, which determines the types of demands most likely to have an impact on decision-making. Then, moving away from formal organisational arrangements, there is the distinct culture that each administrative level generates. Organisational cultures mirror allegiance to an administrative level and thus readiness to promote its interests, at the possible expense of other levels. They also foster distinct worldviews shaped by the features of each administrative level (Trice and Beyer, 1993). Further contributing to different scale-induced cultures are specific geographies, and socioeconomic and value distributions found therein (Dale and Burrell, 2008; Maréchal et al, 2013).

Not all scales of relevance to planning pertain to administrative echelons. The neighbourhood level, which is bereft of the formal institutional structures and processes encountered at the other scales, is a major source of influence on planning and its outcomes, as illustrated in previous chapters. Organisations set up to advance neighbourhood views on planning matters are generally rudimentary and fluid, operational only for the duration of debates around contested issues. It follows that planning stands taken by neighbourhood organisations are, as a rule, neither formulated by experts, nor the outcome of the procedural stages present in the other scales.

Another distinctive trait of neighbourhood mobilisation relative to other scales is its focus on a very narrow range of issues, mirroring its absence of policy-making responsibilities. The neighbourhood scale is sometimes concerned with self-help, but most often it aims at influencing policy (see Chapter 1, this volume). In this regard its influence is felt when it filters up to the scales of planning related to the state apparatus. Finally, more so than other scales, neighbourhood mobilisation lends itself to the achievement of consensual positions. There are two reasons for this. First, the consensus potential is enhanced by the relative socioeconomic and value homogeneity found at the neighbourhood level. Second, mobilisation takes place over local issues experienced by all or most neighbourhood residents. The immediate nature of these issues often dissociates them from divisive society-wide political contentions.

The Growth Plan

In the early 2000s the Progressive Conservative (PC) government of the Canadian province of Ontario, then in its second term, was confronted with two leading issues concerning development in the Toronto urban region. These were: rapidly rising levels of traffic congestion and the environmental consequences of imminent urban growth in a sector, the Oak Ridges Moraine, known for its environmental sensitivity (the headwater of most Toronto region rivers) and natural beauty (a blend of hills and lakes). Given its anti-regulation slant, one could have expected the PC government to ignore these issues and allow development to continue with minimum interference. These matters, however, were raised by two groups at the core of the PC political constituency (Taylor, 2013). Among all complaints voiced about traffic congestion, those emanating from business associations were most successful at seizing the attention of the government. While the most virulent opposition to the urbanisation of the Oak Ridges Moraine came from environmental groups, their cause was widely supported by outer-suburban residents, an important source of PC electoral support (STORM, nd). Ideology was overshadowed by the need to address obstacles to economic efficiency and the reality of electoral politics.

In 2002, the PC government set up a panel composed largely of local politicians and representatives of the development industry and the environmental movement to frame, under the advice of consultants and provincial experts, a development strategy for an extensive Toronto-focused region with a population of 7.5 million, labelled the Greater Golden Horseshoe (GGH). The strategy was mostly concerned with controlling sprawl and alleviating traffic congestion. When it gained power in 2003, the Liberal Party (a centrist formation) adopted wholesale the strategy and formalised it into the Growth Plan, which was adopted in 2006 (Ontario, 2006). Its main constitutive elements consist of the creation of a green belt containing the Oak Ridges Moraine, the setting of urban growth boundaries, the apportioning of 40 per cent of new development within existing built areas, and the establishment of a nodal network. A parallel plan, The Big Move, adopted in 2008, proposed an ambitious public transit infrastructure consistent with the principles of the Growth Plan (Metrolinx, 2008).[1]

In Canada, provincial governments have jurisdiction over municipal administrations, land use planning and urban transportation (which explains the absence of any mention of the federal level), although responsibility for urban planning is delegated to municipal administrations, with oversight from the province. The implementation of the Growth Plan thus relies heavily on regional and municipal planning.[2] This is why the province has adopted planning directives targeted at regional and municipal governments (Ontario, 2006, 34–8). Strict prescriptions, including the density thresholds they must meet for their official plans to be approved by the province, are imposed on these administrations. Still, they are not mere executers of provincial planning dictates. It is largely up to municipal administrations to determine how to achieve Growth Plan objectives and meet its density thresholds within their territory. Moreover, regional and municipal administrations have felt free to express their views on provincial planning policy. It is easy to see how such an administrative setting is susceptible to scaling effects.

The object of the case study is the formulation and implementation of the Growth Plan across different scales, from the province to the Region of Waterloo, the City of Waterloo and that of a specific City of Waterloo neighbourhood. The Region of Waterloo is located 100 km west of the City of Toronto and posts a population of 553,000. The City of Waterloo, with a population of 99,000, is one of its three urban municipalities. It is the fastest growing city in the Region of Waterloo thanks to its information technology and university-based economy. The neighbourhood under investigation is mostly a single-family housing area at the edge of downtown Waterloo. Information for the case study originates from a survey of newspapers, a review of planning and other documents presenting the views of agencies and actors involved at the different scales, and interviews with planners from the provincial, regional and municipal levels, who took part in the formulation or implementation of the Growth Plan.

Scaling and the formulation and implementation of the Growth Plan

The province of Ontario

The impetus for the adoption of the Growth Plan was both economic and electoral. As expected given the jurisdictions of the province, the pursuit of the Growth Plan mirrored concerns about the GGH as well as province-wide repercussions. Economically, the plan was seen as essential to the competitiveness of the Toronto region, perceived as threatened by the economic consequences of deteriorating traffic congestion. From the perspective of the provincial government, the economic traction of Toronto means that impediments to its economy reverberate across the province. In the words of a provincial level planner:

> In the same way that Toronto and the GGH are economically important to the nation, they are even more important to the province...If the heart fails nothing else does as well as it can. (Provincial Planner 1)

There was equally an electoral motivation to the policies addressing traffic congestion, which attempt to abate time spent commuting, although it is perhaps in the case of measures hemming in urban sprawl that the effects of electoral concerns are clearest. While obviously sensitive to the high public sector costs of servicing this form of development, the provincial government was also attentive to interest groups and public opinion opposing sprawl. If the province played up positive local impacts of Growth Plan measures, with an eye on individual provincial legislature seats from the GGH, it also emphasised their regional and province-wide benefits.

The province relies on two approaches to implement the urban goals of the Growth Plan: directives assuring regional and municipal planning compliance with Growth Plan objectives, and direct provincial investments, earmarked mostly for public transit. To secure regional and municipal planning conformity with the Growth Plan, the province has set quantified thresholds which municipalities must meet. As a provincial level planner has noted, there is, however, a danger that regional and municipal administrations will plan according to these metrics rather than the spirit of the Growth Plan.

> We spend a lot of time debating what is the land budget and dancing on the head of a pin. We spend all of our resources and debates on that as opposed to how can we make the downtown better [or] how can we make intensification more viable. (Provincial Planner 2)

It is essential that public transit investments are closely coordinated with the other dimensions of the Growth Plan. New transit services are indeed required to produce accessibility gradients capable of propelling intensification. When such development does materialise, public transit must be in place to avoid density-induced traffic congestion, which fuels NIMBY reactions aimed at this form of growth. Public transit investments are, however, especially vulnerable to the juggling by the province of competing priorities, as economic cycles and restructuring take place. These circumstances cause the spending capacity of the government and individual ministries and programmes to fluctuate.

> At the provincial level...you're competing with education and health. These are two biggies! And then on the transportation side, with roads. (Provincial Planner 2)

For example, in the wake of the 2008 recession the province endured concurrently shrinking fiscal entries and ballooning social expenditures, and participated in efforts to rescue two of the North American automobile companies, both with considerable production in Ontario. Weakened financial capacity caused the province to delay its public transit development agenda (Spears, 2010). In a similar vein, the entire Growth Plan initiative is vulnerable to a change of provincial administration. Even if the two main parties have adhered to the Growth Plan at different stages of its evolution, in opposition, the PC party has returned to its hard-edged anti-regulation free-market ideology.

Region of Waterloo

The Region of Waterloo has long been committed to sustainable urban development. It was the first in Ontario to adopt an urban growth boundary and protect environmentally sensitive policy areas. It is presently launching the construction of a 19 km long light rail transit line, which will run the length of a corridor designated for intensification. Two factors explain the strong adherence of this regional government to the sustainability credo. First, a number of its areas of intervention are compatible with sustainable approaches. Regional-level planning is responsible for the delineation of the built perimeter, a mandate that lends itself to the adoption of urban growth boundaries. Another regional jurisdiction is public transit, an ideal candidate for the promotion of transportation and urban form sustainability. The second factor is the nature of the Region of Waterloo electoral system. Regional Council includes the mayors of the four rural and three urban municipalities constituting the Region of Waterloo as well as a specified number of councillors elected at-large within each urban municipality. This set-up leaves Regional Council without ward-level representation, which creates conditions conducive to the consideration of region- and city-wide issues, at the expense of perceived adverse neighbourhood repercussions, such as traffic diversion and side effects of intensification.

Not surprisingly, the Region of Waterloo adhered from the very start to the principles of the Growth Plan. At the time, certain Region of Waterloo planners were of the opinion that a number of core Growth Plan proposals had been inspired by planning practice in the region (Region of Waterloo Planner 1). The Region of Waterloo in fact appeared even more committed than the province to the implementation of the Growth Plan. An interviewed regional planner echoed these sentiments by wishing for more direct provincial involvement to assure the implementation of the plan.

> Once the province approves, our plans and policies are supposed to reflect the Growth Plan. That's pretty much the extent of the province's involvement in our plan. They don't review any decision-making after they review the plan. They don't review any development application, site plan, any kind of detailed development. They're out of the picture. (Region of Waterloo Planner 2)

Region of Waterloo officials and planners felt betrayed when the Ontario Municipal Board (a quasi-judicial provincial tribunal adjudicating on planning litigations) recently contradicted the spirit of the Growth Plan by ruling against a Region of Waterloo policy constraining peripheral development (Pender, 2013). The sustainable urban development aspirations of the Region of Waterloo are also frustrated by local municipalities. Eager to stimulate growth within their territory, they readily accommodate dispersed automobile-dependent developments.

You have municipalities competing against each other and sometimes making decisions on the basis of trying to attract that growth. This is one of the obstacles preventing an effective sustainable strategy across the region. (Region of Waterloo Planner 2)

Given the limited range of Region of Waterloo jurisdictions, provincial delegation of responsibilities for the Growth Plan and the self-interested behaviour of local municipalities, it should come as no surprise that the region has difficulties carrying out its urban sustainable development agenda. Transportation modal shares (under 4 per cent of journeys) and urban morphology in the Waterloo metropolitan area remain consistent with the dispersed model. The ambivalence of Region of Waterloo policy-making also accounts for this situation. It both promotes sustainable urban development and, under pressure from local municipalities and the development industry, and exposed to the habits and preferences of a large share of the population, it accommodates dispersed development. For example, at the very time it pursues the intensification of the LRT corridor, it makes large tracks of suburban land available for car-oriented shopping dominated by large single-storey specialised outlets in a sea of parking.

City of Waterloo

There are important distinctions between City of Waterloo and Region of Waterloo perspectives on urban development. For one, the Mayor of Waterloo is hostile to the LRT due to its cost, the construction and traffic disruptions it will cause and citizen objections, and the City of Waterloo backs off on intensification projects when confronted to challenges from near-by residents (Desmond, 2013; The Record, 2013). More so than the region, the City of Waterloo pays attention to neighbourhood scale reactions to planning proposals. The political system of the City of Waterloo, where council is composed of the mayor and seven councillors, each representing a ward of approximately 15,000 persons, goes a long way in explaining this difference of attitudes. When the political career of council members rides on amiable relations with neighbourhood-based citizen groups, local issues tend to assume prominence on council agendas. The City of Waterloo is torn between contradictory urban development pressures. On the one hand, intensification is a mainstay of its planning objectives, reflecting compliance with provincial and Region of Waterloo directives, along with the realisation that with little undeveloped land left, future growth within the city will inevitably take the form of redevelopment. On the other hand, the electoral system forces it to heed the apprehensions of residents about intensification.

Because of their heavy dependence on property taxes, municipalities are highly sensitive to the real estate market and the preferences of developers. As a City of Waterloo planner contends, it is a waste of municipal resources to zone areas for sustainable urban development formulas if devoid of market appeal and/or unable to interest developers. Fallow land does not generate property tax revenues.

> Our nodes and corridors framework…have opportunities for higher density residential development. And so by default, they all have the potential to be mixed-use areas. It's just whether or not there is consumer preference for this style of housing, whether developers are willing to take this risk. (City of Waterloo Planner 1)

CORE: A city of Waterloo neighbourhood organisation

The land-use intensification and public transit strategies advanced by the Growth Plan have triggered neighbourhood objections in Toronto, where such developments are far more advanced than in the Region of Waterloo. It is not unusual for intensification projects to be greeted by NIMBY-type movements. The iconic reaction against the type of public transportation approach pursued by the province has been the Toronto St Clair Avenue West neighbourhood opposition to a new light rail transit line, which was nonetheless built. The local movement objected to the ensuing disruption of automobile circulation and perceived adverse consequences on street-front retailing. During the 2011 Toronto mayoral campaign, successful candidate, Rob Ford, pointed to St Clair West as an example of a so-called 'war on the car' about to afflict other parts of Toronto slated for new LRT infrastructures.

It is to be expected that the materialisation of development compatible with the Growth Plan in the Region of Waterloo will steer the same type of neighbourhood agitation as witnessed in Toronto. The focus here is on an early neighbourhood reaction of this nature in the City of Waterloo: CORE – Conserve Our Residential Environment – which groups 226 households from an upper middle-class residential area comprising largely pre-Second World War homes. The neighbourhood is adjacent to Uptown Waterloo (the City of Waterloo downtown), which is part of the regionally defined intensification corridor about to host the LRT. At present, there are three residential towers under construction (and six more projected) at the edge of the area represented by CORE. CORE defines its mission as follows:

> Our mandate is to conserve the residential environment of historic Uptown Waterloo neighbourhoods that have earned the right to protection and which play a pivotal role in keeping Uptown stable, vibrant and diverse. If we realise our goal, those who have built these successful neighbourhoods will not be disowned, and the rest of Waterloo will have an irreplaceable endowment to enjoy and treasure. (CORE, 2013b)

CORE was set up in 2012 in reaction to the proposed location of high voltage wiring through the neighbourhood to supply electricity to nearby high-density developments. The proposal was perceived as an unwelcome intrusion in the neighbourhood as all electric wiring is overhead. Trees would have to be cut or trimmed to prevent interference with the new cables. Soon after, residents expressed worries that traffic generated by these new developments or diverted by the dedication of car lanes to the LRT would cut through the neighbourhood. Members of CORE also voiced concern about overshadow effects of new high-rise buildings and incompatibility between these structures and adjacent heritage single-family homes. Attitudes ranged from apprehension of the consequences of intensification to all-out opposition to any high-rise development, in a context of uncertainty about the number and size of such projects in the future.

> It is important to keep in mind that these are first of an unknown number of future buildings. They are being shoehorned onto parcels of land adjacent to existing low-density historic neighbourhoods. The mass of these buildings will literally overshadow zoned density. (CORE, 2013a)

In the absence of formal administrative structure tied to the state apparatus, the influence of neighbourhood movements hinges on their ability to project the image of a local consensus over their objectives. In order to prevent stoking political divisions in a neighbourhood whose votes in the 2011 provincial election were split between the Liberals (48 per cent), the Progressive Conservatives (27.2 per cent) and the centre-left New Democratic Party (20.8 per cent), CORE raises either concrete local issues, such as the ones described above, or upholds uncontroversial principles. The foremost such principle is the protection of the heritage nature of the neighbourhood. It is noteworthy that CORE steers clear of middle-range issues, such as debates around the validity of the Growth Plan, which could have a divisive political effect and thus jeopardise its consensual aspirations. CORE has forged a close relationship with the city councillor representing the ward in which it is located. The councillor has defended its views at council meetings and made CORE aware of planned actions of the city affecting the neighbourhood.

Scaling, neighbourhood mobilisation and the limits of planning

The chapter has shown that by dividing reality into segments and providing conditions for specific views of these segments, scaling fosters the emergence of communities of interest specific to each scale. The case study has revealed distinctions between four scales with an interest in, and impact on, the Growth Plan and its implementation. Differences of attitudes towards this planning exercise were linked to the mandate and the position in the state apparatus of administrative levels associated with three of the scales. Geographical scopes and attendant socioeconomic distributions of all four scales also reverberated on their stands towards the Growth Plan.

Scaling comes out as a source of fragmentation imperilling integrative planning. Not only are scaling-induced segmentations the outcome of administrative levels and the organisational cultures, interest bases and worldviews these levels spawn, but issues related to scales also provide opportunities for political expression for social divisions engendered by the structure of society. Geographies of scaling intersect with societal divisions and, when they lead to mobilisation around issues arising from inter-scalar dissonance, they contribute to the coalescence of these divisions into social movements. For example, such dissonance afforded occasions for non-partisan political expression to the upper-middle-class residents of the investigated City of Waterloo neighbourhood. Inter-scalar dissonance caused them to pull together to safeguard the historical character and tranquility of their neighbourhood, and stave off perceived threats to property values.

Findings side with writings that question the integrative nature of planning (Allmendinger and Tewdwr-Jones, 2002; Tewdwr-Jones and Allmendinger, 1998). The argument of the chapter regarding the impacts of scaling is therefore at odds with theorists who either celebrate the integrative nature of planning processes or propose means of achieving such results (for example, Healey, 1997). The perspective taken here is that fragmentations arising from scaling (and societal structure) are inescapable impediments to the integrative ideals of planning.

As a factor of fragmentation, scaling interferes with dialogical planning. Effects of scaling indeed run counter to the prerequisites – shared culture, interests and worldview – of impartial communication and consensual outcomes, at the heart of dialogical planning. With more immediate relevance to the case study, scaling can also hinder the pursuit of strategies that are wide-scale and consistent over time, by making it difficult for different actors, impregnated with the values of their respective scale, to come together around common objectives and the elaborate processes required to meet planning objectives.

From the perspective of the case study the main tension between scales of planning opposes plans developed by experts and adopted by politicians at the upper administrative scales, and public reactions expressed at, and shaped by, the neighbourhood scale. When conditions to carry political weight at the municipal level – apparent consensus, capacity to mobilise a large number of residents and mount political actions – are present, such reactions can influence municipal policy-making. Their impact is diluted as one climbs the scales, however. Contrary to the situation prevailing in small municipal wards, neighbourhood mobilisation has a limited impact on the election of members of the provincial legislature in constituencies where the population is generally well in excess of 100,000 residents. Another factor of dilution is the wider spectrum of responsibilities at upper echelons of governments. Voters are more likely to make their choice at provincial elections on the grounds of the performance of a government regarding healthcare, education and the management of the economy, than of neighbourhood issues.

Ultimately, the chapter is about obstructions to the capacity of planning, or by extension the state, to mount ambitious interventions to address societal crises. The chapter is thus in agreement with the association Brenner establishes between scaling and the ongoing transition to neoliberalism. Just as his interpretation portrays scaling as a factor of nation-state capacity depletion in the neoliberal age, the chapter links scaling with a weakened planning capacity to address urban problems (Brenner, 2004). Since planning constitutes in its own right an important form of state intervention, both this chapter and the work of Brenner concentrate on the relation between scaling and diminished state capacity. In fact, the identification of connections between heightened effects of scaling on planning and the progression of neoliberalism further advances this meeting of views. Neoliberalism begets deeper social polarisation, which then intersects with geographies of scaling to impair integrative planning processes and large coordinated planning interventions (Brenner and Theodore, 2002). The neighbourhood mobilisation scale constitutes a foremost channel transmitting the effects of polarisation to the planning process. Deeper social divisions, accompanied with reduced adherence to common values, further differentiate neighbourhoods while impeding the acceptance of planning strategies at this level. Standardised approaches adopted by large-scale planning strategies are often incongruent with increasingly diversified neighbourhood realities. These divisions impair the effectiveness of dialogical efforts seeking the agreement of the public over major planning initiatives. They also exacerbate the potential for clashes between planning expertise and views voiced by the public.

Notes

[1] For convenience, references in the chapter to the content of the Growth Plan also pertain to that of The Big Move plan.

[2] In Ontario, there are both single and dual tier municipal administrations, with municipal responsibilities vested either in one local government or shared between a local and a regional administration.

References

Allmendinger, P, Tewdwr-Jones, M, 2002, The communicative turn in urban planning: Unraveling paradigmatic, imperialistic and moralistic dimensions, *Space and Polity* 6, 5–24

Atkinson, G, Oleson, T, 1996, Urban sprawl as a path dependent process, *Journal of Economic Issues* 30, 609–15

Brenner, N, 2000, The urban question: Reflections on Henri Lefebvre, urban theory and the politics of scale, *International Journal of Urban and Regional Research* 24, 361–98

Brenner, N, 2001, The limits of scale? Methodological reflections on scalar structuration, *Progress in Human Geography* 25, 591–614

Brenner, N, 2004, *New state spaces, urban governance and the rescaling of statehood*, Oxford: Oxford University Press

Brenner, N, 2009, Open questions on state rescaling, *Cambridge Journal of Regions, Economy and Society* 2, 123–39

Brenner, N, Theodore, N, 2002, Cities and the geographies of 'actually existing neoliberalism', *Antipode* 34, 349–79

Burchell, RW, 2005, *Sprawl costs: Economic impacts of unchecked development*, Washington, DC: Island Press

Carruthers, JI, Ulfarsson, GF, 2003, Urban sprawl and the cost of public services, *Environment and Planning B* 30, 503–22

CORE (Conserve Our Residential Environment), 2013a, *Presentation to Waterloo Council by CORE*, 14 June, www.facebook.com/CoreWaterloo

CORE (Conserve Our Residential Environment), 2013b, *It has now been one year...*, 16 August, www.facebook.com/CoreWaterloo

Dale, K, Burrell, G, 2008, *The spaces of organization and the organization of space: Power, identity and materiality at work*, Basingstoke: Palgrave Macmillan

Desmond, P, 2013, Region approves purchase of Bombardier LRT, *Waterloo Region Record*, 11 July

Downs, A, 2005, Smart growth: Why we discuss it more than we do it, *Journal of the American Planning Association* 71, 367–78

Filion, P, 2010, Reorienting urban development? Structural obstruction to new urban forms, *International Journal of Urban and Regional Research* 34, 1–19

Forester, J, 1989, *Planning in the Face of Power*, Berkeley, CA: University of California Press

Forester, J, 1999, *The deliberative practitioner: Encouraging participatory planning processes*, Cambridge, MA: MIT Press

Habermas, J, 1984, *The theory of communicative action, Volume 1: Reason and the rationalization of society*, Boston, MA: Beacon Press

Healey, P, 1992, Planning through debate: The communicative turn in planning theory, *Town Planning Review* 62, 143–63

Healey, P, 1997, *Collaborative planning: Shaping places in fragmented societies*, Vancouver, BC: UBC Press

Healey, P, 1998, Building institutional capacity through collaborative approaches to urban planning, *Environment and Planning A*, 30, 1531–46

Healey, P, 1999, Deconstructing new communicative planning theory: A reply to Tewdwr-Jones and Allmendinger, *Environment and Planning A*, 31, 1129–35

Huxley, M, 2000, Institutional analysis, communicative planning, and shaping places, *Journal of Planning Education and Research* 19, 111–21

Innes, JE, 1996, Planning through consensus building: A new view of the comprehensive planning ideal, *Journal of the American Planning Association* 62, 460–72

Kunstler, JH, 1993, *The geography of nowhere: The rise and decline of America's Man-made landscape*, New York: Free Press

McGuirk, PM, 2001, Situating communicative planning theory: Context, power, and knowledge, *Environment and Planning A* 33, 195–217

Maréchal, G, Linstead, S, Munro, I, 2013, The territorial organization: History, divergence and possibilities, *Culture and Organizations* 19, 185–208

Marshall, A, 2000, *How cities work: Suburbs, sprawl, and the roads not taken*, Austin, TX: University of Texas Press

Marshall, JD, Brauer, M, Frank, LD, 2009, Healthy neighborhoods: Walkability and air pollution, *Environmental Health Perspectives* 117, 1752–9

Marston, SA, Smith, N, 2001, States, scales and households: Limits to scale thinking? A response to Brenner, *Progress in Human Geography* 25, 615–19

Metrolinx, 2008, *The big move: Transforming transportation in the Greater Toronto and Hamilton Area*, Toronto, Ontario: Metrolinx

Mouffe, C, 2000, *The democratic paradox*, London: Verso

Neumann, RP, 2009, Political economy: Theorizing scale, *Progress in Human Geography* 25, 615–19

Ontario (Government of, Ministry of Infrastructure Renewal), 2006, *Growth plan for the Greater Golden Horseshoe*, Toronto, Ontario: Queen's Printer for Ontario

Pender, T, 2013, Region defends actions to curb sprawl: Council votes to appeal decision opening more lands to development, *Waterloo Region Record*, 30 January

Richardson, HW, Bae, C-H, 2004, *Urban sprawl in Western Europe and the United States*, Aldershot: Ashgate

Smith, N, 1995, Remaking scale: Competition and cooperation in prenational and postnational Europe, in H Eskelinen, F Snickars (eds) *Competitive European peripheries*, pp 59–74, Berlin: Springer

Spears, J, 2010, Ontario will delay transit projects as deficit soars, *Toronto Star*, 25 March

STORM (Save the Oak Ridges Moraine Coalition) (nd) *About STORM*, www.stormcoalition.org/pages/about.html

Swyngedouw, E, 1997, Neither global nor local: 'Glocalization' and the politics of scale, in K Cox (ed) *Spaces of Globalization*, pp 137–66, New York: Guilford

Taylor, Z, 2013, Right-wing populism and the curious revival of regional planning in Toronto, *Society for American City and Regional Planning History*, Biennial Conference, October, Toronto, Ontario

Tewdwr-Jones, M, Allmendinger, P, 1998, Deconstructing communicative rationality: A critique of Habermas collaborative planning, *Environment and Planning A* 30, 1975–89

The Record (Waterloo Region), 2013, Waterloo not ruling out new ideas for Uptown, *Waterloo Region Record*, 29 June

Trice, HS, Beyer, JM, 1993, *The cultures of work organizations*, Englewood Cliffs, NJ: Prentice Hall

Waterloo (Region of), 2011, *Regional official plan*, Kitchener, Ontario: Region of Waterloo

15

Flexible local planning: linking community initiative with municipal planning in Volda, Norway

Jørgen Amdam

Introduction

Comprehensive municipal land-use and 'community strategic planning' have been a part of local political and administrative responsibilities in Norway since 1965, although many Norwegian municipalities encounter significant challenges around the design of effective planning processes, decision-making and implementation. A number of tensions undermine the efficacy of plans and some of these centre on the interface between strategic priority and the local needs sometimes expressed through community action. In this chapter, I will use the Volda municipality – together with results from national research – to expose the shortcomings of local planning in Norway and its *interactions* with strategic national priorities, local needs and community action. Complexity theories are used to explain these shortcomings and also to point to potential remedies, paying attention in particular to the appropriate level at which services are planned and delivered. The chapter will use the idea of 'complex adaptive systems' to examine the blurring between the public and private in municipal planning and as a framework for thinking about the processes needed to link community initiative with the orthodoxies and instruments of municipal planning.

The chapter is concerned primarily with linkages and with formulating public policy, and producing plans that are operable across different scales. In focusing on scales of responsibility, I will contrast national and regional priorities with the initiatives from action groups, and from local organisations and communities which seek to strengthen civil society and localise municipal functions, providing a counterbalance to regional and national directive. In light of the inherent complexities of planning and delivery systems (see Rittel and Webber, 1973), I will spotlight the role of community actors and civil society in working with the local, regional and national state to resolve critical challenges and ensure more tailored service outcomes.

Complex rural challenges and changes

Norway is sparsely populated, having just 16 inhabitants per square kilometre. Moreover, less than a fifth (19 per cent) of the country's land area is populated, with the remaining 80 per cent completely devoid of people. Although characteristically rural – and subject to typical rural pressures such as depopulation, economic fragility and the erosion of vital public and private services – Norway's rural areas are in some respects atypical, being significantly influenced by the oil economy. This economy has generated pockets of affluence and areas in which the resident population is growing and there is significant demand for new housing, either for permanent or seasonal occupancy.

Image 15.1: The landscape of Volda municipality

© Jørgen Amdam

Volda municipality is located on the west coast of the country, in the county of Møre og Romsdal. It had a population of just over 8,800 in 2013, with 6,000 residents in the centre and the remainder spread across the municipality's rural hinterland. Total population rose by

11 per cent between 2001 and 2011, although the number of people living in the hinterland dropped by 10 per cent during the same period. This increased degree of concentration is accentuated by the presence of Volda University College with its 2,500 resident students (Volda Kommune, 2012b).

Norway's west coast communities have traditionally been dependent on agriculture and other primary industries, including fishing. This generated a land- or resource-based culture reflected in a degree of homogeneity in local communities: differences between communities were bigger than differences within them (Gammelsæter et al, 2004). This situation has changed in recent years, however, with economic shifts bringing greater heterogeneity in the social make-up, signalled by new commuting patterns, the search for employment across a greater range of sectors, and patterns of movement, social-contact and sociability that appear more suburban than traditionally rural. There is greater outward complexity in communities, manifest in different occupations, interests, networks, social relations and leisure pursuits.

These more complex communities present conventional planning with a critical challenge: that challenge is one of connectivity and of ensuring that a greater diversity of aspiration and need is acknowledged by public policy and planning, and that communities become co-producers of programmes, projects and other interventions that are alive to the reality of social complexity. One way to begin thinking about this challenge is to view Volda's communities as components within a 'complex adaptive system' (Innes and Booher, 2010), which provides a means of 'reading' the scale links and relationships in a locality, and also a way of thinking through how planning might itself negotiate this complexity.

Innes and Booher (2010) have identified the key features of complex adaptive systems (see Table 15.1) and this provides a useful descriptor of the context for local planning. The view of planning being embedded in, and inseparable from, a broader operating system (that transcends scale and cuts across sectors) is reminiscent of Friedmann's theory of a 'transactive planning' (Friedmann, 1973; see also Parker, Chapter 10, this volume) that is necessarily part of an open society in which, in one way or another, we are all of us planners but with varying influence on processes, decisions and actions (Gallent and Robinson, 2013). The remainder of this chapter is split into two sections. In the first section, Innes and Booher's descriptors of a complex adaptive system are used to show how rural communities are embedded in the local system alongside conventional planning processes. In the second section, it is argued that convention must give way to 'flexible local planning'

Table 15.1: Features of complex adaptive systems

Features	Summary descriptions
Agents	The system comprises large numbers of individual agents connected through multiple networks.
Interactions	The agents interact dynamically, exchanging information and energy, based on heuristics that organise the interactions locally. Even if specific agents only interact with a few others, the effects propagate through the system. As a result the system has a memory that is not located at a specific place, but is distributed throughout the system.
Non-linearity	The interactions are non-linear, interactive, recursive, and self-referential. There are many direct and indirect feedback loops.
System behaviour	The system is open, the behaviour of the system is determined by the interactions, not the components, and the behaviour of the system cannot be understood by looking at the components. It can only be understood by looking at the interactions. Coherent and novel patterns of order emerge.
Robustness and adaptation	The system displays both the capacity to maintain its viability and the capacity to evolve. With sufficient diversity the heuristics will evolve, the agents will adapt to each other, and the system can reorganise its internal structure without the intervention of an outside agent.

Source: Innes and Booher, 2010, 32

that is able to work with open local and regional systems, delivering cooperation and collaboration in the face of potential conflict and diversity of interest.

Volda as a complex adaptive system

Agents and stakeholders

The inhabitants of any place are bearers of individual values, norms, intentions, knowledge and resources that are critical for planning processes (Healey, 2006), making them important stakeholders in local development and planning. 'Stakeholders' tend to be defined by the direct economic or social interest they have in planning decisions and in consequent outcomes (Amdam and Veggeland, 2011). Conventional planning processes have often sought a controlled and formalised input from different stakeholders, but it becomes apparent in many situations that the input of participants into the planning process can seldom be stage-managed in the way that policy-makers might wish.

Community stakeholders are often part of strong and well-developed social networks, pursuing key agendas around schools, healthcare, roads and other services. They display a readiness to mobilise if their interests appear threatened. In his study of Volda in the 1960s, Caulkins (1994) found a strong tendency towards community-level organisation, but low levels of participation in municipal or regional bodies or groups. A repeat study undertaken more recently (Caulkins, 2004) has suggested that community-level voluntary action remains strong in Volda (though it is skewed towards particular groups within communities), but that inhabitants are now better connected to the centre. Young families, in particular, now look beyond their immediate village and participate in groups based in Volda itself, as this is now where they work and where they develop the strongest social ties. Caulkins has been able to show that the rural insularity of the 1960s has given way to greater connectivity across the municipality, which is largely a result of economic shifts. Fifty years ago, planning was administering to the needs of relatively closed, separated communities. Today, it is dealing with a society that is more connected and where the boundaries between places (and between interests) are more perforated.

The municipality is arguably more complex than it was; interests are more varied, as are needs, and hence greater flexibility is required in the planning response. In order to achieve that flexibility, it needs to move away from its emphasis on seeking controlled and formalised input from participants.

Interactions

Planning in Norway started to become more rigid and formalised in the 1960s, however. Legislation in the middle of that decade established new institutions, set up to deal with the needs of rural communities as understood at that time. Before that date, the process of seeking development permission was fairly simple and involved interaction with a couple of local bodies. Since then, however, the system has grown in complexity and today, at least 22 separate permissions are needed to progress a residential development. The system requires great tenacity on the part of applicants, who will spend a considerable amount of time interacting and negotiating with different agencies. Left to operate in this mode, the rigid structures of land-use control will act as a brake on local development. The alternative is to let 'the agents interact dynamically, exchanging information and energy, based on heuristics that organize the interactions locally'. One possible heuristic device here is that of the 'planning project' (Zeote and Spit, 2002) that focuses skills and experience around replicable schemes rather than attempting top-down coordination (or 'comprehensive planning') at the municipal level. The system that has evolved over the last half century has become increasingly linear, however: a strict sequencing of events is required for development to progress.

Nonlinearity

Linear planning models run though a sequence of objectives, alternatives, predicted consequences, decisions and implementation (Allmendinger, 2009; Friedmann 1987). These models try, through the exercise of executive power, to deliver 'comprehensive instrumental local planning' in which participation and other necessary activities are rigidly staged. In a more complex and dynamic society, this kind of comprehensive instrumental planning will seldom work. The instrumental model has some traction for bounded projects, but increasing complexity makes it difficult, or even dangerous, to follow this model in a dynamic and unbounded reality. The challenges that are faced, and the actions that seen to be required, are the product of interactions between a large set of stakeholders who exist within a highly complex system. Information changes all the time and the challenges keep evolving. Problems that are 'solved' reappear in 'new clothes' (R Amdam, 2011) because they are of course 'wicked problems' (Rittel and Webber, 1973) that defy resolution.

Responses therefore need to be non-linear, interactive, recursive and self-referential (Innes and Booher, 2010). The linear process dedicates a fixed quantum of time to each stage before progression to the next stage is triggered. Non-linearity means working at different stages simultaneously; it also means not being constrained by the time scales of regulatory process (see Matthews, Chapter 3, this volume) and, in particular, moving to 'active engagement' with communities and avoiding the containment of 'invited participation' at fixed times. In Volda, local communities have become adept at disrupting the linearity of planning processes by using their network connections to express opposition and dissent, not at the particular outcomes that planning is seeking, but at the manner in which planning tries to make decisions and drive forward processes. Effective planning must deal with this complexity and begin to embed itself in real community processes rather than seeking the quickest – linear – path, which is rarely the line of least resistance.

System behaviour

Regional and local challenges and development problems are not bounded by public or rigid sectoral frameworks, and the borders and networks of regional systems are dynamic compared to static administrative jurisdictions. Economic clusters or flows, in particular, are seldom aligned with administrative boundaries (Porter, 1990; Storper, 1995) and this reality is slowly being acknowledged. At a national level, government in Norway has been wrestling with the challenge of planning different activities across boundaries. Locally, it is recognised that economic systems, and consequent movements of goods, services and people, have become considerably messier over the last few decades. In Volda, only a small fraction of people now derive their incomes from land-based activities. Farming is no longer the dominant activity. Likewise, the proportion employed in the oil industry is low; though that industry plays a key role in wealth generation and in supporting a range of service-sector occupations.

Robustness and adaptation

Volda, then, is characterised by increased social complexity and interconnectedness than was apparent in the 1960s, by more regular interaction by stakeholders (triggered by conflicting and competing demands), by linearity in the planning system that runs contrary to the non-linearity of the complex adaptive system of which stakeholders are now a part, and by unbounded systemic behaviour underpinned by economic change. The situation is a typical one, but poses a critical challenge to the planning orthodoxy. A linear, bureaucratic system, bounded by fixed jurisdictions provides a reasonably good tool for controlling change and limiting development. It is less effective, however, at working with multiple actors (each operating to different timescales) to stimulate new forms of development while balancing different social, economic and environmental interests. For that reason, it is vital that local and regional land-use planning is in a sense responsive and sensitive to community changes and goals: that it becomes flexible and moves away from the mindset of command and control, seeking consensus around visions and content (Amdam and Veggeland, 2011).

The pattern of development pressure in Volda is sporadic. There are few large development sites, but many locations where single-home projects are being progressed. Each one is subject to the linear frameworks and sequence of permissions set out above. There is a general feeling, among actors and commentators, that a very heavy and bureaucratic system – designed for major development – is being imposed in rural areas where development pressures are very light. The centre is using a sledge-hammer to crack a nut: greater discretion and flexibility is needed. There is also a core belief in the wisdom of communities doing more for themselves, while being relieved of the burden of excessive public-sector planning.

Planning for local rural development in Volda

Many of these issues and needs have been acknowledged by Volda's political leaders since the local elections of 2011. A working group with participation from all the political parties and involving all local communities was tasked to recommend new approaches to rural development (Volda Kommune, 2012a). In April 2013, the municipality (or *Kommune*) agreed to:

• support local initiatives and provide administrative assistance to community-led planning and development;
• distinguish between land for agricultural use (and 'modern production') and other land (with relaxed planning) for residential use or new forms of economic activity, where communities take control of development and are freed from the normal regulatory constraints;
• generally devolve responsibility for planning, development, infrastructure investment and the oversight of land transactions to community actors.

The guiding principle has been the transfer of power and responsibility to communities, who are thereafter supported by the municipality, which maintains a dialogue with those communities around the challenges faced in the wider area. Different communities, however, have responded in different ways to the opportunities presented by the policy shift. Those with a tradition of internal cooperation and external linkage (a store of bonding and bridging social capital) (see Rydin, Chapter 2, this volume) have been quick off the mark. Others, marked out by serious internal conflicts and little communication with the municipality, have been slower to respond to the change and will doubtless need additional support.

This difference points to a broader challenge with community-led action and control. In a world of top-down planning, bureaucracy has a levelling effect: the benefits or problems it brings tends to be evenly felt, although in Volda the new planning strategy is more *reactive* to community desire and needs. If there is no clear expression of those needs and desires, then there is a risk that the municipality will not *react*: very proactive communities (with abundant social capital) will grab the attention of the centre and receive a great deal of support for their community-based initiatives. Quieter, less proactive, communities can slip beneath the radar. They may not have the capacity to take control of their own development and may therefore fall behind.

While the extension of powers to general development and planning is new, many communities already have a track-record of controlling certain local services. Half of all kindergartens in Volda are 'voluntary controlled' and a social enterprise was responsible for the building of a new sports stadium in 2012. These have been provided through an existing mechanism whereby the municipality gifts land to community groups, acts as guarantor for bank loans, assists in the planning process and, where necessary, will rent space in new facilities in order to guarantee income to meet running costs. So there was already a willingness to support community action before 2013, but the new approach is more comprehensive and extends into all areas of planning and rural development; it seeks a consistent bottom-up perspective in decision-making.

Advocates of collaborative planning approaches (for example, Healey, 2006; Forester, 1993; 1999; and Innes and Booher, 2010) point to the many principles that need to be adhered to if public policy is to respond to the challenge of social complexity. There should, for example, be a routine sharing of information between partners, open dialogue, avoidance of expert privilege, and a transformation of the planner into a 'reflective practitioner', able to respond to different situations as they arise. Principles, however, do not suggest a one-size-fits-all model. Rather, they need to be applied in different ways to suit different contexts. The concept of 'flexible and communicative local planning' (hereafter just 'flexible local planning') has emerged from a number of studies in Volda and across Norway (J Amdam, 2000; 2001a; 2001b; 2003; Amdam and Amdam, 2000; R Amdam, 1997; 2011) and represents an attempt to bridge the instrumental and communicative (that is, district-wide and community-based) aspects of planning, dealing with scale and with the tension between top-down priority and local ambition.

In previous work, five key attributes of flexible local planning have been set out, starting with the mobilisation of stakeholders, the organisation of those stakeholders and the development of tactics, implementation, and then a series of feedback loops that use formative learning to continually adapt this process to develop context and the interplay with that context (see Amdam and Amdam, 2000; R Amdam, 2005). The model is shown in Figure 15.1, and is not dissimilar to the strategic, tactical and operative planning described in the Norwegian Planning and Building Law 2008. The key feature of this flexible

Figure 15.1: Model for flexible and communicative local planning

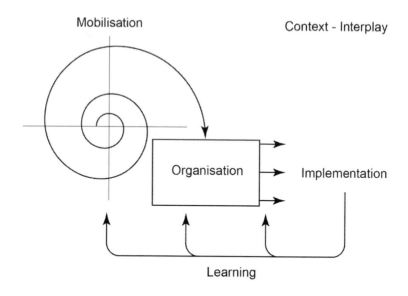

Source: Jørgen Amdam

local planning is the adaptation of process to context. It tries to adjust in response to continual feedback, mobilising new stakeholders as necessary, shifting its organisation and tactics, and therefore seeking new ways of implementation. It has a project focus and represents a form of 'situational' or adaptive planning that attempts to combine the (non-linear) principles of self-governed local development with the orthodoxies of more process-driven (and linear) instrumental planning. I now examine how these five attributes come together in Volda.

The mobilisation of stakeholders (1)

Dynamic, complex systems tend to defy simple coordination. Stakeholders are self-selecting and will mobilise in response to sporadic triggers and not necessarily at the instruction of local government, although municipalities can play a part in creating the conditions for 'active citizenship', by creating the frameworks and opportunities for continual involvement in political and planning processes. Finding a way to draw out local knowledge is key to flexible local planning, and the path to uncovering that local knowledge begins with the creation of arenas in which the norms, values and interests of different groups can be expressed in open dialogue. Open dialogue, which is accessible to all stakeholders, needs to replace the private dialogue (between private interests, political leaders and the planning profession) that has characterised past planning processes. This private dialogue happens behind closed doors, and when the decisions it supports are finally revealed to the wider community, it becomes a source of conflict. Open dialogue, however, exposes the interests and rationales that drive decisions, enhancing democracy and aiding community development (Amdam and Amdam, 2000).

This process points to the need for a 'moral discourse' which underpins consensus-building (Amdam, 2000; R Amdam, 1997; 2001) and which delivers trust within the process, a key principle of collaborative planning. There are, of course, many techniques for delivering this mobilisation, including community workshops. Workshops, however, are most successful in communities where interaction is an everyday feature of community life and where there is the necessary 'interactive infrastructure' (see Kilpatrick et al, Chapter 5, this volume) of meeting spaces and hubs where people regularly come together to engage in open dialogue. That infrastructure provides a platform and context for mobilisation, though the municipality may need to be more pro-active in seeding that mobilisation and consequent dialogue in some instances.

As in many planning systems, the Volda Municipality must perform a balancing act between its strategic role and its desire to harness local community energies in support of specific projects and outcomes. Its dealings with communities needs to take place within a strategic framework, that deals with the 'municipality as a community' (that is, its social development and wellbeing), its future land-use needs, and the particular projects that will contribute towards the achievement of broader goals (that is, area-based policies). Volda currently has a raft of inherited and emergent strategic-level plans: a comprehensive ('community') plan from 1998, a strategic land-use plan for the hinterland from the same year, a plan for the town of Volda from 2010, and area-based plans for specific rural communities which have adoption dates from between 1990 and 2000. On top of these, there are also a number of service or thematic plans – dealing with sports, childcare, climate change mitigation, healthcare, social care, water supply, and a range of social issues – that are regularly renewed, but which are public-sector led.

The context for communicative local planning in Volda is not an easy one. The municipality is tasked to maintain its strategic planning function. It is facing pressure to produce a new raft of strategic plans – dealing with policing, traffic safety, sports, climate, health and housing – on a time-scale that would make it difficult to connect with community and strategic priorities. The speed at which new plans can be drawn up has, however, been limited by a dearth of planning capacity within the municipality and by economic uncertainties. This has provided communities with an opportunity to work with local planners on a shared timescale. It now seems certain that community input into Volda's future community vision and its land-use policies will be significant.

Organisation and tactics (2)

Shared knowledge must become the basis for planning strategies, programmes and projects. The open dialogue described above needs to be steered to resolve conflicts and bring all stakeholders to agreement around common interests (R Amdam, 2001; 2005). This suggests particular organisational needs. For some projects, community groups may be able to take responsibility for planning and implementation. This will certainly be the case for small residential schemes, but for more complex projects – where there may be greater scope for conflict – the organisational needs will be different. 'Owners' of tasks will need to be identified, responsibilities discussed and the whole process framed in order to achieve an acceptable outcome. There may be some independent mediation in this process (similar to that described by Gallent, Chapter 16, this volume), and in some situations, the current author has been involved in framing the process, encouraging community actors to think about:

• what they can and should do for themselves;
• what they cannot do, who outside the community might take responsibility, and how they can motivate others and influence outcomes;
• what they must do in partnership, who the partners might be, and how they might work with those partners. (Amdam and Amdam, 2000)

It is also the case, however, that Volda municipality plays a key facilitation role, accepting the responsibility it has under Norwegian law. Finding the tactics needed to implement plans, including working with community stakeholders to overcome local barriers, is a key responsibility, although this is made more difficult by a recent history of rapidly shifting national priorities. There is no feed-back loop from community input to those high-level priorities, so the municipality will regularly find itself pursuing goals with its community partners that are suddenly mismatched against infrastructure, rural development or social policies cascading down from national government. This is not of course an unusual predicament for local partners. Communication across the local/community scales is far easier to achieve than genuinely bottom-up national policy. The key problem facing Volda, and other parts of Norway, however, is the degree of prescription contained in national policy and the tendency for that policy to have very particular and unwelcome local outcomes. In 2011, for example, a new school was opened in one of Volda's remoter rural communities where just six children have been born in the last five years. The school cost €10 million and was part of a municipal programme of upgrading, guided by national priority. Elsewhere in the municipality, another school – built in 1976 and providing education for 400 pupils – has been condemned as unsafe, largely because of a lack of maintenance.

Implementation (3)

In theory, effective mobilisation (drawing out key knowledge) and a suitable organisation of tactics will lay the foundations for the implementation of projects that enjoy broad support. At that point, the communicative processes can give way to some form of conventional delivery in instances where projects are not small-scale and community-led, although implementation presents its own challenges. Beyond agreeing what should be done, community actors need to play a role in deciding how it should be done. A common flash-point in the planning process has been disagreement around implementation, or how to achieve an agreed goal. The success of flexible local planning depends on dialogue that continues through the planning and implementation phases. Figure 15.1 points to active learning during mobilisation (learning about which groups to mobilise and ways to motivate them), organisation (learning about context and situational tactics), and implementation (maintaining the dialogue with users as plans become delivered projects). In instances where implementation is not in the hands of the community, those communities have formed groups to oversee delivery. In recent years, there has been considerable tension between these groups and the municipality. The squeeze on public budgets over the last five years has meant that agreed projects have not always been delivered in a way that has been entirely acceptable to communities. In 2014, Volda municipality must reduce spending on public services by 10 per cent, or €4 million. This follows on from similar cuts since 2009, which have affected, among other services, childcare and schools in Volda's rural areas. Communities have become frustrated by the mismatch between agreed and actual service provision and have learnt that investment in a collaborative process does not guarantee the services they need. The dialogue that is now happening in the municipality, however, does of course help communities understand the pressure on public finances and acts as a further catalyst for the many voluntary initiatives, some focused on child care, that have sprung up in recent years. There is increased understanding not only of what communities 'can and should do for themselves', but also of what they *must*, in some instances, do for themselves. Crisis, and the costs of public service provision, provide an impetus for self-help (see also Kilpatrick et al, Chapter 5, this volume).

Learning (4)

Learning is central to flexible local planning. Learning happens through 'interactions [that] are non-linear, interactive, recursive, and self-referential'. It happens continually within a collaborative process, shaping tactics and informing implementation, although learning needs to happen through open dialogue, with knowledge being shared across partners. With the sharing of knowledge comes the possibility of building consensus (as partners come to understand the challenges, opportunities and constraints of a situation), but where knowledge becomes concentrated, the balance of power in a process shifts. Stöhr (1990) and Friedmann (1987; 1992) have shown that the 'monopolisation of power' poses a significant danger to collaborative processes. Knowledge may be used selectively – by political, expert or even community elites – to coerce others and achieve particular outcomes. There is no foolproof way of preventing this from happening, but if flexible local planning is to have any chance of succeeding (in the building of consensus or in the achievement of acceptable outcomes) significant effort needs to be expended on the learning process, on bringing stakeholders together, on accessing new voices and opinions, and on ensuring that there is very broad awareness of the contextual challenges that planning faces.

As an epilogue to this point, it seems clear today that the learning process in Volda has not worked as well as it might have done. The openness of the municipality to community input significantly raised the expectation of better and more comprehensive service provision in Volda's rural hinterland, although it is now apparent that there will be a withdrawal of many services in light of funding cuts. Collaborative processes rely on the honesty and sincerity of partners, who need to be clear about constraints. This is a prerequisite to building trust across networks (Innes and Booher, 2010) and in Volda that trust has been denuded by recent experiences: by platitudes not followed up with investment.

Interplay with context (5)

Flexible local planning is *situational* planning. It is situated in its physical and socio-cultural context, and attempts to read that context (through open dialogue) and adapt to it, although there is much within and outwith that context that can threaten its success. It aims towards consensus-building and the avoidance of outcomes based solely on the exercise of executive power, but can these outcomes really be avoided? In Volda, the context for education was dissected by key public and community partners during their open dialogue, and through that dialogue they came to an understanding of necessary response. That did not, however, prevent a top-down intervention that has oversupplied educational provision in one location and caused a crisis of under-supply in another. There are always stakeholders, inside or outside the planning community, which elect not to involve themselves in consensus-building processes, and which have power over resources, processes or other stakeholders. They act either in self-interest or in strategic interest, which may not align with needs or the objectives that emerge from community action.

This is not to say, however, that communities are always able to easily agree objectives, build consensus around necessary action, or engage in self-help. They have different capacities. In Volda, some rural communities have a long and positive history of voluntary action. For these communities, more sustained engagement with the municipality is yielding significant benefits, and it seems natural for them to ask what they can do for themselves and how they can work with others to address local needs or take control of development outcomes. The 'cultural' context for flexible local planning is uneven: in contrast to those communities which are proactive, there are others which are more accustomed to sitting back and waiting for solutions to arrive from the centre. Put simply, some communities are rich in the capacity to take control, but others are comparatively poorer. The processes outlined in this chapter are without doubt most successful in those communities more inclined towards voluntary action. This can create an unevenness in service provision, either because some communities do more and achieve more, or because communities demand different types of intervention. As an example, two schools in two villages just 7 km apart have recently opened. The first is a municipal-controlled school delivered as a public-sector led project. The second is a community-controlled school. Residents in the two villages wanted different forms of provision and were not able to work together towards a shared outcome. Either of the schools could have met local need, but the result has been over-provision and a further stretching of budgets. Perhaps either stronger or weaker intervention was needed: stronger intervention to deliver a single municipal-controlled school, or weaker intervention (and more limited investment) to force cooperation and a solution between the villages.

It could be argued that the challenge here is dual-mode operation, or perhaps that insufficient attention was given to the cooperation needed between these communities. The focus in this chapter has been placed on links between community actors and a district-wide public planning process, but lateral cooperation between communities at the same level is also important. Planners have a role in helping resolve conflict and acting as agents of change, but it is difficult to reconcile competing values (Forester, 1993; Sager, 1994) of the type that played a part in delivering the school provision outcome above. What we see in this case, however, is also a failure to learn, and therefore to cooperate, motivate and organise. Failures in collaborative planning are perhaps inevitable in an 'uncollaborative world' (Brand and Gaffikin, 2007).

Conclusions

Public local planning in Norway can be reorganised so that it functions as flexible planning, embracing different stakeholders and their particular challenges and actions across scales. The success of this type of planning is dependent, in part, on a change of political and administrative attitude and leadership, and also on establishing a reflective process that is able to adapt to different circumstances. What I have described is a strategic decision to seed and support community action as a particular approach to project implementation, and an extension of established planning processes in Norway. 'Self-governed local development' is a recent phenomenon that builds on the past successes achieved through voluntary action. It also responds to the appetite that some communities have displayed for greater local control. Unlike simple acts of voluntarism, however, this seeded community action has raised the expectation of external support and investment. Because it has arrived at the same time as public spending cuts, it has been unfairly associated with frustration and failure. As a response to more varied needs, however, the approach of flexible local planning – shared knowledge through open dialogue, feeding into programmes that are alive to the complexity of the problems being addressed – seems to be a reasonable one.

In Volda, the administrative and political leadership has come to accept the underlying wisdom of this approach: of assigning communities a more significant role in addressing their own needs, although it is also accepted that the jump from theory to practice is not easy. A very significant challenge in Volda has been the undermining of localised solutions by uncoordinated state interventions that often seem to come out of nowhere to jeopardise faith in the local partnerships. Similarly, municipal budgets are often asynchronous with the investments needed to support some local projects.

There is, however, a feeling in Volda – and elsewhere in Norway – that a loosening of planning control and responsibility at the interface with communities is the right trajectory. This approach has grown from the bottom-up; not necessarily from communities themselves but from local government. It was Volda itself that recommended and implemented a new approach to rural development. Well-functioning, flexible, communicative and participatory planning will, however, remain a dream rather than a reality until national government frees the local state from many of the strictures, planning and budgetary, that still shape its relationship with community action.

References

Allmendinger, P, 2009, *Planning theory*, Basingstoke: Palgrave-Macmillan

Amdam, J, 2000, Confidence building in local planning and development: Some experience from Norway, *European Planning Studies* 8, 5, 581–600

Amdam, J, 2001a, The politics of local land-use planning in Norway, in R Byron, J Hutson (eds) *Community development on the North Atlantic margin*, Ashgate: Aldershot

Amdam, J, 2001b, Flexibility in regional planning, in T Herrschel, P Tallberg (eds) *The role of regions? Networks, scale, territory*, Sweden: Kristianstads boktrykkeri

Amdam, J, 2003, Structure and strategy for regional learning and innovation: Challenges for regional planning, *European Planning Studies* 11, 6, 429–60

Amdam, J, Amdam, R, 2000, *Kommunikativ planlegging*, Oslo: Samlaget

Amdam, J, Veggeland, N, 2011, *Teorier om samfunnsstyring og planlegging*, Oslo: Universitetsforlaget

Amdam, R, 1997, Empowerment planning in local communities: Some experiences from combining communicative and instrumental rationality in local planning in Norway, *International Planning Studies* 2, 3, 329–45

Amdam, R, 2001, Empowering new regional political institutions: A Norwegian case, *Planning Theory and Practice* 2, 2, 169–85

Amdam, R, 2005, *Planlegging som handling*, Oslo: Universitetsforlaget

Amdam, R, 2011, *Planning in health promotion work: An empowerment model*, Routledge studies in public health, London: Routledge

Brand, R, Gaffikin, F, 2007, Collaborative planning in an uncollaborative world, *Planning Theory* 6, 3, 282–313

Caulkins, DD, 1994, Norwegians: Cooperative individualists, in M Farber, C Ember, D Levinson (eds) *Portraits of culture, ethnographic originals, Volume 3*, pp 1–30, Prentice Hall, NJ: Upper Saddle River

Caulkins, DD, 2004, Organizational memberships and crosscutting ties: Bonding or bridging social capital?, in S Prakash, P Selle (eds) *Investigating social capital*, London: SAGE

Forester, J, 1993, *Critical theory, public policy and planning practice: Toward a critical pragmatism*, Albany, NY: University of New York Press

Forester, J, 1999, *The deliberative practitioner: Encouraging participatory planning processes*, Cambridge MA: MIT Press

Friedmann, J, 1973, *Re-tracking America: A theory of transactive planning*, New York City: Anchor Press/Doubleday

Friedmann, J, 1987, *Planning in the public domain*, Princeton, NJ: Princeton University Press

Friedmann, J, 1992, *Empowerment: The politics of alternative development*, Cambridge, MA and Oxford, UK: Blackwell Publishers

Gallent, N, Robinson, S, 2013, *Neighbourhood planning: Communities, networks and governance*, Bristol: Policy Press

Gammelsæter, H, Bukve, O, Løseth, A, 2004, *Nord-Vestlandet – liv laga?*, Ålesund: Sunnmørsposten forlag

Healey, P, 2006, *Collaborative planning: Shaping places in fragmented societies*, Basingstoke: Palgrave-Macmillan

Healey, P, de Magalhaes, C, Madanipour, A, 1999, Institutional capacity-building, Urban Planning and urban regeneration projects, *Futura (Journal of the Finnish Society for Futures Studies)* 3, 117–37

Innes, JE, Booher, DE, 2010, *Planning with complexity: An introduction to collaborative rationality for public policy*, London and New York: Routledge

Porter, M, 1990, *The competitive advantage of nations*, London: Macmillan

Rittel, H, Webber, M, 1973, Dilemmas in a general theory of planning, *Policy Sciences* 4, 155–69

Sager, T, 1994, *Communicative planning theory*, Aldershot: Avebury

Storper, M, 1995, *The regional world: Territorial development in a global economy*, New York City: Guilford

Stöhr, W (ed), 1990, *Global challenge and local response: Initiatives for economic regeneration in contemporary Europe*, London and New York: Mansell

Volda Kommune, 2012a, *Strategi for busetjing på bygdene*, Volda Kommune

Volda Kommune, 2012b, *Kommunal planstrategi for Volda commune 2012–2015*, Volda Kommune

Zoete, PR, Spit, T, 2002, Project planning and regional planning: Linking as a vital challenge, paper presented to *AESOP Conference*, 18–23 July, Volos, Greece

16

Connecting to the citizenry? Support groups in community planning in England

Nick Gallent

Introduction

Politicians in many industrialised nations have sought to connect more directly to the citizenry, accepting that the needs of communities are ever more complex and diverse (Rittel and Webber, 1973; see also Amdam, Chapter 15, this volume) and that, in response, planning and service delivery need to become increasingly sophisticated, cross-sectoral and collaborative endeavours (Marsh and Rhodes, 1992). Such collaboration is not always easy to achieve. Those operating in the traditional 'public' (that is, within government) and 'non-public' realms (that is, voluntary, private and community actors) have tended to form their own discrete groupings, with the former coalescing into 'policy communities' and the latter into 'interest groups', with only weak connectivity between the two (Marsh et al, 2009, 621).

This *weak connectivity*, and the means of overcoming it, provides the focus for this chapter. The observation of Marsh et al (2009) is generally that traditional policy communities have their own ways of working, or operational protocols (operating in Habermas's 'system world': see van der Pennen and Schreuders, Chapter 8, this volume). Moreover, they connect most easily with professional networks and qualified individuals. In contrast, the 'interest groups' bring together non-experts and actors, who feel unconstrained by legal frameworks and who pursue agendas that serve local interests and ambitions. The former operate in the framework of *democracy*: their role is often to give expert and impartial advice to elected representatives, who make decisions and take actions on the back of it. The latter, on the other hand, are part of a *governance* shift that has, in recent decades, challenged representative democracy and the professionalised model of government, of which closed policy communities are an integral part. Owen et al (2007, 50–1) argue that democracy and governance are diametrically opposed concepts. The former is 'top-down', rooted in 'representative authority' and achieves its ends through mandated power. It places great weight on a strategic perspective (arguing the case for a broader public good) and its *modus operandi* is through local authorities, as the instruments of change, who work in partnership with other professional agencies. The local authorities provide accountability while their partners – in fields such as economic development and housing – bring additional expertise to bear on complex problems that the authority alone is unable to resolve. Governance, on the other hand, denotes something that is 'bottom-up'. It begins at a sub-local level and involves unleashing hitherto private energies. Priorities are defined within affected communities (sometimes rejecting abstract ideas of the 'public good' (Campbell and Marshall, 2002) and instead prioritising community goals) and local groups are empowered to take actions against these priorities.

These concepts make reference to broader strategic interests and to local priority; and inherent in their use is the acceptance that the strategic and local need to be *bridged*, in order, as Davies (2008, 18) puts it, to deal adequately with 'the strategic dilemmas integral to governing'. Effective bridging (across scales) requires a means of dealing with the 'diametric opposition' of representative power, in the form of established democratic processes that support executive actions, and the need to assign communities a role as co-producers of public policy, of planning frameworks and of consequent decisions.

Addressing weak connectivity in England

Through the Localism Act 2011, the UK government has established a formal process of 'neighbourhood planning' in England (see Parker, Chapter 10, this volume) and offered a vision of a very simple link, or bridge, between the aspirations of community actors and the priorities of local government. This law gives community groups the opportunity to produce a plan for their area, for residents to approve it by referendum, and for it to be recognised within the local development planning system. That system then embraces the ambitions of communities, but only those ambitions which are compliant with national planning policy and with higher-level plans.

In the decade before this particular piece of legislation, however, discussions concerning the *connectivity* of informal community planning with formal local plan-making – and therefore how the activities (and aspirations) of neighbourhood groups might be drawn into the policy process – were already ongoing. Parish[1] level plans – and other appraisals and statements – were regularly being produced by communities in rural areas. These communities, however, were often frustrated by the apparent unwillingness of local councils to adopt formally the various policy ideas and positions contained in those plans. Councils, for their part, argued that the content of parish plans tended to be inactionable: many of their ideas were ultra vires – outside the remit of land-use planning (Gallent et al, 2008). This led commentators to argue that the existing system of parish planning was flawed, raising expectations, but ultimately alienating communities who came to believe that their voices were being ignored.

Two answers to this problem came forward. First, it was suggested that it was wrong to treat parish plans as plans at all; that they gave much broader signals as to the aspirations of a community and as such, they should provide the community-level intelligence for the last Labour government's 'community strategies' (Bishop, 2007). Those strategies, which aimed to articulate broad goals and frame a district's, or borough's, suite of corporate, service-delivery and land-use plans, were a more natural home for ideas and feelings on how an area should be shaped in the future and how, for example, services should be provided. In the language of the time, community aspiration sat more easily with the broader concept of 'place shaping' (Lyons, 2007) than the legalistic mind-set of statutory planning. Community strategies – produced by strategic local partnerships (LSPs) or public, private and community actors – would provide a bridge to the planning system, however, and, in time, communities would come to detect the impact of their own plans on the decisions reached by local planning departments.

An alternative view also came forward, however, that has left its imprint on the emergent neighbourhood planning arrangements in England: that parish plans could be aligned with local statutory planning. This would be possible if, through instrumental framing, the white noise of general ambition could be filtered from parish plans and they became more focused land-use documents. This could happen if planning teams had the resources to support plan production; to advise on content, and to test the soundness of parish plans, ensuring that nothing ultra vires slipped through the net of strict regulatory control. Proponents of the much softer bridging approach argued, however, that this level of control would remove power from the hands of communities, curbing their enthusiasm, and removing much of the reason why people get involved in the local activism that spawns parish and other community plans. Rather than being straightforward plans, they are accounts of local ambition: they signal a community's priorities and its hopes for the future. Their value extends beyond the land-use control function – they are a means of harnessing local energies and bringing communities together around agreed agendas.

Despite these differences, there was general agreement that better plans might be forthcoming if communities received some form of external support, although for those objecting to a tightening of control over planning at the community level, this support needed to be independent of local government. It should not seek to frame ambition within the bounds of the planning system, or try to align parish plans with a pre-determined vision of how a place should look in five, ten or twenty years' time. Harmonisation between informal and formal planning should not mean the former becoming more like the latter: rather, a fundamentally different relationship between the two needed to be brokered.

Support groups in community planning

Building effective bridges between 'strategic top-down and the very local bottom-up in decision making' should, according to Owen et al (2007, 72), result in the proper retention

> at the strategic level [of] such responsibilities as the coordination of service delivery, targeting of need and securing of economies of scale [while allocating] significantly increased responsibilities to very local communities, encouraging the deployment there of local knowledge, understanding, energy and skills.

There has been no single model for supporting community planning in England: rather, areas have tended to develop their own arrangements; though many have experimented with assistance through community liaison officers, embedded in local councils; through dedicated support groups attached to Rural Community Councils; and through wider Community Support Networks, often comprising volunteers who have gained some expertise in their own communities and who offer this expertise to groups just starting out (Owen et al, 2007).

The notion of bridging captures the idea that one point (the local bottom-up) needs to be connected to another (the strategic top-down), but support for community planning is not motivated solely by this desire to bridge (or by the goal of influencing policy frameworks or ensuring that responsibilities are shared or delegated downwards). Support may seek to loosen dependencies, creating the conditions in which communities become self-sustaining. The role of those working *with* communities is summarised by Weil (2005, 239) who emphasises the need

> to (a) work with communities to plan for strengthening community social and physical infrastructure, (b) engage in mutual work and learning with community members, (c) develop supportive services, (d) establish sustainable social and economic development programs, and (e) promote strong and broad participation to develop resources and improve the quality of local community life.

While these functions can be performed by local government, there is a risk that public sector objectives will become an overriding consideration and that the community is steered, or 'stage managed', to comply with public sector agendas and goals. Other researchers have observed how skilled intermediaries – with a variety of backgrounds and allegiances – can expose the mutual benefits that arise from collaborative working arrangements (Owens, 2005; Booher and Innes, 2002), but those embedded within the public sector may impose a particular value-set, which leads to an 'instrumental framing' in which certain orthodoxies prevail and the broader aspirations of communities are lost or diminished (Radaelli, 1995; Owens, 2005). Against Weil's functions, this might mean that infrastructure investments reflect local government priorities, mutual learning becomes the *education* of community members to accept the priorities and constraints of public policy (Gallent and Robinson, 2012) and participation remains consultation on a limited set of service options. In short, those embedded in local councils may be unable to act as independent arbitrators, unless freed from management constraint and given free rein to work with communities to whatever end – which may be unlikely.

The alternative is for the functions outlined by Weil to be performed by a body or individual that is entirely independent of local government. Developing Weil's summary, the key goals of community support might be as follows:

- to 'build capacity within local systems' (MacCallum et al, 2009), first, to deliver an enhanced social community infrastructure and thereafter to deliver a physical infrastructure (possibly through the acquisition of local assets) which has only become possible because of an enhanced capacity for the community to work collectively. Summarising the work of Castelloe (1999), Weil (2005, 239) argues that community support should aim to develop 'social capital and community competence to construct and enlarge collective efficacy for community revitalisation';extending this capacity-building role, to ensure that communities come to understand their place in a wider environment of actors, gaining also an appreciation of the orthodoxies of the public sector without being constrained by them. Support groups have a 'teaching and coaching' role within communities (Orchard and Peryman, 2012) and equally, a responsibility to ensure that other actors are made aware of what communities have to offer the decision-making process. Support groups can form a vital learning bridge, facilitating a genuine dialogue; this might lead to a related goal to deliver supportive services, tailored more clearly to what communities actually need. If needs are more complex, and communities less homogenous, then communication with users becomes vital to ensuring that services provide the right support in the right places. The *exchange* of information is key to developing these supportive services; and linked to this,

- developing programmes and patterns of development that support the way that communities would wish to develop, ensuring that planning happens *with* communities rather than to them (see Ross, 1955). Again, this is dependent on putting an effective learning bridge in place; though Weil (2005, 239) suggests that 'community practitioners' must play a role in advocating a community's interests, stressing the value of participative approaches in decision-making; and

- achieve all of the above through strong and broad participation, often by introducing facilitation expertise (Orchard and Peryman, 2012) in order to maintain momentum in community-based activity, to connect to a broader spectrum of groups (within that community), and to generally ensure that participative processes are a genuine enhancement to local democracy – by avoiding a narrowing of the community voice to only highly specific interests.

A rearrangement of the above is perhaps needed in order to see the lifecycle of support given to communities. This might begin with a focus on internal dynamics: (a) democratising and bringing more groups into the frame of participative processes, which may be part of a wider effort to (b) build capacity within local systems. Having received this support, communities are likely to venture into a range of localised activities, independent of other traditional actors. Equally, however, they may connect to these traditional actors through the (c) learning bridge, which provides a means to shape and deliver (d) supportive services and (e) effectively advocate community interest to the planning system and onward to development interests. For some commentators, (e) can only be achieved where a partnership structure, including community support, provides 'technical support and transparency concerning integration with formal (council) processes' (Orchard and Peryman, 2012, 48) but this then re-introduces the challenge of stage-management, which a supported approach to community planning, using independent arbitrators, seeks to avoid. That said, there is often a great deal of technical support and expertise within support groups, which remains independent.

Research in the Ashford growth area

The largely rural Borough of Ashford is located in the county of Kent in South East England. It had a resident population of 118,000 in 2011 (ONS, 2011). Almost 70 per cent of these residents live in either Ashford itself or Tenterden. The remaining population is distributed across the borough's villages and rural hinterland. Ashford Borough is divided into 39 civil parishes. While the area is generally affluent, it displays pockets of income deprivation, particularly in its urban wards, although this deprivation is masked by broader statistics, which show that economic activity in the borough (at 65 per cent) exceeds the national average and unemployment (at 1.3 per cent) is a whole percentage point below the figure for England (ONS, 2009). The proportion of top socio-economic groups (defined by the UK Census) residing in the borough, however, is less than that of the South East region as a whole (27.7 compared with 31.9 per cent in 2009).

Ashford itself is a market town, set within a traditional agricultural area that has experienced an industrial and commercial transformation in recent years. This is in large part due to its location on the Channel Tunnel Rail Link and its good road connections to London. In 2006, roughly 56,000 people were employed in the borough and approximately the same number commuted to jobs outside of Ashford, many to the capital. Commuting is an important feature of life within Ashford. In a recent typology tracking economic, political and demographic diversity across rural England, Lowe and Ward (2007) classified the borough as a 'dynamic commuter area' and an 'extension of the wealthy suburbs' of the Greater London conurbation, with a significant concentration of 'dynamic commuter residents' who tend to be articulate and well-connected into networks of power and influence, and quite prepared to engage with the politico-administrative system at local, regional and national levels. They [are] particularly resistant to further encroachments in terms of land-use and other developments which might undermine the rural idyll into which they have bought. (Lowe and Ward, 2007, no page number)

Because residents are articulate and 'well-connected' – displaying some of the same characteristics as Matthews' Cheshire households (Chapter 3, this volume) – such areas may be characterised by a propensity towards active engagement with issues around planning and development. Ashford has, in recent years, faced numerous challenges on this front, being designated a Growth Area by the Labour Government in 2003 (ODPM, 2003). This followed on from a study commissioned by the Regional Assembly two years earlier which aimed to test the growth potential of the Borough. That study concluded that over the next 15 years, 35,000 new residents and 18,000 new jobs could be accommodated in and around the town. After 2003, the Borough Council began working with English Partnerships (a national housing and regeneration agency) on a 'Greater Ashford Development Framework' which, over a 30-year period between 2001 and 2031, anticipated the town growing by 31,000 new homes and 28,000 new jobs. The borough's consequent local plan set out a requirement to deliver approximately 15,500 dwellings on greenfield sites within two major urban extensions.

Like many growth proposals, those around Ashford provoked the usual concerns and anxieties that accompany potentially dramatic and unsettling change. Ashford was chosen as a case study of *connectivity* between community interests and policy makers because of the impending change in the Borough and concerns over the extent of existing communication (Gallent and Robinson, 2012). That study, conducted during 2009 and 2010, focused broadly on the relationships forged between community groups (in ten parishes) and those responsible for developing policy and delivering growth. It looked more specifically at the brokering of those relationships and the role of a key support group: *Action with communities in rural Kent.*

Besides focusing on three directly affected parishes (Great Chart with Singleton, Shadoxhurst and Mersham and Sevington), the study also examined seven other parishes around Ashford, which either bordered the extensions or appeared more remote from the direct effects of the proposed new housing and infrastructure. These ten parishes are

Image 16.1: Picturesque Woodchurch, typical of the case study villages (author)

© Nick Gallent

shown in Figure 16.1. During the course of the study, interviews were conducted with representatives of these parish councils, including the parish clerks and/or the parish council chairs alongside either ordinary council members or coopted individuals involved in the preparation of parish plans. These interviews addressed three themes: arrangements within the community for formulating plans (who provided leadership, the extent of involvement, community capacity); connectivity to policy actors and experiences of shaping local policy frameworks (especially the local plan); and the nature of dialogue with external actors and the enhancements to local democracy possible through a focus on neighbourhood-based action. Key to the first two themes, and linking to the third, was the role of support bodies in facilitating community planning and in bridging between community and policy groups. All interviews were recorded, transcribed and analysed according to these three major themes.

The research also focused on connectivity to the communities from the perspective of key policy actors. Interviews were conducted with officers of the Borough Council (from Planning Strategy, Development Control, Housing and the officer providing secretariat support to the Local Strategic Partnership), from the Kent Highways Authority, from the Regional Development Agency, and with representatives from the special delivery vehicle ('Ashford's Future') set up to deliver the

Figure 16.1: Ashford and the ten case-study parishes

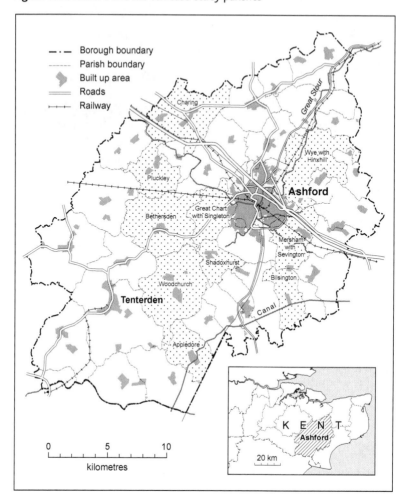

Growth Area's key projects. These interviews focused on two themes: the practicalities and the value of connecting to community groups.

The final focus of the research was the support provided to communities, and to policy actors, by Action with Communities in Rural Kent (ACRK). Thus the research took triangulated evidence on independent support for community planning, focusing on the separate points of 'strategic top-down and the very local bottom-up in decision making' and on the potential bridge between these points.[2] In the remainder of this chapter, the critical roles of this support group are examined against the framework developed earlier.

Support groups in community planning

Democratising community planning

Support in 'democratising' community planning (that is, helping Parish Councils reach out to different sections of a community through facilitation) (Orchard and Peryman, 2012) and assistance in 'building capacity' in local systems (MacCallum et al, 2009) are two sides of the same coin. The latter can refer either to the capacities introduced by the support group itself (its injection of expertise) or to the way in which 'hub' groups (in this case, parish councils) are encouraged to reach out to the wider community, and to latent ideas and skills. ACRK has used parish councils as community entry-points, behind which there are likely to be a broader set of interests, opinions and capacities. The starting point for widening engagement in the Ashford area was frequently a facilitated 'community exercise', often using a mix of standard methods and approaches observed in neighbouring villages. Rather than merely giving communities a shopping list of ways that parish councils might connect to residents, ACRK instead highlighted the techniques that had worked in other locations, putting parish councils in contact with one another to facilitate learning and raise awareness of the wider operational environment. As well as drawing out lessons on the production and format of village appraisals, Parish Plans and Village Design Statements (VDS), ACRK used regular seminars to showcase good practice. The parish council at Wye undertook a pre-plan appraisal. After forming a Parish Plan Steering Group and designing a questionnaire (with ACRK's help), the latter was delivered by hand by 45 'patch workers' who also collected the questionnaire by hand and who achieved a 60 per cent response rate. The efforts and successes at Wye were held up as good practice to other parishes thinking about producing a plan.

The broader set of interests behind parish councils is not always easy to access, however, and there is a risk that support groups will connect only to a limited set of community interests (Orchard and Peryman, 2012). The councils, or clerks to those councils, may act as 'gatekeepers' (ACRK interviewee) and represent either a narrow set of views or a particular interpretation of community opinion or priority. The study pointed to two important obstacles confronting those who would seek to democratise community planning. The first is a philosophical one – parish councils or equivalent forums may come to view themselves as another part of the hierarchy of local government, 'representing' residents through electoral mandate: and because parish councils suffer a notoriously low (or highly variable) voter turnout (Woods et al, 2003), and many members are coopted rather than elected, the democratic credentials of councils may be doubted. This means that councils need to accept that their mandate is weak and engage in more *active* democracy. This leads to a practical obstacle – how to find the resources needed to engage in that active democracy. ACRK's task was two-fold and involved: winning the philosophical argument and thereafter working with councils to engage more residents: the aim of the latter being to enhance democracy through community planning *and* build capacity for community projects and revitalisation (Castelloe, 1999).

Building capacity in rural communities

> Parish council capacity is very limited because your councillors are volunteers and your clerk is part-time, and I haven't met a parish clerk who doesn't feel that there is a host of things [that] could be done in their parish, but they just haven't got the capacity to do it. It's a continuing cry, a plea. (Wye with Hinxhill interviewee)

Initially, this 'cry' goes out through personal networks with friends and neighbours coopted onto parish councils, although the pattern of coopting commonly pulls in retired people, whose connectivity to current (and broader) professional networks may be weak. Moreover, coopting may further undermine the democratic credentials of councils or accentuate perceptions of irrelevance, if their demographic becomes obviously skewed. Attention was drawn to this issue in Wye, where the majority of parish councillors were said to be those with 'time on their hands'. Getting residents of working age involved had proven difficult and had limited the parish's capacity for 'reaching out':

> Reaching out is often about professional networking and of course if you're working in the fields of planning or whatever, or education, then of course you have that professional network to hand. We don't necessarily have that advantage because of the age profile.

'Getting moving' on projects, for Wye and for other parishes, had sometimes proven difficult. Both time and knowledge had been limiting factors, but on numerous occasions the cry for help from communities had been answered by ACRK. It had helped communities launch key initiatives around parish visioning and planning, advising on how to broaden interest and in so doing, introduce new capacity to core community groups. It had substituted for the missing professional networking, and it had often worked with parish councils to promote more widely the benefits of community planning and, through 'mini consultation exercises' – which aimed to 'flush out likes and dislikes' around community development – it aimed to 'create a buzz' and in doing so 'harness the volunteers' (ACRK interviewee). Building this capacity for community planning was described by ACRK as the primary mission for many communities, ahead of influencing the policies and behaviours of service providers. With greater capacity, communities often believed that they could deliver results for themselves. For this reason, assistance with mobilising support and raising enthusiasm was seen as crucial.

In Appledore, an open day for residents that aimed to gather ideas on a 10-year vision for the village had only happened after the chairman of the parish council had attended a seminar event run by ACRK on how to mobilise community interest, and how to communicate in different ways with different groups. This led to the drawing up of a mission statement which set the twin aims of producing a plan that would be an internal 'guide for the future' and also be recognised and adopted by the Borough Council. Following the seminar, it was through ACRK that Appledore Parish Council was able to access funding to begin the process of drawing up its Parish Plan.

While parish councils tended to look inward for some of the technical skills needed to produce plans (for example, desk-top publishing), they tended to look to ACRK when they needed help with local surveys or with understanding aspects of the planning system. Yet the support group remained keen that parishes did not view community planning as a narrow and strictly technical exercise, lest this limited interest in the process. Rather, ACRK was keen to sell the idea of Parish Plan production as an *informal* process, owned by the whole community, and with which a broad spectrum of people might engage. In Wye, when ACRK had presented the case for drawing up a Parish Plan:

> they said 'look, it's called Parish Planning, but it's not planning'. It's not strictly the old fashioned idea of planning, it's a parish appraisal, so it's appraising everything in the parish that you want appraised. It's up to the people to decide what they want to appraise and the issues they want to deal with, so you appraise them and then you draw up an action plan and that action plan will basically guide and then give a mandate to your parish council and other groups

in the village – because some of the actions may not be [for] a parish council. They may be appropriate for some of these community organisations to get on with.

ACRK promoted the idea of appraisal (underpinning Parish Plans) as a widely shared undertaking that eventually gave a steer to the parish council. The 'mandate' which the council ended up with should be the product of broad involvement, with local enthusiasm, rather than expert input, driving community planning and giving communities their core capacity.

Providing a learning bridge

As in other parts of England, the creation of the Local Strategic Partnership (LSP) – introduced at the beginning of this chapter – was viewed by policy-makers as a key vehicle for better connecting residents' interests with policy formulation and service delivery (Morphet, 2008, 120). Indeed, interviewed officers suggested that enhanced connectivity with communities had been achieved through systemic changes in local government and in planning during the 2000s (LSP, Planning Strategy, Planning DC interviewees): a view that was generally refuted by parish councils, which viewed the planning system as increasingly complex, remote and inaccessible. The representative of the LSP claimed, however, that the partnership brought together 'voluntary and community' sector actors with key 'agency stakeholders' and was therefore functioning according to its design. It was pointed out that the Vice Chairman of the Ashford Community Network, claiming to represent 800 community groups (including Parish Councils) and eight black and minority ethnic groups, sat on the LSP. The community networks represented on the LSP were said to provide a good 'functional interface' (LSP interviewee) with Ashford's communities, offering an effective learning bridge between parish councils and higher-level policy actors, giving the former a voice in decision-making.

This view was rejected by the parish councils who argued that the 'voluntary and community' actors in question were in fact membership associations which, while advancing the need for a local perspective, were themselves detached from any *particular* local view. Hence, the LSP sought representation of the local, but had no direct connection to the parishes. In the 2000s, it had been implied that communities and neighbourhoods able to connect with the LSP would have a direct hand in 'place shaping' (see Lyons, 2007) and would be far more likely to receive the services they needed, although none of the parishes in the study recalled any dialogue with the LSP and few were certain of its function. Many parish councils were surprised to learn that the partnership had responsibility for drawing up a 'community strategy' (for the Borough as a whole), which seemed to some oddly named and without any clear connection to Ashford's 'real communities'. Again, second-hand 'representation from networks' was said to paint too general a picture of the needs of communities, ignoring inevitable differences.

This local analysis of the failure of LSPs to connect to socio-spatial communities (and to form an effective bridge to policy communities) is repeated elsewhere. Given the shared community focus of partnerships and parish councils, albeit at different spatial scales, Owen et al (2007) argued that a fit should be sought between Community Strategies produced by the LSP and the content of community plans, adding that this could be realised through the appointment of liaison officers, tasked to work with communities (Owen et al, 2007, 69). Referring to a number of local studies across England, these authors perceived 'an acceptance that the community strategy could help broker the policies and decisions required by many bodies to address very local problems' (2007, 70). Despite this perception, however, Owen et al observed 'very little traffic' on these 'bridges' between community and policy actors and these same findings emerge from Ashford.

While the LSP's direct connectivity to policy-making was strong, its connectivity to the parish level appeared weak. For that reason, rather than simply sitting on the LSP, ACRK chose to actively teach the partnership's members exactly what community planning at the parish level involved and how it might benefit policy-making. ACRK gave a presentation on this subject to LSP members (including Kent County Council, the Primary Care Trust, the police, and the County Highways Authority) in 2008 and this was the start of its 'bridging' focus, which then involved regular attendance at workshops and rural conferences (Planning Strategy interviewee) – where its role was first to educate service providers as to the value of parish plans for understanding local service needs, and second the development of a 'mediation' function, helping specific service providers understand the signals emerging from plans, and helping communities ensure that the right information (useful to providers) was set out in those plans.

Specifically, ACRK worked with other RCCs in the South East of England to establish a database of parish plan content, which housing officers expected would help them better understand housing needs and future project investments (Housing interviewee). More broadly, this database formed a key part of ACRK's 'bridging work', which tried to 'make links between the Parish Plans and the various service providers'. This was an on-line database and included entries for every (parish) Action Plan produced in Kent. It listed all the actions proposed and, for Ashford, indexed these actions against the Community Strategy and the Vision for Kent (a joint Community Strategy undertaken by all the county's local authorities and their partners). The intention was to ensure that service providers could quickly reference a community's aspirations, perhaps be guided by them when seeking to make interventions in that area, and could, as appropriate, also be guided by local data gathered by parish councils. In this way, service providers would benefit from a fine-grained disaggregation of spatial data, and communities would find a way to convey their own aspirations to local and regional stakeholders. The system appeared useful and was being actively promoted:

> we're doing work now to promote the use of that [database] to the service providers [and] we've had meetings with the police and with the fire service. Clean Kent from KCC were here this morning looking at fly-tipping data and we had a developer – actually one of four bidders in Shepway and Dover – looking to find out what communities close to [a new] school development would find useful to have [associated] with that development, so there is a bit of interest and that seems to be picking up.

Beyond that particular resource, ACRK had also brought communities and service providers directly together with a view to increasing awareness of provider responsibilities. In one parish, residents had been supplying the serial numbers of washing machines and other white goods found abandoned in fields and hedgerows to Environmental Services and the police, hoping that the owners might be traced and prosecuted. This prompted ACRK to bring service providers and communities together, with the hope that any data collected by Parish Councils would be useable and could be acted on. This involved ACRK acting as an intermediary, reporting back to the parishes on the sorts of data useful to housing, DC, the police and so on. The advice given to communities was spelt out:

> if you ask these questions in this way [through a local appraisal] the data may be more useful to this service provider if that's who you're trying to influence.

The notion that ACRK would act as a liaison, and as a 'critical friend', was extended into the whole process of Parish Plan production and, as the Pluckley group observed, the support group was quick to impress on communities the potential to influence borough and county thinking through the production of a plan that was able to 'push the right buttons' (that is, by containing the right evidence) and could win the 'approval' of the local authority (Pluckley interviewee). Hence the learning bridge, that ACRK itself claimed to be providing, became both a channel of communication – through the database – *and* a means of ensuring that parishes understood the 'game rules'.

As many parish respondents observed, however, community planning is as much about *self-help* (through mobilising local energies around agreed projects) as issuing a *call for help* (through the production of plans that are intended to guide external interventions). Communities generally wanted service providers and policy-makers to learn from, or adopt, positions taken in Parish Plans, but they also wanted these plans to provide a focus and a drive for community action.

Shaping supportive services

The shaping of services that support community development (Orchard and Peryman, 2012) happens through the 'learning bridge', with ACRK helping service providers better understand the needs of communities. For example, in the case of rural housing projects, it was ACRK (as well as dedicated Rural Housing Enablers) that liaised between parish councils and Ashford Borough, helping the former gather evidence (through local surveys) on their housing needs and helping the Borough understand the aspirations of communities and the type and location of housing development that would be acceptable (Housing interviewee). Indeed, the support group had often provided 'an impartial assessment of potential [housing] sites', which both the communities and housing officers valued. More generally, ACRK (and English Rural Housing Association) had been highly effective in 'doing very close liaison...and then wider community consultation'. This liaison proved essential as some parishes were said to be 'a bit reluctant in terms of concerns that even a small scheme might lead to greater development' and others worried about how homes 'might be allocated'. On these points, ACRK and other trusted intermediaries were able to calm nerves and provide a bridge to the local authority, ensuring that new investments in local needs housing were possible.

Advocating community interest to the planning system

Finally, Action with Communities in Rural Kent was an avid proponent of community interest *per se*, and instrumental in promoting that interest to the planning system. These two forms of advocacy – internal and external – are distinct. ACRK was keen to insulate communities in the early stages of community plan production from external influence, aiming to ensure that the plans produced were a genuine articulation of community ambition. For example, it was ACRK that advised Bilsington to only seek the views of Ashford Borough Council on its Parish Plan once the community was 'further down the line' (with the production of its plan) and once it had more fully 'set out its stall'. This struck the parish council chairman as odd given that the Borough Council had been apparently supportive of communities' efforts to draw up Parish Plans. The advice from ACRK hinted at a concern that parishes produced their own, un-doctored, plans before engaging with the local authority – which would take a view on admissible content that could affect the early development of those plans. This advice reflected a concern that plans should not be subject to any 'instrumental framing' (Radaelli, 1995), at least not in the formative stages of their production.

More generally, ACRK have been an enthusiastic advocate of the articulation of community interest through *internal* parish planning, which is then externalised through the promotion of Parish Plans within the broader planning system. The group have an officer whose role is to link with all Chief Planning Officers in Kent, and who has recently been pushing the value to the planning system of the Parish Planning Database and therefore the added value brought to the planning system by community planning. The same officer has regular contact with the Kent LSPs, which come together in a Kent Partnership Support Group in order to promote a county-wide Vision for Kent. The same advocacy role is played by other Rural Community Councils in other parts of England, which come together under the umbrella of the Rural Community Action Network (RCAN). All the RCCs – of which ACRK is one – aim to provide advocacy and influence with regional partners. Interestingly, ACRK has found that its advocacy function cannot be fulfilled merely through membership of the LSP, which proved to have weak direct connectivity to rural residents and communities. Advocacy needs to be more than representation; it needs to be actively pursued through specific initiatives (the database in this case) and through the pro-active education of partners on either side of the community planning support bridge.

Conclusions

Government-led mechanisms for enhancing connectivity between community stakeholders and policy makers have not always proven effective. The apparent failure of the LSP model in England (which appeared *passive* in its engagement with actual place communities) is reconfirmed by the case study presented in this chapter. Although this same general picture of failure has been drawn by other researchers (Owen et al, 2007), what stands out from this study is that support for neighbourhood planning, within communities and beyond them, in terms of remedying weak connectivity, must be active support. Groups like ACRK are most effective when they have the resources at their disposal to work *with* communities around promoting neighbourhood democracy, building local capacity and connecting to policy (and beyond that, advocating community-level interest and the value of active engagement with neighbourhoods to service providers). The general model of effective community support, outlined by Weil (2005), fits the English situation. It is a good descriptor of the essential tasks of support bodies. Beyond that descriptor, which emphasises a loosening of dependencies, the idea of support groups providing an essential learning bridge – as an antidote to weak connectivity – seems central to the evolution of effective community planning. It is essential because services need to respect the complex and diverse needs of communities and because what happens within communities – the visible manifestation of a shift towards broader participative governance through active engagement – needs some alignment or agreement with the meta-governance processes (achieved through representative democracy) that deliver the broader operational environment. Collaborative governance needs to work with the mandated power wielded by higher structures. The idea of the 'learning bridge' goes beyond the 'teaching and coaching' role of support groups (Orchard and Peryman, 2012), occurring between scales, seeking vertical connectivity based on mutual understanding through dialogue, trust and clarity of expectation.

This broad conclusion needs to be read in two contexts, however. The first is the particular and recent evolution of community planning in England, which is occurring today with little additional investment in bridging activity, and which supposes that 'neighbourhood development planning' can become more like the 'old fashioned idea of planning' and therefore achieve a simpler and easier link to local plans at a district or borough level, owing to a narrowing focus on matters of land use and development form. The second is the reality that 'community development' – or the underlying mobilisation of community interest – is not solely motivated by the desire to plan and to influence. Communities want to do more for themselves and, as illustrated in this study and elsewhere in this book, are achieving notable successes. Support groups in community planning, where they have the means to be active, have a vital role to play in supporting communities in the ways in which they would wish to be supported. Governments that are serious about community development and 'localism' (in planning, service delivery, self-help and so forth) need to recognise the need to make crucial investments to achieve these goals.

Acknowledgements

The research on which this chapter draws was supported by the Economic and Social Research Council. Field work assistance was provided by Steve Robinson.

Notes

[1] Parishes are the smallest unit of local government in England and generally found in rural areas.

[2] ACRK is a voluntary organisation that was previously known as the Rural Community Council (RCC) for Kent and Medway. The first RCC was established in Oxfordshire in 1921, and by 1986 each county in England had its own RCC, which have been described by Leavett (1985) as independent voluntary organisations which bring 'together a wide range of other voluntary bodies, local authorities and statutory agencies to promote and support voluntary action to alleviate the social and economic problems of rural communities'. The RCCs operate under the umbrella of Action with Communities in Rural England (ACRE), which is now part of a Rural Community Action Network (RCAN). ACRK's general aims are the same as all RCCs: to provide direct advice and support to community organisations; to stimulate community action, particularly voluntary action, and encourage good practice; to develop and manage demonstration projects; to provide professional support and advice to key service providers; and to raise awareness of rural issues and influence decision makers (see www.ruralkent.org.uk). It aims to work with communities, and with service providers, acting as a bridge between the two.

References

Bishop, J, 2007, Plans without planners?, *Town and Country Planning* 76, 340–44

Booher, D, Innes, J, 2002, Network power in collaborative planning, *Journal of Planning Education and Research* 21, 221–36

Campbell, H, Marshall, R, 2002, Utilitarianism's bad breath? A re-evaluation of the public interest justification for planning, *Planning Theory* 1, 2, 163–87

Castelloe, PE, 1999, *Community change and community practice: An organic model of community practice*, Digital Dissertation AAT 9943191 (quoted by Weil, M, 2005, Social planning with communities: theory and practice, in M Weil (ed) *The handbook of community practice*, pp 215–43, Thousand Oaks, CA: SAGE)

Davies, JS, 2008, Double-devolution or double-dealing? The local government White Paper and the Lyons Review, *Local Government Studies* 34, 1, 3–22

Gallent, N, Robinson, S, 2012, *Neighbourhood planning: Communities, networks and governance*, Bristol: The Policy Press

Gallent, N, Morphet, J, Tewdwr-Jones, M, 2008, Parish plans and the spatial planning approach in England, *Town Planning Review* 79, 1, 1–27

Leavett, A, 1985, *Role and relationships of RCCs: Review on behalf of the Development Commission*, London: Development Commission

Lowe, P, Ward, N, 2007, Rural futures: A socio-graphical approach to scenario analysis, paper presented at the *Institute for Advanced Studies Annual Research Programme*, 9–10 January, Lancaster: Lancaster University

Lyons, M, 2007, *Place-shaping: A shared ambition for the future of local government. Executive summary*, London: The Stationary Office

MacCallum, D, Moulaert, F, Hillier, J, 2009, *Social innovation and territorial development*, Abingdon: Ashgate

Marsh, D, Rhodes, R, 1992, Policy networks in British government: A critique of existing approaches, in D Marsh, R Rhodes, R (eds) *Policy networks in British government*, Oxford: Clarendon Press

Marsh, D, Toke, D, Belfrage, C, Tepe, D, McGough, S, 2009, Policy networks and the distinction between insider and outsider groups: The case of the Countryside Alliance, *Public Administration* 87, 3, 621–38

Morphet, J, 2008, *Modern local government*, London: SAGE

ODPM (Office of the Deputy Prime Minister), 2003, *Sustainable communities: Building for the future*, London: HMSO

ONS (Office for National Statistics), 2009, 2011, Neighbourhood Statistics, www.neighbourhood.statistics.gov.uk /dissemination/

Orchard, S, Peryman, B, 2012, Facilitating community involvement in community–council master planning, *Lincoln Planning Review* 3, 2, 41–50

Owens, S, 2005, Making a difference? Some perspectives on environmental research and policy, *Transactions of the Institute of British Geographers New Series* 30, 287–92

Owen, S, Moseley, M, Courtney, P, 2007, Bridging the gap: An attempt to reconcile strategic planning and very local community-based planning in rural England, *Local Government Studies* 33, 49–76

Radaelli, CM, 1995, The role of knowledge in the policy process, *Journal of European Public Policy* 2, 2, 159–83

Rittel, H, Webber, M, 1973, Dilemmas in a general theory of planning, *Policy Sciences* 4, 155–69

Ross, MG, 1955, *Community organization: Theory, principles and practice*, New York: Harper and Row

Weil, M, 2005, Social planning with communities: Theory and practice, in M Weil (ed) *The handbook of community practice*, pp 215–43, Thousand Oaks, CA: SAGE

Woods, M, Edwards, WJ, Anderson, J, Gardner, G, 2003, *Participation, power and rural governance in England and Wales: ESRC final report*, Swindon: Economic and Social Research Council

17

Reflections on community action and planning

Daniela Ciaffi and Nick Gallent

Introduction

We have sought in this book to sequence community action and planning; to show how it begins, the stages of its progression, and its outcomes for communities themselves and for the broader policy-making environment. In the first chapter, the capacities and values of socio-spatial communities were connected to their tendency to mobilise, to take action against everyday challenges, and in some instances to plan for their future wellbeing. The discussions of 'foundational' ideas that then followed, in the second and third chapters, emphasised the importance of social capital as a framing idea, and also the argument – often contested – that through dialogue different actors can find clear paths through conflict and be guided by a 'collaborative rationality'. There was clearly a great deal of idealism in the opening chapter, and also an element of proposed linearity. Much of that idealism is stripped away by Rydin in Chapter 2 who argues that communities may come together for a range of positive or negative reasons, and in Chapter 3 (and again in Chapter 14), the simple linearity of community planning and of collaborative action is broken down and found to be lacking in many respects. The reality is that community action and planning can be conceptualised in a number of different ways. The contributors to this book have applied a range of perspectives: the idea of social capital has proved useful for some, but not all; collaborative and deliberative planning have offered some authors a way in to this area, but others see critical limits in the extent to which collaborative rationality explains changing power relationships in situations of apparently 'networked' governance.

Different perspectives have brought different insights, but analyses have also been coloured by the particular experiences of specific places and what community action appears to have delivered on the ground, relative to local constraints within each case study. Some of the contributors have clearly been more optimistic than others, seeing huge opportunities for an extension of such action in the years ahead. Others are more reticent, arguing that social fractures and state centrism will continue to limit what can be achieved *within* neighbourhoods.

The purpose of this final chapter is to draw together some of the key reflections on community action and planning that have emerged from the last 16 chapters. We begin by looking again at the *contexts* for action; whether there is any commonality in the apparently very different politics, policy environments and places dealt with by each of the contributors. The focus then shifts to the *drivers* – which transform potential into actual mobilisation – alongside the inhibitors of action. *Trust*, within communities and across scales, is then identified as an important commodity which triggers social mobilisation, sustains it, and can turn piecemeal cooperation into an effective form of networked governance. The chapter then ends with *reflections*, drawn from the case studies, on the future trajectory of community action and planning on the ground.

Context and crisis

It is now seven years since the beginning of the financial crisis affecting the economies of the global north, and the world economy more broadly. The majority of the contributors to this book have drawn attention to the 'difficult times' that communities have faced during this period, to the impacts of spending cuts and the withering of welfare states across many countries. The context of crisis – and the consequent struggles that communities face – is crucial for seeding community action. It does this in two ways: communities begin to look inwards for support mechanisms; and governments call on citizens to accept greater responsibility for themselves and for their neighbourhoods or villages. Desperation – or at least the resort to self-help – comes together with welfare austerity to broker a new relationship between citizens and the state; and new conceptions of citizenship follow.

Although the withdrawal of welfare and key services is felt broadly across societies, it has the greatest impact among vulnerable groups, particularly in locations where those groups already experience disadvantage. In Chapter 5 Kilpatrick and colleagues paint a vivid picture of isolated farming and fishing communities in Australia, arguing that these had always been 'vulnerable to the unpredictability of climate and global economic forces' but that a recent 'accumulation of factors' constituted especially 'difficult times', leading to an acceptance that communities needed to come together and do more for themselves. In a very different context, Wolf-Powers in Chapter 12 traces 'neighbourhood activism' in New York City to the Oil Crisis of the 1970s and to the consequent calamity in the private rental sector, with landlords no longer being able to 'provide basic services to their buildings'. This set the context for occupation of buildings by activists and eventually their reuse as 'multi-family structures'. In the Netherlands, a deterioration of the public housing stock (and of some private housing within New Towns) combined with reduced spending on social welfare created the conditions in which 'active citizens' (characterised as innovators and 'everyday fixers', see van der Pennen and Schreuders, Chapter 8) emerged as agents of change, occupying the space left by a withdrawal of funding from local government.

Crisis creates a fertile context for community action, but it also provides a trigger (or a reason) to rethink the overall architecture of planning. As van der Pennen and Schreuders observed in the Netherlands, there has been a growing polemic against the welfare state of which aspects of central planning are a crucial part. Austerity politics provide a context in which to rethink top-down solutions to a variety of social problems, with devolution of responsibility to communities often seen as an important component of a 'third' or a 'fourth' way in social welfare delivery. In such situations, it is sometimes the case that the aspirations of communities (to do more) and states (to devolve more) meet at a mid-point. Indeed, Parker (Chapter 10) observes a 'strong theoretical challenge to traditional planning…particularly in the US and then in the UK' which has been paralleled by 'an upsurge in self-organisation and efforts to plan from below'. Episodic protest against normative planning processes became organised challenges and ultimately an accommodation of 'community participation in structural terms'. Participation in what remains top-down intervention can, for some participants, however, remain unsatisfactory and will not satiate the desire for effective control over processes or assets. Messaoudène and colleagues observe in Chapter 6 in their study of Marseille that 'participatory planning' is a long way from the image of genuinely 'communitarian' planning offered in Chapter 1, and Dandekar and Main's case study of community-based participation in southern California, in Chapter 9, reinforces the point that community ambitions are constrained by both internal (capacity) and external (political) factors.

In instances of strong political support – where the local state embraces the ambitions of citizens, in whatever form those ambitions might take – the outcomes can, however, be quite remarkable. Hamiduddin and Daseking, in Chapter 13, argue that the City of

Freiburg gave its citizens 'a strong hand in the physical shaping of the city' and through community self-build, '1,100 new homes have been delivered since 1993'. Similarly remarkable results were achieved on the Isle of Gigha. Land reform across Scotland gave residents there the opportunity to buy the entire physical assets of their community, including the island itself. In Chapter 7 Satsangi argues that this single act, although a long time in gestation, set the community on an entirely new development trajectory: one characterised by self-determination.

Self-determination as a concept obviously encompasses democratic ambitions. Across all the case studies there is a sense that the 'crisis' confronting communities is as much a democratic as an economic one, although that crisis of democracy was felt most readily in Barcelona. Vilà explains in Chapter 4 that although the top priority of the neighbourhood movements 'has been the physical improvement of the city's neighbourhoods', they have also been concerned with the 'attainment of democracy' – initially under the Spanish dictatorship, and then eventually with regards to shaping urban policy and decision-making. In all of the case studies, communities appeared to want to take more decisions for themselves. Messaoudène and colleagues follow a similar analytical path to Vilà, arguing that urban struggles against poverty and poor living conditions alongside the fight for democratic rights have been the crucial contextual ingredients for community action and planning. Certainly, these ingredients have underpinned more militant actions in places like Marseille, Barcelona and New York City. The crisis in 'representative democracy' (highlighted by Messaoudène and colleagues) is recognisable in all of the presented studies, however, whether it was a product of electoral apathy (in France and elsewhere), the strengthening of top-down planning (in England) or just having a 'bad laird' (in Scotland).

The contributors to this book have shown that in different contexts, different forms of community action and planning have taken root. We suggested in the opening chapter that a distinction can be drawn between 'communitarian planning as a by-product of community life (with its focus on social goods) and (implanted or hijacked) community planning as a product of the state's search for legitimacy – through extended interaction that delivers a less contentious vision of "what urban change should be like"'. The reaction of remoter Australian communities to 'difficult times' exemplifies the first type, but even in instances where the state attempts to connect or seed community action – as in the case of post-earthquake L'Aquila in 2009 – a local tendency towards self-help (and a distrust of intervention) may ensure that communities continue to act for themselves and on their own terms. Between action motivated by self-help and action seeded by the state, however, there seem to be other intermediate models. A more 'relational' form of community action appears to have emerged in the Dutch New Towns, and which exists in order to tap public resources. It is not seeded by the state, but emerges because an environment is created that makes it advantageous for communities to mobilise. In the Netherlands, van der Pennen and Schreuders attribute the rise of 'relational community action' (or a 'fourth way') to the presence of what they call 'everyday fixers' and what Kilpatrick and colleagues refer to as 'boundary crossers'. This intermediate context for community action – between self-help and seeding – is created where there is the right 'interactional infrastructure' and where the local state is receptive to sharing resources and devolving control.

Drivers and inhibitors

The drivers, or the inhibitors, of community action are of course selectively present in different contexts. In many instances those contexts – of socio-economic hardship, lack of political rights, or of perceived external threat – provide the drivers, but it is also the case that different rationalities aid the transition to, and reinforce, different ways of working and alternative democratic practices. This is most clearly articulated by van der Pennen and Schreuders when describing their conception of the 'fourth way', which

> harnesses the power of active citizens in an equal partnership with government institutions: rather than stimulating *action,* the state works alongside community actors building flat, horizontal rather than vertical, relationships. It stimulates (by creating the conditions in which communities can flourish and by signalling its support for collective action) but then works with those actors towards key social, economic and environmental goals.

In this instance, local governance becomes a nurturing framework for community mobilisation; it provides the opportunities that make collective action worthwhile. Communities know that the actions they choose to take will be supported, and that support therefore gives impetus to the process. Although these types of local relationships aid community action, others can impede it, however. In England, Parker argues for a need to bridge 'the accompanying mindsets or rationalities that can frustrate the vertical integration of ideas, needs and interests'.

Echoing the concerns of Filion, who draws attention in Chapter 14 to the 'scaling' issues that limit the ambitions of communities within his study of the City of Waterloo in Ontario Province, Parker suggests that there is a need to 'find ways to learn from the community development model and to focus effort at vertical two-way integration of knowledge and needs at global, national and local/neighbourhood scale'. A distinction needs to be drawn here between the immediacy of community action and the longer term of community planning. In England, planning as a community development exercise (setting goals and delivering against these through local projects) has been replaced by community planning as a segment of statutory planning. Therefore, the enthusiasm with which communities embrace planning at this scale is driven or inhibited by perceptions of how far it (that is, planning, and therefore community actors) can influence higher policy and strategic decisions. In some respects, the English situation has become unique, with the absorption (from 2011) of community plans (or 'neighbourhood development plans') where they exist into a broader framework comprising local, district-wide, development plans. In a sense, community planning in England is no longer merely an extension of community action, and enthusiasm for 'getting into planning' does not correlate with any wider enthusiasm for community activism. Community groups may be frustrated by the limits placed on their planning ambitions without losing faith in the power of community action.

Past research in England has drawn attention to what is attainable from 'entrepreneurial social enterprise' (see, for example, Moseley, 2000) and in all the case studies in this book, it is the expectation of what is *possible* that triggers community action, and it is then tangible returns on time and effort invested that sustains it. These include health benefits in Australia, and critical improvements in the physical urban environment for residents in the French, Dutch, New York and German examples. It is also an ethos, described by residents of Gigha, of self-reliance and the idea that 'we should support ourselves: we can't rely on whatever government agent'. Achievement through self-reliance is a powerful driver, although there is a regular return to the idea that the state must play some role in creating the opportunities for, and framing, that self-reliance. In Scotland, land reform delivered that opportunity and in Volda there was general agreement to 'devolve responsibility for planning, development, infrastructure investment, and the oversight of land transactions to community actors'. Freeing community-based development from 'normal regulatory constraints' (Amdam, Chapter 15) is a way of catalysing action. In England, the current equivalent is the 'community right to build' and the bypassing of those 'normal regulatory constraints' through localised adjustment of permitted development rights.

In all the case studies, however, drivers and inhibitors coexist. Local planning frameworks are often adjusted to support community development, but the wider structures of planning (and the government structures in which these are embedded) generate persistent friction with community ambition. Beyond the 'scaling' issues highlighted by Filion in Canada, there is the ever-present tension between notions of a broader public good and the 'community good' pursued at a neighbourhood scale. Public policy is, in many instances, hard-wired to prioritise strategic interests (and contested notions of the public good) and finds it difficult to work through or with communities. Again, however, these inhibitors are only significant if community planning is understood by reference to statutory regulation and if its success is dependent on penetration into normative systems that are external to the level of the community. In England, there is a blurring between community and public planning. Elsewhere, the division is more clear-cut, although everywhere the ambition to plan and deliver services (in the areas of housing, health, economic development and so on) seems to suggest an eventual shift – at different speeds in different places – to greater connectivity between these divided planning sectors. At the point of connection, the tension between strategy and community aspiration becomes an apparent impediment to community development: the two can seem inseparable. This, however, is very much a planning perspective and one which is informed by the English experience.

In the case studies contained in this book, local or national government lends varying degrees of support to community action, but how far the community can act is dependent on internal dynamics and capacities. This is most vividly illustrated by Messaoudène and colleagues in Marseille. In that city, communities fractured along ethnic lines, or diffuse communities that associate by ethnicity rather than place, are slow to mobilise and are seldom able to shape development outcomes. Extreme poverty and population churn (of the type seen in Marseille in the last 20 years and in Barcelona 40 years ago) can 'saturate' a city's 'physical capacities' while leaving it with few of the social capacities needed to mobilise a response. The great challenge faced in Marseille has been the influx of poor migrants from North Africa and further afield. While the North Africans mobilised to fight racism in the 1980s, and have since won some victories against poorly conceived urban policy interventions, other migrants have struggled to integrate or come together as communities. The lack of integration means that 'boundary crossers' have been slow to emerge and communities, such as they are, lack the skills and knowledge needed to help themselves. The degree to which social capital, or the resource potential of relationships, underpins (and is even the 'primordial soup' of) community action is not discussed in every chapter. There is evidently some disagreement over 'social capital' as a concept or, more probably, as a descriptor for the interactional processes that constitute 'community life'. It is clear, however, that all the contributions (directly, or by implication) make a connection between some sort of community capacity and Matthews' use of 'time and belonging' to explain what communities do (Chapter 3). Communities are variously said to have 'energy', to be 'energised', to have a 'power to act' (which is constituted within a 'neighbourhood'), to be 'empowered', to have 'momentum' or to have a capacity to contribute to, or shape, their environment. The idea of social capital has become mainstreamed within US, UK and Australian literature: Parker places skills and knowledge at the heart of community planning in England and invokes the idea of 'bridging' as a means of reconciling different mindsets and rationalities. Social capital is a framing idea in the contributions from Wolf-Powers and from Dandekar and Main. It is also central to Kilpatrick and colleagues' understanding of community action in farming and fishing communities. Elsewhere, a lack of key capacity is used to explain community inertia or a failure to influence.

The drivers of community action range from the obvious *prompts* – the big challenges that suddenly appear on the horizon or the clear affronts to community and individual rights – through different rationalities (community and state), support structures and incentives, all the way to the *foundations* for action that exist in community dynamics. If it is accepted that 'community' interaction (or some sense of collective unity or affinity) is the basis of all action then providing opportunities for interaction becomes critical. Kilpatrick and colleagues emphasise the importance of support groups providing 'a social connection opportunity'; van der Pennen and Schreuders place similar emphasis on generating 'familiar trust' in the public domain by ensuring that communities have the spaces they need to promote 'neighbourhood' engagement. Community development – aspects of which are examined by Gallent in Chapter 16 – is a crucial platform for all community planning and action. At the heart of community development, and its onward extension into activism, is the concept of trust.

Trust in (and beyond) the community

Trust, within communities and across scales, is a crucial commodity, triggering social mobilisation, sustaining it, and sometimes turning piecemeal cooperation into an effective form of networked governance. Trust as a concept figures in the majority of contributions to this book. *Scale* relationships in planning are, as Parker points out, dependent on the degree of trust societies have in democracy. The ability to work *across lay and professional boundaries* depends, as Gallent argues, on the existence of trusted intermediaries. Similarly, Kilpatrick and colleagues' 'boundary crossers' commanded the trust of individuals across social and professional networks. This was also the case for community organisations in New York City, whose effective advocacy of different neighbourhood interests depended on winning local trust; the same was true of community coordinators in Palermo, the 'everyday fixers' in Almere, and the President of the Tenants' Committee in Bassens. Trust across scales; trust in advocates and community leaders; and familiar trust within communities: these forms of trust are all vital. It has been observed previously that trust is fundamental to collaborative rationality. The dialogue on which networks depend must be 'authentic' in the sense of being transparent and trustworthy. This is fundamental to the working of the social networks that support community development or the extended networks that connect communities to external resources and structures. Trust is a product of repeated interaction. It is the familiar trust described above and provides the glue needed to build the neighbourhood or larger coalitions that have the means and the skills required to carry forward community ambitions and projects.

In Barcelona, the 'neighbourhood movement has been characterised by its open structure' and by its readiness to build relationships with other entities, organisations and movements that share the objective of improving life in the city and defending social rights'. These movements became a clear expression of community capacity, with their expansion made possible by open dialogue with other groups. They were successful in winning and retaining trust. All such bodies, however, need to take care to maintain their independence, sometimes from the political and systemic failings that community action is seeking to remedy. In New York City, suspicions have arisen that community-based housing groups 'have become too fully assimilated into a government and market prescribed status quo' and have today become 'too busy correcting market and state failures to question or challenge the social system that produces them'. In that case, trust is being eroded and faith in the power of community action to deliver positive change is being undermined. Perhaps the key lesson here is that over recent decades, the trust that society once placed in government has been redirected, in many instances, to the informal sector. Many of the inequities and injustices that exist in the world today are thought to be 'institutionalised' and it is only through direct action, which steers clear of those institutions, that redress will be achieved. But this of course raises important questions for 'community action'. First, to what extent does trust in that action depend on the maintenance of clear boundaries between it and the state in its various guises? Second, are the most effective forms of community action those which retain their independence and, in all likelihood, remain small scale? Third, to what extent can mediated action deal with the problem of state interference and the loss of independence and trust?

It is probably the case that action that becomes 'too fully assimilated into [any] government and market status quo' – for example, community-based housing groups in New York City or neighbourhood planning processes in England – will lose some of the social and political benefits of its independence, though it will probably gain other useful attributes. Internationally, what we might see emerge in the years ahead are different forms of community action and planning: some that are relatively isolated from state influence, some that are 'relational' and enjoy the sponsorship of local government, and some that become integrated into traditional governance structures, either because they actively seek penetration into those structures or because the 'energy' and legitimacy they represent is courted by the state.

Although the tendency towards community action has been characterised in this book as part of a universal governance shift, underpinned by very substantial and fundamental changes in society in the global north and beyond, we suggested right at the start that the particular ambitions of community action (including the ambition to 'plan' and the nature of that planning) vary between different places 'with outcomes being coloured by underlying cultural drivers'. In this book we have tried to steer a discussion of the various contexts, drivers and outcomes of community action and planning, introducing contributions from a range of countries. These contributions have drawn attention to some important and reasonably ubiquitous attributes of community action and planning: the importance of coordination and leadership from key individuals, for example; tapping into the right resources and skills; partnerships across sectors based on trust; the ability to directly shape outcomes in all instances, and meaningful influence over strategy in some. Communities come together to achieve *something*. This something can be immediate or long term; it can be something very basic (asserting and acquiring a right, for example) or it can be complex and involve sustained action and engineering fundamental changes in the physical or political environment. Community action is itself something very simple, but also fundamental to questions of democracy, governance, governmentality and planning. Certainly, it has now come of age. While it continues to achieve its local victories, it has also become the focus of efforts, in many countries, to renew democracy and to find better ways of planning for, and providing services to, all kinds of places and all sorts of community. Assimilation is now the big risk for community action and planning, and whether that assimilation – into the old institutions of government – will undermine its vitality. But if that happens and if some networks and structures are lost, others will rise to challenge the institutional injustices which have always been the target of community action.

Reference

Moseley, M, 2000, England's village services in the 1990s: Entrepreneurialism, community involvement and the state, in *Town Planning Review* 74, 1, 415–33

Index

References to figures, tables and images are shown in *italics*